PENGUIN BOOKS

AN ADVENTUROUS LIFE

Sir James Hardy with Rob Mundle

Sir James Hardy is well known for his contribution to the sporting and business life of Australia. He represented his country in the Olympics and in the challenge for the America's Cup. He is part of the famous Hardy wine company. Sir James now lives in Sydney with his wife Joan.

Rob Mundle was the first cadet journalist employed by *The Australian* in Sydney in its first year of publication in 1964. After training as a general reporter he combined his career with his sport and went on to be recognised in Australia, and internationally, as a leading authority on sailing. He met Jim Hardy early on in his life and they have established a solid friendship.

Rob now lives with his wife in Sydney, runs his own promotions company and works as a freelance journalist.

AN ADVENTUROUS LIFE

Sir James Hardy with Rob Mundle

PENGUIN BOOKS

Penguin Books Australia Ltd
487 Maroondah Highway, PO Box 257
Ringwood, Victoria 3134, Australia
Penguin Books Ltd
Harmondsworth, Middlesex, England
Viking Penguin, A Division of Penguin Books USA Inc.
375 Hudson Street, New York, New York 10014, USA
Penguin Books Canada Limited
10 Alcorn Avenue, Toronto, Ontario, Canada M4V 1E4
Penguin Books (N.Z.) Ltd
182–190 Wairau Road, Auckland 10, New Zealand

First published by Margaret Gee Publishing, 1993
This edition published by Penguin Books Australia, 1995
2 4 6 8 10 9 7 5 3 1
Copyright © Robert Mundle and Sir James Hardy, 1993

Typeset in Goudy Oldstyle by Midland Typesetters
Made and printed in Australia by Australian Print Group

National Library of Australia
Cataloguing-in-Publication data:

Hardy, James, Sir, 1932– .
An adventurous life.

ISBN 0 14 024804 8.

1. Hardy, James, Sir, 1932– . 2. Vintners–Australia–
Biography. 3. Sailors–Australia–Biography.
I. Mundle, Rob. II. Title.

Contents

Dedication

To my lovely wife, Joannie, family and friends, who have encouraged
me to relate my many and varied experiences in life.

James G. Hardy.

To Christine, my darling wife, for all her love,
support and encouragement.

Rob Mundle

CHAPTER ONE

Hell on High Water

IT TOOK JUST one pitch black night and the mother of all storms in the middle of the Irish Sea in 1979 to change my life. It was the Fastnet Race from England to the Irish coast and return where, suddenly, staying alive and hoping I would see tomorrow was far more important than what had happened yesterday or last year. On that horrible night the wind was raging at around 70 knots and huge foaming black seas sent from Satan were threatening to engulf our yacht. That night there was death in our sport. Fifteen fellow competitors would die at the hands of the storm.

For almost a decade prior to this I had been wallowing in a sea of self pity. The America's Cup, yachting's holy grail and the ultimate prize in my chosen sport, had been mine for the taking. But I had failed, and in doing so I had, to my mind, not lived up to the expectations of my country, syndicate head Sir Frank Packer or anyone else associated with that 1970 Cup campaign.

I couldn't get over losing. I was convinced we would win. We had the yacht, the people and everything else going for us, including the fact that the Americans had a slow boat in the modified *Intrepid*. But at the end of it all we didn't have the Cup. Someone had to take the blame, and that person was me. So I let the loss plague my mind like a cancerous growth year after year. I had great difficulty talking about it so took my leave from the high profile side of sailing and found my solace by disappearing over the horizon on ocean yacht races.

There I didn't have to answer to anyone. It was my boat and if I won a race then it was good. If I lost . . . who cared?

Now it was the Fastnet race that in a matter of hours would become known as the Fastnet disaster. Our struggle to survive in that maelstrom and complete the 603 nautical mile course was frightening enough. But it was to become a chilling experience via the yacht's radio, which was jammed with calls for assistance. Yachts were sinking, people were being lost overboard and there was nothing we could do to help. Nothing was being said officially on the race radio frequencies, but we knew it was inevitable people would die. Here we were battling the same horrifying storm and I was in charge of the yacht. I was responsible for the lives of nine others and caring just as much about my own. We were all asking if we would be the next to confront disaster.

Time and time again a wall of water with a massive foaming crest would descend on our yacht, burying it. We hung on. The thin ropes between our safety harnesses and fixtures on the deck were like umbilical cords between mother and child. They were the difference between life and death. Death, I kept saying to myself over and over again. I couldn't believe there was death in our sport. Sure guys got hurt sailing on the odd occasion . . . but you didn't die. This wasn't motor racing, where dicing with death was an accepted risk.

I remember saying to myself: 'What the hell have I been doing all these years worrying about losing the bloody America's Cup?' It was as though it was some big deal. Hell, it was just another boat race compared to what was happening there and then. Those death-dealing seas were leaving children without fathers. Loved ones who had gone sailing for the fun of it wouldn't be returning home after that night.

To face death in that storm was to face reality. The shock of the situation was in fact cleansing me of ten years of melancholy. Losing the America's Cup didn't matter any more. While I steered our small yacht, sometimes over and often through the raging seas, I was reminded how many times I'd felt sorry for myself and said: 'If only . . . ' Hell, if the dog hadn't stopped for a piss we would have had hare for dinner. What did it matter.

To this day the trauma of the 1979 Fastnet disaster has created a most powerful bond between myself and the rest of the crew aboard the Australian Admiral's Cup team yacht, *Impetuous*. It placed a new value on life and friendship for all of us. I'm sure that at some stage during that night each one of us thought there was a chance we could die.

We knew there was a blow coming when we set sail from Cowes, on the Isle of Wight, for the race across the Irish Sea, around the Rock and back to Plymouth. But tradition said this was a demanding race, one of the world's classic offshore encounters, so the thought of a 30 knot north-westerly wind caused us about as much concern as a southerly buster during a Sydney–Hobart race.

That all changed when the front line of the storm charged like a locomotive out of the ink black night and flattened our yacht with a 50 knot squall. The only difference between this and a locomotive was that there was no warning. In an instant we had gone from a pleasant night time sailing experience to one that called on every skill of each crew member. There was no frivolity from that moment because our sole aim was to keep racing the boat. We had gone into that final race of the Admiral's Cup in third place on points, knowing that a good result in the Fastnet would give us a shot at winning what was the ocean racing world championship.

We had two things at the forefront of our minds as soon as we were hit by the squall—our own safety and the survival of the yacht. Safety harnesses went on straight away and everyone worked frantically at reducing our sail area. It was when my co-helmsman, Hugh Treharne, a great, great sailor, called on me to make a decision on what jib we should set that I really recognised the gravity of the situation. He wanted a split-second decision, and the right one, from the man who as the eldest and most experienced on board was immediately recognised as the leader. "Which jib do you want, Jim? Which jib? Quickly," he shouted at me across the howl of the wind, which had the sails flogging and cracking like whips. "The storm jib, Hughie," I shouted back, and in a flash it was on deck and heading for the bow.

All the time *Impetuous* was lying at an angle of around 45° and struggling to come upright. It was like one of those bob-up toys, but this one was staying down because of the pressure of the wind on the sails and rigging. The crew were having trouble keeping a foothold on the wet and sloping deck as the yacht bucked and tossed over the rapidly building seas. They were battling to set the storm

3

jib and reef the mainsail to about one-third the size it had been minutes earlier. At that stage we all still had our minds very much on the race, my major concern being that the sails wouldn't hold together. The mainsail was flogging wildly and the rig and yacht were shaking violently, like they were being hit by an earthquake. Would we be joining the large number of boats in the 303 yacht fleet whose rigs had already failed, or would we get through unscathed?

Through nothing short of great skill the crew had the boat under control and the sails trimmed very quickly for an ideal course towards Fastnet Rock. There was no thought of heading home, especially with the Admiral's Cup at stake. But conditions were deteriorating, with the wind strengthening instead of abating and the seas beginning to come at us out of the dark in ever increasing volume. We expected to reach Fastnet Rock somewhere between 1 am and 2 am and then make the now anxiously awaited turn for home. It was during this approach to the Rock that the first of many high water marks came. Tension and anxiety were building in the crew. Soon after midnight half the crew spotted a light to leeward, below our supposed course to the Rock. They became convinced it was Fastnet and that we were sailing way off course. You could feel the crew splitting. The pressure was coming on me to make a judgment, to either change course for the light they could see or continue on the current track. I had only one option and that was to stick by the navigator, Phil Eadie. He had plotted our position and given me a course to the Rock. I knew I had done my best to steer that course in those conditions, realising all the time that if we wobbled off course five or ten degrees we could be in big trouble.

We pressed on with the wind increasing to around 60 knots and the seas becoming mountainous. A combination of spray and rain was peppering our faces like buckshot and our wet weather gear was doing more to keep the water in than out. We were soaked through and bitterly cold but there was nothing we could do about it. Co-owner John Crisp, being all too aware of the seriousness of the situation, asked what he could do to make my life on the helm easier. I said: "Just keep wiping the compass so I can see our course." So for the rest of our slog to the Rock there was John in the cockpit alongside me wiping the water off the compass with an old sock.

Phil Eadie was busy continually checking our position and course. It was a nightmare for him down below, jammed into his small navigation area, trying to plot our position while the yacht was being bucked everywhere by the seas. To make things worse, everything below was wet, including his charts. You just couldn't stop water from gushing into the cabin area. Phil also couldn't stop water from getting into the tray under his chart table. It all got too much for him when he lifted the chart table and found everything in the tray swimming around: charts, pencils, books and all sorts of navigational aids. He rummaged the bilge of the yacht, found a battery-operated drill and took to the bottom of the tray with great gusto. Voilá— drain holes.

It was around 12.30 am when we spotted it. There, right on our bow, was the loom of the Fastnet Rock lighthouse. There was elation among the crew because soon we would no longer be hammering into the teeth of this gale. We would be turning the corner and heading for home.

Little did we know what that would really mean.

If you have ever put your head out of a car window when travelling at 70 miles an hour you'll have an appreciation of how strong the wind was as we sailed towards our turning point. On top of that the seas, which were breaking, were higher than five storey buildings. That's big by any calculation, but when you're confronting them in a 42 foot yacht they take on monumental proportions. I remember one huge, breaking wave rolling out of the darkness towards us. It was breaking as far as you could see either side of the yacht. We had no choice but to just aim the yacht at it and hope for the best. It was like sailing through the surf, the white wall of water completely submerging the yacht. We hung on and *Impetuous* slowly surfaced like a submarine surfacing from the depths with water pouring off its decks.

It was Hugh's turn to steer as we neared the Rock and as we made our final approach we began to realise our efforts and determination to press on were being rewarded. Other yachts in the race were beginning to converge on the Rock and they were all bigger than *Impetuous*. We were obviously doing well on handicap, so with some common sense and good seamanship and an element of luck we could turn in a good result for our team.

The magnitude of the dangers we faced in that gale were no more evident than when we closed on the Rock. There was this massive lighthouse sitting on top of an equally large and craggy piece of rock in the middle of the ocean that was being pounded by the giant seas. The impact from the waves crashing onto this mighty monolith resulted in the spray going over the top of the lighthouse, something like 200 feet above sea level. The whole scene was made more eerie and awesome by the sweep of the lighthouse light, which was penetrating the pitch black night and illuminating the action. I had to share the sight with Ken Down, who was below deck at the time, because this was something you would never forget. "Ken, you've got to come and look at this," I shouted to him. He stuck his head out of the companionway and looked at the scene, somewhat awestruck. "Thank you for showing me, Jim," he said. "I never want to see it again." With that he disappeared below like a rabbit down a burrow. I don't think he's been ocean racing since.

Rounding the Fastnet Rock in such a terrible gale was a daunting experience. This was a race, so every unnecessary metre we sailed beyond the rock before turning to sail around it was time wasted. But our enthusiasm to get on the course for the finish and sail hard towards a good placing on handicap had to be tempered by good seamanship. A mishap at that moment, like broken rigging or a blown-out sail, could spell disaster. A wave could pick up our yacht and hurl it onto the rocks, taking us with it. On top of that we had larger yachts bearing down on us. They were on a collision course and holding right-of-way under the race rules. Hugh, monitoring the progress of every approaching yacht, was constantly calling on Phil to take a compass bearing on the light and to tell him the second it was safe to tack. When Phil shouted "OK," Hugh's call to tack the yacht could hardly be heard above the roar of those giant waves crashing onto the rocks and the howl of the wind. I think we all said a little prayer then, hoping nothing would go wrong. The yacht was getting tossed around all over the ocean and the atmosphere was made even more dramatic with the regular sweep of the towering lighthouse light, which lit up our sails on an otherwise beastly black night.

ROB BROWN – crew member: "Apart from Jim's great leadership that night it was the actual rounding of Fastnet Rock that sticks in my mind. Not once did we lose sight of the fact that we were in a race, something that was never more apparent than at that time. The teamwork between Jim, Hugh and Phil was magnificent.

*They knew that if we tacked-to round Fastnet the second it was
safe to do so then we would make considerable gains on our more
conservative opponents, who were giving it a wide berth. We were
little more than one hundred metres away from the rocks when
we tacked and made our turn towards home. I remember it being
like riding on one of those merry-go-round horses you see at a
fun fair, but instead of a horse it was a yacht going up and down
near vertically. And the rise and fall wasn't just half a metre. It
was more like between fifteen and twenty metres. Then came the
spume as we sailed around the lee side of Fastnet Rock. The wild
wind and the waves had churned up a spume that was like soap
suds about a metre deep on the surface of the ocean. We had
no choice but to sail through it and as we did it was blowing
up into our faces then straight up the mainsail. It was an amazing
thing to experience."*

Once around Fastnet we thought things would get a little easier
as the wind and waves would be coming from behind and not ahead.
But those expectations were quickly dashed. We were now in danger
of being completely overwhelmed by the giant waves as they roared
up from behind. If you can picture a surfboat going down the near
vertical face of a huge wave and being tossed upside down as the
wave broke, you have an idea of what we faced. The big difference
was that the waves we were trying to negotiate were between 50
and 60 feet high. Our concerns about being rolled upside down were
to be justified at the end of the race when we learned of other
yachts being rolled completely, 360 degrees, by the force of those
immense and haunting black waves. To go below deck to rest on
the yacht was to enter a nightmare. It was a waste of time trying
to find dry clothes because everything was wet. You just collapsed
cold and wet on top of equally wet bags of sails on the cabin floor,
or onto a sopping wet bunk, and tried to sleep. For food you just
grabbed a chocolate bar or the like. There was no way you could
cook or do anything else in those conditions.

*GRAEME LAMBERT – co-owner: "I have many vivid memories
of that race, some funny, some frightening. It was Jim who provided
us with one of the most memorable, one that was somewhat symbolic
of just how bad life on board really was. We hadn't been around*

Fastnet Rock for long when he went below to rest. A few minutes later the hatchway slid back and Jim handed up a tea towel that was all bunched up. 'Here, get rid of this over the side,' he said nonchalantly. The smell was rather repulsive. 'What is it?' I asked as I went to throw it overboard. 'Shit,' he replied in a very distinguished manner as he went back below. 'I had to have a crap somewhere. The head (toilet) can't be used in this weather, so that was my only alternative'."

As the night wore on we gained more confidence and believed we would get through the storm. We even decided to set a slightly larger jib because we felt the wind had decreased slightly and we could make more speed. How wrong that was. After about an hour we just couldn't control the boat. The gale was our master once more. We were doing ten knots all the time but I couldn't steer the yacht where I wanted it to go, for the safest course was down the front of those waves. We either took the big jib off or suffered the full wrath of the storm. I had no alternative but to get two of the younger blokes, Rob Brown and Phil Walsh, to go to the bow in the dark and take the sail down. It was a horrible moment, having to ask them to put their lives on the line for the safety of the yacht. I knew that if something broke while they were up there, or their safety harnesses failed, they were gone. There was no way in the world we could turn around in those conditions and get back to them. It flashed through my mind that I was responsible if we lost them overboard. The entire crew planned the move with meticulous care, knowing one mistake could see one or both of those guys go over the side. The situation wasn't helped by the fact that having two grown men on the bow as we hurtled down those waves made the yacht far more difficult to steer and more vulnerable to the possibility of nosediving. Somehow, I'm not sure how, Rob and Phil managed to hang on to the flogging sail and get it to the deck. They crawled along the deck and back to the cockpit, where Phil bellowed above the noise and mayhem: "I've broken all my fingers." All I could say, as we negotiated our way down another watery cliff face, was: "You'd better just sit there for a minute and we'll look at your fingers when we get a chance. It's a bit hectic here at the moment." As it turned out his fingers weren't broken, just battered and badly bruised from trying to hang on to the flogging sail.

8

The yacht became a lot easier to control after that so I suggested to Graeme Lambert that we continue sailing under mainsail alone: "Graeme, I have won a few races by being a bit conservative," I said. "We are still doing ten knots and I can now steer the boat where I want it to go. I think we should stay with just the mainsail set for a while." I vividly remember Graeme saying to me, his eyes wide and white as we hurtled down yet another liquid mountain: "Just keep doing what you are doing, Jim. Please, keep doing what you're doing."

While we were having our share of problems, drama was beginning to unfold around us. The radio was becoming choked with calls for assistance. Yachts were losing rudders and masts. We knew it was getting serious when all communications were cancelled and an emergency frequency took control. At that time it was obvious yachts were sinking and we became convinced lives were being lost. But we still weren't mentally prepared for the news we would hear soon after sunrise. Fifteen of our fellow sailors had been claimed by this monstrous storm. A pall of shock, sadness and disbelief descended over our yacht.

Being aware of the dramas this storm was dealing other yachts made us even more cautious. I feared we would lose our rig or rudder, two events beyond our control. It was very important that we kept our spirits high and stayed alert to minimise the chance of a mistake that would bring disaster. I was back on the helm for the watch between 3 am and 6 am, the most tiring watch at the best of times because you anxiously watch for the signs of first light. To help stay alert and remind everyone we were sailing as a team in the worst sailing conditions imaginable, I recited poetry at the top of my voice for all to hear. One memorable piece came from Lord Byron's 'Childe Harold's Pilgrimage':

"Roll on thou deep and dark blue ocean—Roll!
Ten thousand fleets sweep over thee in vain;
Man marks the earth with ruin
His control stops with the shore . . . "

How true it was. Once again I was being reminded that the ocean is the master and without its consent we cannot survive.

Somehow some of the crew managed to get a sense of humour rolling. The night before this race had started our team captain, Syd

Fischer, brought all the Australian crews together in Cowes to watch a motivational film by a leading American football coach, which I had brought with me from Australia. Part of this film had the football team saying in unison: "We are a symbol of national excellence. We are the greatest. We have pride in our own performance." Well, here we were at the height of this incredible storm, rocketing down the faces of these huge waves like a tumbleweed bowling down a cliff, and the young blokes, surrounded by mayhem, were sitting on the side of the yacht soaked through and hanging on for dear life, shouting: "Pride in performance. We are a symbol of national excellence." Well, funny or not, I think it helped those guys cope. It was a case of: "We are here and we can do it." If nothing else it gave them something to hang on to mentally. It was like reaffirmation.

> HUGH TREHARNE – co-skipper: "I knew things were bad, but it wasn't until sunrise, after I had taken over the helm from Jim, that I could really come to grips with the magnitude of the conditions we had survived that night. As the sun rose, its rays penetrated a small gap between the cloud line and the horizon and came at us horizontally. It only shone for a few minutes, then it disappeared behind the clouds. But during those few minutes we must have seen the sun rise fifty or more times. When the yacht was at the top of the wave we would see the sun. Then we would surf down the incredibly steep faces of the waves and go into shadow. What I remember most was that when we were in the troughs the waves were casting a shadow over the mainsail that went to within just a few feet of the top of the mast. That was fair indication that even at that stage, when the storm was abating, the waves were more than 45 feet high."

By morning the extent of the horror that had swept the fleet was becoming evident. The news services were crammed with reports of the loss of life, the carnage—24 yachts had been abandoned and more than 130 sailors had been plucked from the sea. The skies were continually buzzing with search and rescue helicopters and aircraft. But the race had not been called off so we had to keep our minds and yacht in racing mode, something that would help ease the shock of the previous night. With the wind strength decreasing we ventured to set a small spinnaker. By early afternoon we were the first to set a proper storm spinnaker. Later, back at the finish in Plymouth, we were to hear we'd given our rivals around us plenty to talk about when the spinnaker went up. The Italians, still sailing very cautiously at the time, saw our multi-coloured sail pop on the horizon. They couldn't identify the yacht, but amongst themselves agreed: "It can only be those crazy Australians."

Crazy or not, it helped. All three Australian team yachts survived the hiding the storm handed out and scored sufficient points to take the Admiral's Cup. But there was no jubilation, no celebration. Our concerns were only for those who had died during the race, and their families. The realisation of what had happened during what was just another boat race left an indelible mark on our lives.

KEN DOWN - crew member: "We all felt so empty and helpless at the finish of the race. The loss of life was hard to comprehend. It was Jim who realised that there and then, as we motored from the finish line back to the dock in Plymouth, there was one small tribute we could make to those who had died. He unfurled our Australian ensign on its staff and rigged it at half mast. We moved into the dock with our flag at half mast. What more could we do? What more could we say? Nothing. Jim had said it all with one simple gesture."

The indelible mark the Fastnet disaster left on me came in the form of a refreshing new outlook on life. To have come face to face with death was to realise what really mattered. I had made my own life miserable just because I had lost what was really nothing more than another yacht race, the America's Cup. That didn't matter any more. There were far more important things to care about. My priorities had changed. I could now revel in success and cope with disappointment. I had the strength to contend with the low points, like the end of my marriage, and the collapse of our famous wine company, Thomas Hardy and Sons, which had been in the family for more than a century. I was to gain an even greater appreciation of the strength my youngest son, Richard, had shown in struggling through life with his disabilities following an accident as a child.

I knew after that awful experience on the Irish Sea that while

11

life wasn't going to be all wine and roses I could go on and face the world, enjoying life to the fullest. The sea of self pity I'd been sailing on for so long was gone. In the years ahead I was to appreciate what were previously inconceivable levels of happiness and satisfaction, especially through new love, a knighthood, wonderful friends and our magnificent win in the America's Cup in 1983.

CHAPTER TWO

From the Beginning

THROUGHOUT MY LIFE I have stretched my mind to its boundaries in search of a memory of my father, Tom Mayfield Hardy. I was almost six when he died, so I have always thought there was a chance that somewhere in my memory bank there was an image or an imprint of him. I do have memories of people from the period, like our maid Totie, who would take me for a walk. Family outings up to the Tintara winery, when my father must have been there, are in my mind. We would go up to what was called the scrub section, among beautiful blue gums, for a picnic. There were dams there so we would go fishing with nets for yabbies. The nets were rings of fencing wire with netting stretched across. There were three strings attached to them to keep them level when you pulled them up. We would tie a piece of meat in the middle of the net, lower it to the bottom of the dam and wait. The excitement, the anticipation, waiting for that net to be pulled to the surface always got to me. When the time came and the net surfaced with the yabbies on it with their big claws going chomp, chomp, chomp, I couldn't cope. I would take off like buggery thinking those bloody yabbies would get me. I'm sure I shared that fun with father and gave him plenty of laughs, but I can't find him in my images of those days.

I can also still, very clearly, see my father's grey Chrysler motor car with burgundy leather upholstery and two big spare wheels, one mounted in each mudguard up the front. What a magnificent car that was. I think if you pulled a dozen cars out from that era today

13

I would pick it, though I wouldn't know what my father looked like. I'd ask: "Who are you?" if he was there.

When I was very young my mother, Eileen Clara Hardy, and father were somewhat separate from us, the children. They were the grown-ups and ate in the dining room while the children, my two brothers Tom and David, sister Pam and I, ate in the kitchen with the maid. Later in life one of our maids was to relate a lovely story about me and my father. Apparently he came into the kitchen one day while we were eating and started talking to me about something or other. God knows what it was, but when he left I stood my ground. "Why did he have to come in here?" I asked the maid with considerable consternation. "This is not his room, it's our room. He should stay in the grown-up's room." I knew my place in the home when it was meal time so he should know his place.

Brother David enjoys telling another story from the same era involving a lamb chop. We had a lovely tennis court on the northern side of the house which, when it wasn't being used for tennis, had a long wire clothesline stretching right across it. It was one of those clotheslines where, after you had hung the clothes out, you used a clothes prop, a tree sapling with a fork at one end, to hold up the middle of the line so the clothes didn't drag on the ground. David came home one day to be greeted by the sight of me on the tennis court wearing a harness-like thing around my chest. Stretching from the harness at the back of my neck up to the wire clothesline was a rope that had a dog clip attaching it to the line. The line was long enough for me to have the full run of the court, but I couldn't get out. To stop me from getting hungry while I was out there playing the maid had pinned a lamb chop on a little piece of string to my shirt. Apparently I had been getting up to mischief around the house that day and creating merry hell. The harness, the lamb chop and the tennis court made a logical cure-all for the maid. Solution as it was then, if a parent did something like that to a child today, a psychologist would say I was an abused child. I don't think it did me any harm.

My first solid memory in life, one that I hold vividly to this day, came just before my sixth birthday. I was standing outside our home watching some men from the upper Tintara winery unloading large slate paving stones, which were to be laid around the outside of the house. Some had holes in them because it was the slate from the big vats at the winery that were being demolished. My mother came out looking very distressed, and took me by the hand around to the western side of the house. I could show you the exact location today. There she told me my father had been killed in a plane crash and said we would now have to really stick together as a family. I was old enough to realise I wouldn't be seeing him that night, he wasn't coming home any more. The date was 25 October, 1938, just two days before brother Tom's fourteenth birthday. News of the crash was tough on him. He was on his way home from school when he saw the newspaper posters at Adelaide railway station headlining the crash. He feared the worst, then knew Dad was gone when a friend came up to him on the train and asked: "Was your father Tom Hardy, the wine man?" Tom apparently contained his emotion while on the train then cried all the way from the station to the house.

As well as claiming my father, the crash took some of Australia's other leading wine industry men, Louis H. Gramp of Gramp and Son and Sidney Hill Smith of H. Smith and Sons, of Yalumba. Also on board was federal politician Charles Hawker. The group was en route to Canberra for a meeting between the government and wine industry representatives. They were among fourteen passengers who boarded the Australian National Airways Douglas DC-2 aircraft Kyeema at Adelaide's Parafield airport for the two hour twenty minute flight to Melbourne. In an ironic twist of fate it was a navigation error on the part of the crew that killed my father, the first person in Australia to hold a Master Yachtsman's Certificate recognising his ability as a seaman and outstanding navigator. Family friends told me that if Dad had been navigating the crash wouldn't have happened. The investigation into the crash found the crew had radioed Melbourne to report they were "passing Daylesford" on course for Melbourne when in fact they were some 25 miles closer to Melbourne's Essendon airport. What was thought to be Daylesford was probably Sunbury or Gisborne. The thick cloud that then confronted the plane was of little concern to the pilot, as he was confident he knew his position. He began his descent towards where he believed Essendon airport was located. But the plane was already well past Essendon and it crashed into Mount Dandenong at 1.45 pm, its expected time of arrival in Melbourne. No one survived.

It wasn't until a few years ago, on the fiftieth anniversary of the crash, that I was comfortable enough to make a pilgrimage to the crash site in the Dandenongs and establish another emotional link with my father. It was an eerie experience—the forest seemed silent—standing there almost in the shadow of Mt Dandenong and surrounding cliffs. An obelisk with a brass plaque listing details of the crash and carrying the names of the victims marked the spot. Nearby there was the stump of a huge old tree, about six feet across. It was all that remained of the tree the plane hit as it crashed. I stood there and took it all in, the incredible depth of the silence that day and how it must have been all those years ago.

The day after the crash was terrible for me. I came home from the nearby Hopetoun pre-school to a sight that is still with me as clear as a bell. Flowers. I've never seen so many flowers in all my living days. They were stacked outside the house, along the path to the front fence, they were all through the house, filling every room, and all the way up to the top sitting room where my father's coffin was lying on a huge wooden table. Holy Moses, from that day on, coffins and cut flowers—I can't stand the sight of them. As soon as I see cut flowers, as nice as they might appear, they take me back to that moment. Cut flowers to me are dead flowers. I love them in flower beds, but I can't stand to see them dying in vases. It reminds me of my father's death. It's a strange reaction that's stayed with me all these years.

On top of that, having the coffin at home was quite horrible. I know it was traditional at the time, but I didn't handle it well at all. Since then I've never liked that top room in the house, and I have bad memories associated with anything looking like the carpet in that room. Later in life, when brother Tom and his wife Barbara lived in the house, I used to go to Adelaide from Sydney twice a month and stay with them while I attended board meetings. Wouldn't you know it, they set up a bed for me in the top room. For some unknown reason I couldn't say I didn't want to stay there, but I tell you I didn't ever sleep too well once I turned out the light. It was eerie—there was a thick silence in the room, and the memories just kept flooding back.

Our family house was nothing short of large. Father built it originally to accommodate himself and his four sisters, none of whom were married at the time. It was built from sandstone, or freestone as it was called in Adelaide, and sat very impressively at the cliff edge right above the beach at Seacliff. Sitting very prominently and proudly at the front was its name, "Nunkeri", Aboriginal for "beautiful view". It was a very interesting home to me because it was a little different from the other homes in the area. It had a concrete lintel right around it, above every window. The first metre of the base of each wall was blue stone, making it look a very solid and proud house. There was a bedroom for my parents, a sitting room, the top room, and bedrooms for all the aunts. They moved out over the years until only Aunt Madeline was left, and she was to become the equivalent of a foster mother to us. Until then we had been cared for by maids. Originally, near the rear of the house, there was a large billiard room. After my father and friends founded the Brighton and Seacliff Yacht Club, Mum decided billiards were for the club and that the room would become another bedroom for the expanding family. In fact, with it being on the warm northern side of the house, it became the nursery and my brothers, sister and I were born in that room. As each of us grew up and departed the nursery, we slept in other parts of the house. There was certainly no shortage of bedrooms, but in later years Tom, David and I slept in what we called the sleep-out, the western side of the fully enclosed verandah that encompassed the house. Our tennis court, which was adjacent to the house, was for me the world's biggest play pen. In later years, the activities associated with the court, via Mum's weekly tennis parties, were to have a considerable influence on our lives.

Aunt Madeline, who was with us until after Hitler's war, was tough and kept us under control. With there being no life insurance in those days, or direct benefits coming from the company to my mother following Father's death, she had to work to make ends meet. Her income came in the form of a very small stipend from Thomas Hardy and Sons, where she acted as a hostess, entertaining guests at the winery. Mum was always a very active woman with church, bridge, the Overseas League, tennis, golf and other social activities keeping her on the run. Even with Father gone there were always so many people about, so it wasn't often that I'd see my mother one on one. Auntie Madeline always seemed to be about the place to care for us. Mum, being an ever-popular and gregarious woman, was either out or had friends calling to see her. People used to say they thought our home was like a railway station. All this did nothing to alter the fact that I had great respect for my mother. I thought

17

she was a most interesting woman to talk to. She was a very warm, curious, and alert woman who gave her time and energy to people and they gave theirs in return. She had plenty of stories and experiences to relate to me.

As is the case in so many families, the youngest tends to be a little more spoiled than the older brothers and sisters, and I was no exception. I believed being the youngest, and possibly because there was no father in the house, I held a divine right to throw the occasional tantrum to achieve an objective, like being able to stay up that little bit longer at night or having my brothers involve me in their games when I was the last person they wanted around. I used to be able to get my own way with my mother, often crying my way to success. But Madeline was awake up to me. She put my tantrums down to over-tiredness and more than once sent me to bed for all of Saturday afternoon. In reality I saw Aunty Madeline as a lovely woman who at nights would read *Dr Doolittle* to me for as long as I would brush her hair.

Looking back on it all I can say is that I had a super childhood. The only thing I really hated was when Pam, who was two years older than me, made me go with her when she took her prams and dolls on make-believe picnics. We were playing mothers and fathers and I was forced to push her stupid little pram. She would lay out a make-believe picnic and I'd have to endure all this silly talk and pretend fun. I would have given anything to be somewhere else. Apart from those episodes, being brought up in that part of Adelaide, right at the end of Maitland Terrace with the beach at the bottom of the cliff and bush and a gully behind the house, would have answered any youngster's dreams about a fun place to live. My days were absolutely full of fun and adventure. I never had a moment where I didn't have something whirling around in my mind. I was always off collecting bird's eggs, using old pram parts and bits of wood to build what we called "bitzers", which were billycarts, to race down the zigzag path to the beach or into the gully. The zigzag was quite an amazing thing, demanding considerable skill to negotiate in the bitzers, which we steered using our feet and bits of rope attached to the front axle. For us kids it was one of those fortunate mistakes made by the British when they were doing the original surveys for that part of Adelaide. Maitland Terrace was shown on the town plan to extend right down to the beach simply because the people doing the survey forgot to tell the people back in England drawing up the town plan that there was a cliff along the waterfront. So when the roadmakers got as far as our house they came to an abrupt halt, threw away the plans and built a zigzag footpath down the cliff face. It was a great bonus for the local kids. This was the time when I was first introduced to alcohol, not by mouth, but by Mother. Pure alcohol dabbed on cuts and grazes gained while falling from a bitzer or bike really did sting. Mind you, Mum didn't discourage us from drinking wine at an early age. The woman who started most days with a glass of our finest champagne taught us to enjoy wine in moderation. While most kids in the district were right in to raspberry cordial in those days, my mother let my mates and me drink claret and lemonade or hock and lemonade. That made my parties in the backyard very popular and I do remember getting just a touch tipsy when I broke Mum's rules. But still, it was a lot better than raspberry cordial.

My quest for excitement and adventure led to me entering the local history books at a very young age. Hopetoun Pre-school, which was a mile from home, has a history book that shows Jim Hardy "was excused" from the school because I was just too boisterous . . . all part of being a bit spoiled I guess. I used to jump the school fence and take myself off on adventures during the day. The Misses Fleming, who ran the school, usually found me down under the railway lines in the cattle pit near Brighton station. There I was, in my eyes, defying death, just watching these old steam trains hauling goods trucks roar overhead. It was exciting for me but my absence got to be a bit too much for the Fleming spinsters so they, you could say, "suggested" to Mother that I leave their little private school and go to Brighton Public School next door. That was fine by me because I was then going to school with the big boys. At that school I was to make lifelong friends in David Walker and Jim Macpherson and become noted for the contents of my lunchbox each day—a boiled egg, a raw potato and a little salt wrapped in greaseproof paper. Raw potatoes were my big deal. Most kids liked apples. I liked raw potatoes.

I look back at those days at Brighton and laugh, thinking about me being so proud in my black and yellow uniform, marching around the streets as a member of the school fife band. I was never very good on the flute, though my earnest attempts to extract some form of musical note from the thing was enough to get me chosen for the band. Arbor Day was always a big day for the band, marching through Brighton to various sights where we planted trees. I must look down near the Hove railway station one day to see if my trees survived. That was also the era when you formed gangs, mainly through rivalry between the suburbs. The Brighton boys were always seen as being toughies, while we kids from Seacliff were outcasts. Usually it just involved chucking rocks at each other and using shanghais to repel invaders. The shanghais were best because you could keep the Brighton kids at a distance, but it was always hard to get suitable rubber for shanghais. On the odd occasion we got into fisticuffs. I was never big on that. Forever the diplomat, I always seemed to talk my way out of a good stoush.

It was also a big deal to dig huts on the vacant land at the back of our house. There weren't a lot of suitable trees around for us to use for treehouses, so we decided we should go down instead of up. It was bloody tough work digging into the hard soil on those vacant lots with a pick and shovel. We would put old galvanised iron sheets over the top for a roof and cover that with dirt. We had covered trenches to adjoining huts. The only time we faced a problem was when we dug a six-foot deep hut against a fence near the wall of the neighbour's house. Mr and Mrs White weren't too impressed when they came out and saw their home teetering on the edge of this huge hole we'd dug. We thought they were very inconsiderate when they ordered us to fill it in and move our desires to dig well away from their property. We used to play war games in the trenches and that gave me the chance to wear some of my father's 9th Light Horse Regiment army clothes for the action. He had his name tags on them so I very proudly became Lieutenant Tom M. Hardy. Some nights we would be allowed to stay in the huts and I'd get to sleep in his war issue sleeping bag. The local kids would all band together, get some food and sleeping gear and make it a great night. That was when we learned how you should never turn the wick of a hurricane lamp up too high. Our fear of the dark on our first night staying in the hut resulted in us having the wicks really high to give maximum light. However, it also created maximum smoke, so much so that the next scene had all of us coughing and wheezing and running up for some fresh air.

Like a lot of youngsters, the railway provided maximum

fascination for me. As well as there being an ordinary rail line serving the goods yards, the Brighton Cement company had its own line about one mile long running from their factory down to the Marino railway station. It was operated by cable and became a super thing if you could ride on it. Whenever we knew it was running my mates and I would rush across the gully and hide behind the bushes, waiting for the small railway trucks to come down. Then, as they approached, we'd run out, leap on board and ride them all the way to the bottom, where they'd automatically tip off their load of cement before being hauled back up the hill. There were big signs everywhere saying "Keep Off!" so that made it a greater challenge. Every so often the blokes from the cement works would spot us and come after us. We'd leap off the trucks and run like buggery through the bush, giggling our heads off, heading for the safety of home. After that my mate Bob Ransom and I decided it was time to hit the big league and head for the main railway line. One day we walked across to Kingston Park, where there was a small road bridge going over the rail line right at the top of the steep rise from South Brighton to Seacliff and Marino. I'd observed from the bridge that the old steam train would sometimes slip a bit on the rails before it got to Marino at the very height of the climb, so we decided to make things more entertaining. Our trick was to take some grease, put it on the train lines, then sit back and watch the action. I know it sounds irresponsible these days, but we were smart enough then to plan it for when the train was going uphill, and not trying to stop on its way down to Seacliff. Anyway, there we were behind the bushes beside the track watching the train struggle up the rise, steam and smoke puffing out everywhere. Then it got to the grease. Boy oh boy, did it slip. The poor thing, it was roaring on the one spot. Next thing the driver released sand out of the chutes, pouring it onto the tracks in a bid to get traction. No luck. Much to our delight we had scored a direct hit. We couldn't have created more laughs, for us, if we had tried. After a few minutes the driver gave up and let the train roll about 50 yards back down the line. Then the poor fireman got off and came up the hill with a bucket of boiling water and waste cotton rag. The next scene was him down on his hands and knees washing the line. I laughed until it hurt, all the time thinking: "If he spots me I am dead, I am dead. I am right on the edge of super danger here."

There was seemingly endless mischief to be had in those days when I was between seven and ten years of age. Today I cringe at the thought of some of the things we used to do. Hunting for birds' eggs was high on our agenda each spring. We would really get annoyed when we slipped our hands up into those little nests and found we were too late—the buggers had hatched. They were mainly common birds, like starlings and sparrows, which I had learned from my outings to the vineyards with Mum and the family were pests because they ate the grapes. If you wanted to look on the positive side, my mates and I helped keep the starling and sparrow population down in Adelaide, even if the eggs we sought had hatched. If we found chicks instead of eggs we'd gently pull them out, these featherless, ugly little things with a tiny head and a fat, round little body. You could say we flight tested them, hanging on to their heads and throwing them as hard as we could. The head would part company with the body so all you could see were these little headless bodies soaring through the air. It was great fun then, but it's a horrible thought when you look back on it today.

When we weren't climbing onto roofs or up trees looking for birds' eggs, we'd be up other trees looking for what we called monkey nuts to eat. We also occasionally raided the local orchard, the required skill there being to get the fruit and retreat before the orchard owner peppered your backside with pellets from his saltpetre gun. I suppose that was the only time in my life when I was faster than anyone else on foot because I always escaped the pellets while my mates finished up with stinging backsides. Even our neighbour, Eric Haselgrove, didn't escape our raids. He had a beautiful, perfectly manicured little orchard at the bottom of his property where he used to diligently put brown paper bags over the fruit to stop the starlings from eating it. That only meant the fruit was gift wrapped as far as we were concerned.

Having the beach as well as the bush doubled the fun. We were always eager to get into whatever action was going. There was the time when an old chap named Jack Murray arrived with his horse and scoop on the sandhills near home. His contract was to level the dunes so a house could be built. My mates and I watched with great interest day after day as he skilfully operated a scoop behind one or two powerful draught horses. He was a beaut guy and we used to plague him for a chance to operate the scoop. What we didn't realise was that you had to be really strong to work the thing because it had a big lever that controlled the depth the blade would slice into the sand. He would set us up on the scoop with our hands placed firmly on this big lever, then get the horses moving. The scoop would just go deeper and deeper into the sand then stop because we couldn't control the lever. The horses would keep going, and the lever would take over and fly forward with us still attached. I was catapulted past the horse plenty of times much to the mirth of all around. What old Jack Murray and others were doing in levelling the sand dunes in the district looked good and was providing more real estate for home building. But we were to realise years later that it was actually interfering with nature something awful and causing irreparable damage to the foreshore. As children we would watch one storm wash the sand dunes away, and another bring them back. But once the houses appeared the cycle was interrupted, the flow of the sand had been stopped. The bathing boxes that existed all the way along the coast from Brighton to Seacliff provided the best example of the damage that had been done. They were summer retreats, just small cabins, which people would come and live in overnight to be on the beach front. They were up on stilts and quite secure until the sand dunes started to be levelled then built on. Slowly but surely they were all washed away in the storms. Half of the beach, which was soft, white sand when I was a child, is just pebbles today. The local council now has to truck sand in each summer to replenish the beach.

Along with Jack Murray and his horses, the local milkman, Mr Deere, a wonderful old man who worked with a horse and cart, held a great fascination for me. He would let me ride with him around the streets of Seacliff and Brighton before dawn, delivering the milk. It was always put out by ladle at the front doorstep of each house. My job was to ladle the milk out of his big churn into a smaller container, which he would take up to the houses. Each house would have a note out with the money for one, two or three pints, except for our house, in which case Mum left just a note. Mr Deere would come around to our home and collect the money when he knew Mum had it, always taking time to enjoy a drink or two with her. Inevitably it was something mixed with milk. I really liked that old guy because he always added a little bit more to each order, just for luck, as he would say.

With me gallivanting all over the neighbourhood Mum had trouble getting me home for lunch on more days than one, so she got hold of this dinner gong. She used to stand up on the verandah at home and whack this thing so hard every lunch time I could hear it as far away as Marino Rocks, about half a mile. All the locals would hear it and know it was time for Jim Hardy to go home for lunch. If I was having a good time I didn't exactly rush home, but if I got home after lunch had started I'd be greeted by big brother Tom and his tamarisk stick. He was very much the head of the family after Father died and in turn became a big ogre to me. He was forever whacking my backside with his tamarisk because I was late for this or late for that. I'm sure it was all well deserved, no more so than the time I wrecked his model airplane. Tom built these beautiful little planes out of balsa and fine paper, which was painted with what we called dope to give it strength and take the desired shape, especially over the wings. I came home one day to see this magnificent plane he'd built sitting there in all its glory, painted silver and shining brightly. As far as I was concerned it had "fly me" written all over it, so I thought I'd just give it a bit of a test run off the cliff outside. It was powered by a rubber band so I wound up the propeller, aimed it out from the cliff and let it fly. How beautiful it was to watch, this shiny silver bird making a perfect arc and returning almost to my feet. I just had to do it again, so I gave the propeller a few extra winds to really get the thing going. Well, I must have over-tweaked the whole thing because something went horribly wrong. The plane speared straight over the cliff edge onto the rocks below and smashed into a hundred pieces. It was beyond help, so I just gathered up the bits, took them home and hid them behind the sofa. Sure enough Tom came home looking for his plane. "I don't know where it is," I said, lying through my teeth and not realising that a piece of the evidence was still protruding from behind the sofa. Tom spotted it, discovered the mangled wreckage and belted me until I was bawling. As deserved as that hiding was it didn't make me like him very much. He was eight years older than I was. His big brother-cum-father attitude towards me really became something by the time I was ten and he was eighteen. He was a school prefect at St Peter's College then and they were allowed to cane the kids. I think Tom used me for practice. Brother David was six years older than me and had a lot more time for me and my activities. Whereas

Tom was just my brother, David was my mate. I called him "old Dave". There was a bit of rivalry between Tom and David because whatever Tom was into David wasn't. Tom played cricket, so David took up boxing, and things like that. Actually, in learning to box David gained a new level of respect from Tom. And later in life, when I was in National Service, I was to appreciate the fact that David had learned to box and passed on a few tricks of the trade to me.

In some ways our family was quite close, in other ways we were each quite independent, but there always seemed to be a great deal of family fun and jocularity around the house on most Sunday evenings after Mum's legendary tennis parties. On many of those evenings Mum, her friends and my older brothers played charades. I was considered to be too young, but sometimes they would let me take part for the fun of it. The one charade still sticking in my mind involved the word Tintara, the name of our main vineyard. First the participants came out with metal rubbish can lids, banging them. Their next action was as if they were tarring the road. And finally they were cheering, rah-rah-ing at the football. And to put it all together they fell about as though they were drunk . . . tin-tar-rah. I thought that was very funny and really clever.

We didn't go on a lot of outings as a family, but when we did they were great fun with us all piling into the family car and heading up to the wineries. In those days they used an open fermenting process for the wine so I would look forward to putting my fingers into the vats of what looked like sparkling burgundy and licking them for the taste. The taste at that stage of fermentation was wonderful. It was half sugar and half alcohol, so it was a fun thing to do. I really loved being there at vintage time with all the trucks coming in and unloading tons of grapes. All the activity was very exciting, probably so much so that my first real interest in the business was sparked. Even back then, though, my mother was very good in not letting us feel the winery was any big deal. We were led to believe things were pretty tough, which I think took some pressure off her. Today we realise that while things for our family weren't as good as they had been, we were a lot better off than most people. Regardless of this I learned at a very early age that if I wanted something I had to work for it. This was never more evident than with the approach of Guy Fawkes night in November each year. When my father was

25

alive he apparently treated it as a big deal for us kids, splashing out to buy crackers, sky rockets and all sorts of pretty fireworks and making sure we had a big bonfire arranged. With Dad gone Mum wasn't flushed with funds so if I wanted fireworks I had to find the money. My young mind decided that selling flowers would be the way to go so there I was in the street outside our home with a wonderful array of roses and other fresh garden flowers for sale. When business wasn't coming to me I went to it, hawking my flowers door to door. Roses were one shilling a dozen until one lady said to me "Oh, they're worth more than that. They're worth two shillings." So two shillings it was from that moment on. The only person not pleased with my flower-selling exploits was Mum. She came home one day to realise that my flower supply was coming from her garden. It was bare. Another weekend enterprise I started was a shoe shine business, this time in partnership with my mate Bob Ransom. And how creative we were. We rigged an old pushbike with carpet on the back wheel. While one of us sat on the bike and pedalled like crazy the other would polish the shoes on the spinning carpet. We hung a sign on the hedge outside the house to get the passing trade and also operated in the main street of Seacliff shopping centre.

There's no denying Mum had to work really hard to make ends meet. In 1940, the year I turned eight, her financial burden was lightened considerably through a wonderful gesture from my godfather, Sir James Gosse. He was an old school friend of my father's who went on to head a large company associated with shipping and general merchants in Adelaide. He came to my mother and said, in effect: "I am Jim's godfather and as such it is my role to educate him." So he did just that, paying for my education right through until I left St Peter's College. To make the whole thing legal in his eyes, he also organised with Mum to have me baptised. So, at the age of seven, there I was at St Peter's College with the old Head Master, Reverend Guy Pentreath, holding my head over the font, dripping water on my forehead and doing the Godly deed.

Despite my father being a foundation member and long time Commodore of the Brighton and Seacliff Yacht Club, and even though we lived on the beach front, I had always been a little apprehensive about the water and sailing because I couldn't swim very well. I had played on the beach below home and around the yacht club plenty of times, even once managing to get my backside well and truly kicked because I managed to wreck a weekend club race. I had built a massive sandcastle near the clubhouse during the week and felt that, for the finishing touch, it needed windows. I went rummaging through the yacht club, which was never locked, and decided that the brass bungs that were screwed into the sterns of the Cadet dinghies in the clubhouse would do the job just perfectly. So, armed with a penny I went around half the boats and unscrewed all the bungs. The castle did look absolutely magnificent when it was finished and I stood back and admired it with great pride. Then the lunch gong, or something else, must have distracted me because I rushed off and forgot to put the bungs back in the boats. The next day there was a race and the crews, all assuming the bungs were in place, rigged their boats and sailed out to the course. Next thing there were Cadet dinghies filling up and sinking everywhere. The mystery of the missing bungs was solved when they were found among the remnants of my sand castle. Automatically I was the suspect; I pleaded guilty and got a boot in the backside that I'll never forget. I must have been forgiven soon after, because I was asked to crew on one of the boats to make up the numbers. Until then my only sailing had been a horrible experience with my brother Tom and a cousin at Port Vincent. My mates and I had also built sailing rafts by strapping kerosene drums together with pieces of timber and rigging a square sail on top. They would only sail with the wind, but we didn't care. While we were only sailing off the beach in front of the yacht club our fantasies had us sailing around the world. Anyway, finally I got to race on a real boat, the twenty foot 12 Square Metre Class Sharpie *Unity*, and I have to tell you it was a little overwhelming. I didn't have a clue what was going on—surrounded by three big blokes who were grunting and groaning and doing their best to keep the boat upright. All of a sudden I was gone, straight over the side. I don't know how it happened but I can remember I just kept sinking . . . going down, and down, and down. I can still see this guy coming down after me, his arm outstretched, trying to grab me. There were bubbles everywhere and, after what seemed like a lifetime, he latched on to me. He pulled me to the surface and dumped me into the boat. I was coughing and spluttering and feeling like a direct relation of the proverbial drowned rat. The experience almost cured me, at a very early age, of a sport that was to become a passion later in life. It was a long while before I sailed again.

The chap who saved me, Boy Phillips, went off to the war soon after and sadly lost his life when the Australian ship he was serving on was sunk off the coast of Java.

Even though I was then only eight or nine I realised first hand what the war meant. The army literally moved in and took over our Seacliff home. Because our house was so large and well positioned it was an ideal location for a military headquarters in the area, so the government simply told Mum that the army was taking it over. Serious as this was it became a period of great excitement for me, with barbed wire and tank barriers appearing on the beach and trenches with sand bags around them being dug into the cliff below the house as well as the sandhills. The army built concrete air raid shelters all over the place. It was like one big game going on around the house 24 hours a day. Below our house and behind the sandhills the army put up a line of buildings with bunks in them, probably for medical purposes. The one thing apparent to me, though, was that they never seemed well organised. I had a great laugh when all their defence equipment on the beach, like metal barriers, barbed wire and concrete blocks, was either washed away or stolen. My games led to me experiencing my own version of a war wound. I was chasing around in the sand dunes with some other kids when I tripped and fell into the barbed wire. I finished up with permanent scars on my chest and legs.

The most memorable and certainly most exciting experience came one night when they had a mock battle. The only problem was that the army chaps at Seacliff almost missed it. Their Intelligence told them that the supposed enemy was arriving at 1 am, but they landed at midnight and took the guys at home by surprise. There were army guys just sitting around our living room rolling cigarettes and drinking tea and coffee while the mock enemy was outside the door waiting for the battle to start. Instead of having to fight their way up to our house from the beach, as was the plan, they literally just walked up and knocked on the door. Talk about embarrassment all around— you've never seen people so embarrassed. After that they all returned to their respective positions and turned some great action. The fifteen pound guns were lighting up the darkness as they blasted blanks out towards the bay. As far as I was concerned I was in the real war, even though I was feeling very safe on our verandah. The way the darkness was being penetrated by the light from the cannon flashes was an incredible sight. It wasn't long after that experience that my mate, Dean Patterson, who lived down below, and I rode our pushbikes all the way down to the outer harbour because we'd heard rumours that there was some action there. It was a big deal, riding something like twelve or fifteen miles down and back. The whole area was controlled by the army, but being just a couple of young kids on pushbikes we were able to talk our way through the checkpoints. We could hardly believe what we saw. There was a huge ship tied up at the dock with a massive, gaping hole in the stern. We got the message that it had struck a mine while negotiating the Backstairs Passage between Kangaroo Island and the mainland, so we assumed that the Japanese were on our doorstep. We were to learn later it was a German mine that did the damage because German raiders had laid mines off many parts of the Australian coast. Later in life a guy I had sailing with me, a retired Australian spy, told me that Adelaide, with its high concentration of Prussian Germans living in the Barossa Valley, was to become New Hamburg in Hitler's plan for the new world. Adelaide was apparently a real hot spot for the Germans and at one stage an Adelaide radio station was discovered transmitting messages to German shipping that was in Australian waters.

Australia was well and truly involved with the war at that stage and everyone was doing their thing for the war effort. At Brighton Public School air raid shelters and trenches were dug into the school grounds and we had air raid practice every day. If there was a long siren sounded you had to drop everything and run like crazy out into the school yard and then into your designated air raid shelter. A quick siren meant there was insufficient time to get to the shelter so we had to take cover under the desks and hope for the best. We all wore identification discs with our name and blood type stamped on them. For us kids it was all a bit frightening, yet at the same time it was exciting. If there was a fun side to all this for me it had to be the School Patriotic Fund, or the SPF for short, which was to raise money for the war effort. The aim was to collect everything that could be recycled, like old batteries or lead in any form, any non-ferrous material, even metal buckles and glass and, to my amazement, old bones for fertiliser. The idea was that for each set amount you collected you received a medal in recognition of the achievement and subsequently additional bars. I saw it all as a real challenge and I was into it at

29

a hundred miles an hour. Much to the satisfaction of my ego I finished up with more bars than anyone else in the school, seven in all. I was very proud then, but I must admit now that there were a few people in the district who were mystified by the disappearance of the lead flashing from their roofs. I comforted myself with the knowledge that it was all for the war effort.

With the shadow of the war getting closer and closer to Australia and my mother's struggle to make ends meet financially, there came a dramatic change in my life. Brother Tom was going to Adelaide University, David was still at St Peter's College and Pam was at boarding school. As strange as it might sound, I think it suited Mum and everybody else to get rid of me for a while. I also think she believed that if the worst happened and Adelaide was invaded I had a better chance of survival being away from town. So, like it or not, my bags were packed and I was shipped off to Port Vincent on Yorke Peninsula, to a farm owned by family friends, Mrs Correll, and one of her sons, Jack. Mum had known them for years because the Corrells had been friends with her aunt, who owned the Ventnor Hotel at Port Vincent. We used to go to Port Vincent as a family almost every Christmas and Easter. Jack Correll was to marry his girlfriend, Glad, but while he was always Jack to me she was Aunty Glad. I think they saw and understood Mum's plight at the time and by mutual agreement they became something like foster parents to me.

I had spent a lot of time on the farm when we went to Port Vincent for Christmas holidays, primarily because brother Tom and cousin John Loutit scored great pleasure from scaring the living daylights out of me when they went sailing. They talked me into going out with them on our little Cadet dinghy *Mermaid*, which had been towed across St Vincent's Gulf from Adelaide behind one of the large yachts. That's the first time I actually remember going sailing. They had me believe I would be safe if they tied me into the bow with a piece of old rope. I was young enough and sufficiently naive to believe them and think they were looking after me. Then once we were out on the water they'd start letting the boat tip over, more and more, until the water started coming in over the side. There I was, tied into the bow of this boat, and they were trying to capsize it. The more I screamed the more they laughed and the more they let the boat lean over. Bugger this, I thought, this sailing is no fun, and as soon as we got back to the beach I was off, gone like a rat up a drain pipe, going as fast as I could on my little scooter, heading straight for the sanctuary of the Corrells' farm. I'd play with the sheep dogs and follow old Jack around, probably being a nuisance but in my mind being a great help. My brother had cured me of my desire for the beach and boats. I was much happier on dry land. Actually, it wasn't until I lived on the farm and went out fishing on a boat with Jack one day that I lost my fear of the water. After we put the boat on its mooring off the beach Jack just picked me up, threw me overboard and told me to swim to shore. It was more splashing than swimming for the first few strokes, then I began dog paddling and headed in the right direction. I made it to the sand and from that moment on I realised I could swim. For me being able to swim was an important part of being able to sail. Later in life though I was surprised to learn that one of the world's great sailors, Dennis Conner, couldn't swim. Dennis said to me one day: "In my business, swimming is a sign of failure."

I have little recollection of leaving Seacliff and being shipped off to the farm. I just remember going there in the Sunday Mail newspaper truck, a ride my mother organised with Beavis Taylor, the manager of the newspaper. What a ride that was. The truck was fitted with what was called a gas producer. As the name suggests, it produced gas to power the engine because the war had brought about an acute shortage of petrol. Every hour or so the driver would have to stop the truck to stoke up the charcoal fire that was producing the gas. My next memory was lining up for school. Life for me over the next two years was just as much fun as it had been at home. The kid who lived on the neighbouring property, Ralph Crouch, used to come by every morning with a horse and buggy and the two of us would trot off to school in town. We would leave the horse tied up all day, then after school re-rig it with the bridle and all that stuff then head for home. If for no other reason that school was memorable because that was the time when I started to see girls in a different light. There were a couple of very pretty ones, especially Nita Starkey. She led me to realise that there was more to girls than what I had experienced with my sister Pam over the years. Girls were actually really nice. Nita certainly left that impression because she would bring flavoured ice blocks to school each Wednesday just for me.

It appeared that Mum's fears about Australia becoming a

31

battlefront were close to being a reality. Everyone at the school was well aware that Darwin had been bombed and Sydney had been subjected to an attack by midget submarines. These incidents placed greater emphasis on the SPF, which my new school operated just like the one we had at Brighton. At Port Vincent what you collected for the war effort was quite different to what you collected at Brighton. Over there wool was a priority and I remember Jack's mother saying that while I couldn't take wool from the shearing sheds I could collect as much as I liked off the barbed wire fences where the sheep had gone through and left some behind. So there I was out in the paddock after school and at weekends pulling this blessed wool off the barbed wire. And yes, I did get more medals from the school in recognition of my efforts.

I have some wonderful and very comfortable memories of those days on the farm, especially with the sheep dogs. I'd ride around in the back of Jack's old buckboard as we called it—a utility truck— with the dogs. I'd jump out at every gate and open it, then leap back up into the back of the truck and have a great conversation with the dogs. Jack had an old workshop out the back of the farmhouse that was like a toy shop to me. He had some beaut old things that I used to mess around with. I really enjoyed the blacksmith's set-up he had because I could try to make horseshoes on the anvil with the help of this old guy who came to work on the farm. I got right in there with him, right into all the hot and dirty work, operating the mechanical bellows to keep the coke red hot. My evenings were also busy. I'd love to draw a plan of the farm, seeing if I could name every paddock and show what crops there were and where the sheep were grazing at the time.

Looking back on Port Vincent I think it was a real-life adventure that most kids can only dream about. I developed a real love for the land and that was the one reason I went back there to work after I completed National Service. And I think that it was on the beach that a deep down, genuine interest for the sea was sparked. It really was the perfect combination for me. The two years at the farm were just the best.

It was Christmas of 1942 when Mum, my brothers and sister came across to Port Vincent for a holiday. At that stage all the signs were pointing to the Allies winning the war. We'd won the battle of the Coral Sea and the Japanese were being pushed back elsewhere. My mum's assessment of the war situation, and her finances, were such that she decided it was time for me to go home to Seacliff.

CHAPTER THREE

Roots of the Vine

As I HEADED into my teenage years I became increasingly aware that the name Hardy and its relationship with the wine industry really did mean something. Ours was obviously a proud family with a wonderful tradition dating back to the mid 1800s. Today, when I look back over the colourful history of the family and the company, Thomas Hardy and Sons, my pride remains as strong as ever. But I cannot deny a considerable element of sadness and frustration weighs heavily on my shoulders because I was the one at the helm of the company when we were forced to relinquish family control. That is a story in itself, but I do hope our founder, my great grandfather, understands. The one consolation is that the name Hardy remains ever so boldly on each bottle of wine, a tribute to the resourcefulness and talents of those who have preceded me.

At this time, with Australia becoming restless over its ties with Britain and considering a more independent role as a republic in the new century, I see my great grandfather, Thomas Hardy, being the classic example of the character and intestinal fortitude that was needed to pave the way to where Australia stands with such pride today. The man showed ingenuity, tenacity, courage and understanding in establishing and developing the company, in caring for his family, and in making important contributions to the community. The only thing that might be seen as being a little unusual these days is that he was twice married, each time to a first cousin. I guess back then if it was OK for a royal family to do it then it was OK for my great grandfather. I scratch my head thinking about that, but his obvious lack of concern was justified because I'm not aware of any problems flowing through to the family today, although some people might disagree.

I had always been fascinated by our family history, so in 1979, after we had finished that terrible Fastnet Race in Plymouth, I decided the time was ripe for me take a trip to Devon and trace the roots of the vine. I wanted to see where old Thomas Hardy came from originally. I drove up to Honiton with my then wife Anne and on to the little township of Gittisham, where it is said he was born "of yeoman farmer stock" on 12 January 1830. That is what the records show, but after making that trip I believe Gittisham was actually the village he was working in before he came to Australia. There are indications he was actually christened and raised in another part of Devon.

I'll never forget walking around the graveyard in Gittisham, among all the old, weather-beaten, tilting headstones, and finding there were Hardys in those grounds. It was a very emotional experience, just thinking back and trying to imagine what it must have been like living there more than a century ago. I did feel I could touch the soil, that I was part of it, and I was home. The graveyard was adjacent to a very old, quaint and equally weather-beaten stone church with an overwhelming aura of history about it and which was almost overgrown by large, dense oaks and other typically English trees. It had a small school attached to it. The school showed that in those days they taught reading, writing, arithmetic and, incredibly, navigation. Navigation! That really pricked a thought. Devon was a famous seafaring county, so it really wasn't surprising that navigation was part of their education. And, thinking back, I believe that being taught navigation was probably one of the reasons Thomas Hardy had little hesitation in taking on the big trip to South Australia to establish his new life.

The story of Thomas Hardy, the establishment of the company, Thomas Hardy and Sons, and the history of our family is well chronicled in a book that our company commissioned from author Rosemary Burden to celebrate our 125th anniversary in 1978. The book is titled *A Family Tradition in Fine Wine Making*. Reading it certainly inspired me to make the pilgrimage to Devon the following year.

To me it seems somewhat ironic that in the year 1830, when

Thomas Hardy was born, Captain Charles Sturt rowed his whale boat down to the entrance of the Murray River. Sturt wrote glowing reports of that part of South Australia, a region that would some twenty years later become home for my great grandfather. Six years after Sturt made his voyage the British Province of South Australia was proclaimed and, only a matter of days before Thomas Hardy's seventh birthday, which was happening thousands of miles away, Colonel Light pitched a tent and began surveying land for what we now know as Adelaide.

South Australia was the one colony in Australia that was free settled. The absence of convicts, freedom from religious persecution and the promise of self-government was very appealing to the English at the time. Things were tough all round in the Mother Country. Life in the industrialised cities was becoming hell, with slums being an everyday part of life. Poverty was commonplace in the rural areas too because of mechanisation and falling wages. Little wonder many of the rural community saw a new life in the colonies as being their only hope for a decent future for themselves and their families.

It appears great grandfather Hardy served an apprenticeship with a merchant-cum-grocer, possibly in Gittisham or Honiton, in his youth. But his future wasn't in that village; it was over the horizon. With it being almost certain he studied navigation at school, he would have had less fear than many migrants of the dangers associated with undertaking such a long and arduous voyage to the colonies. The journal he kept when he and cousin Johanna Hardy left England aboard the *British Empire* in April 1850 shows he had actually considered migrating to America before deciding on the colony of South Australia. The journal, now held by the South Australian Archives, has an entry for 2 June 1850 that reads: "Twelve months ago I was in London and expected to have been on the road to America by this time, but my mind was changed . . . Whether it is for the best or worst remains to be seen. One thing I can say, I have not yet regretted going this way. Mr. Nutting and Mr. Lawrie, Rector and Steward, considered I have chosen wisely. If I have my health I do not fear."

All the signs are that even though he was only twenty years old when he left England he was very mature for his age, and very well organised. The next few weeks in his journal give a wonderful insight into the man: "Sunday, May 5 . . . On Thursday they altered the serving out of the provisions not to have it so often but more at a time. We are put to our wits end to find out what to put things in. The steward . . . that serves out the provisions wanted a fresh list made out of the quantities of each article for each mess. He asked Mr Hy Bletchford the son of the first constable to make it out, he could not do it. I always on the lookout offered to assist him. His father thanked me and I set about it and did it all myself to the satisfaction of the 3rd Mate Mr Hooper who served us with the provisions. From this slight circumstance I have got acquainted with Mr Bletchford and Mr Hooper. Mr B talks quite familiar with me. He told me what he had been and he farmed in Hampshire but was unfortunate, as he says, but I strongly suspect that he brought up his family above his station, a very common thing nowadays. Johanna . . . has borne the voyage so far most capital. Has not been sick at all . . .

"Tuesday, May 7: . . . I made rolls for the steward this morning, he came down and called me this morning. I got a glass of brandy for it. Made them with soda they were not very light, so my little knowledge of baking is no use to me yet. . . . I wish I had brought some brandy with me as they did not search our boxes as reported but we were hurried away so quick and had no time to get anything. . . . I find the graver Parsons gave me very useful. I marked all our tin articles knives and forks the first night. During the last three or four days the things are all at sixes and sevens, I have got back nearly all of ours. How could I if it was not marked? . . . Talk about studying human nature . . . go on board an immigrant ship that is the place to see some part of it."

The first sign that Thomas Hardy had an interest in education, something which would continue throughout his life, came on Thursday, 9 May: ". . . There was a notice up yesterday to say that all who wished for the office of Teacher must apply in writing to N. Colthurst Esq. . . . I have had a great wish to have the office. I therefore went below and wrote the following letter and gave it to the surgeon. 'I have been advised to apply for the office of Teacher. I therefore beg to offer my services in that capacity. Should you consider me a fit and competent person for the situation I will use my utmost endeavours to give satisfaction. Your obedient, humble servant, Thos Hardy.' If I do not get it I suppose this will not lower me in the surgeon's estimation. I should like the situation well enough . . . three pounds is a consideration.

"Tuesday, May 14: . . . on Saturday the surgeon and captain came into our apartment. The surgeon asked me if my name was Hardy, if I had ever been used to teaching. I told him no but I would do my best. He said he had considered that I should not have sufficient authority over them therefore he had thought proper to give the situation to two of us and if I acquitted myself to his satisfaction he would give me two pounds. I thanked him.

"Thursday, May 16: . . . Began writing a letter to my dear Father and Mother. How often my thoughts wander homeward, but my heart and hopes are in Australia."

Thomas Hardy was obviously an energetic, enthusiastic and committed young man with considerable self discipline. These traits were to be the hallmarks of his exceptional life in the years to come in his new homeland. His journal entry for 14 July gives fair indication of just how active he was on board the ship during the voyage to South Australia: ". . . This is the only leisure time I have for writing. My time is so occupied. I get up about half past six (it is not light before seven), wash and dress, make our pudding, get breakfast which consists of oatmeal porridge. We are got very fond of this, although but few of the English use it . . . As soon as breakfast is over I manage to write about half an hour, which is all the time I can spare. At 12 I come down but can scarcely begin to write it is dinner time. After dinner I have an hour or scarcely so much to spare. After school hours, four o'clock, there is seldom light enough to write below, and there is no convenience to write above beside some of them are so damned impudent they will come and look over what one is writing . . . After tea or supper, I go above and smoke a pipe or two for an hour then below and read or cipher by the lamp until near 9 o'clock when I turn in. This is the usual days routine. My time does not play at all heavy on my hands."

Thomas Hardy also revealed a sense of humour and considerable powers of observation throughout the voyage: ". . . There are some of the girls; as may be expected, of very loose morals. There is one they call 'Off She Goes'. She was in the cabin galley last night with seven or eight sailors all round her taking all manner of liberties with her. She has a plaster on her lip today."

Now if you were heading for a new life in a completely new world you wouldn't be too excited if the place you landed in was named Port Misery. But in Port Misery it was that Thomas Hardy

38

first touched South Australian soil. He wasn't too worried because he knew he had plenty going for him, like thirty pounds, a few personal possessions in a wooden box and a body full of enthusiasm. That was a good start in those days. In his diary entry for Sunday, 18 August he notes: "About the first thing on Friday morning Joha. came to me to say that she had an offer to go to Rapid Bay with a Mr Burrows, a large sheep farmer, at twenty pounds a year wages. As the captain and doctor were satisfied as to the respectability of all parties, I advised her to go. I saw the man that engaged her. He told me the particulars, etc. . . . Yesterday morning I put Johas boxes to rights and bade her adieu."

On Monday, 19 August he left the ship, invested his thirty pounds in the bank and, obviously because of his experience in the grocery business back home, tried unsuccessfully to "get a situation in the grocery line" in Adelaide. However, in a matter of days he had secured work "for seven shillings a week with a prospect of a rise in a short time". His journal continually reveals the colour of life in South Australia in those early days as well as his initial lack of ability as a cattle hand and his early interest in vines: "My work was to be keeping cattle among the hills for some time, then bullock driving and work in the vineyard. Altho it was low wages, I thought, I had better embrace the opportunity as I have no doubt that I shall soon be able to better myself and beside, staying about in town is so expensive . . . I bought a few things and wrote a note to Joha . . . and started about 3 o'clock. Was fortunate enough to overtake a bullock dray, rode nearly all the way out. Got to my masters just as they were going to bed, had supper and turned in along with Paddy the shepherd boy into his watchbox, where I could not sleep a wink all night for the swarms of fleas.

". . . The master went up into the hills with me to show the way. About dinner time, however, I had lost sight of my cattle. I hunted high and low for them. About 4 I went home and found they had been there for three hours before me. Next day I was more lucky, but the day seemed very long. On Monday about 4 o'clock I lost them again. I made sure they were gone home, so home I trudged. No bullocks there. Workman took the pony and rode up in the hills and found the cattle not two hundred yards from where I left them. The master then sent and borrowed two bells to put on them. Since then I have kept them very well.

". . . I hope to learn a little more about vines and fruit trees this summer if I stay here. The man told me that vine cuttings should be about 18 inches long with seven or eight eyes and be planted with one eye above ground and pruned low the first and second year."

The property on which Thomas Hardy took his first job was owned by John Reynell. In later years this property would become known as Chateau Reynella and produce excellent wines. In 1982, 132 years after Thomas Hardy worked there, our company bought Chateau Reynella and located the head office there.

At Christmas in 1850 Thomas Hardy decided it was time to move on. He went south, where farmers were paying between three or four shillings a week more, providing rations and offering much better accommodation. The new job he secured on a sheep farm had him just fourteen miles from Johanna, at Rapid Bay.

In July 1851, just a year after Thomas Hardy landed in South Australia, his life and that of so many other new settlers was to take a dramatic change. It was gold. Strikes were being made in a lot of areas in Victoria, and the lure of the excitement and the thought of striking it rich was too much to resist. For Thomas it wasn't all that hard to get there—on horse, in a buggy or by foot—from South Australia. Unfortunately for him though his life as prospector was short lived. He was fined the princely sum of one pound for not having a digger's licence and spent the night in a lock-up. While he cooled his heels he had time to assess the situation at the gold fields. He saw a bigger opportunity for himself in droving cattle across from South Australia for butchering. All those gold diggers had to be fed and they were willing to pay for a good steak. For a period of eighteen months he did very nicely financially, moving cattle from South Australia into the Victorian goldfields.

By 1853 he had given up the droving and married his cousin Johanna who, it appears from the somewhat vague records, was a few years his senior. I still scratch my head thinking about marrying cousins. It does sound a bit like the Royal family. But evidently, in the Common Prayer Book, you can't marry a second cousin but it is OK to marry a first cousin, although even that is not recommended. I believe that in those days they were awake to the fact that if there were bad genes it would show up in later generations. All I can say is that great grandfather Tom and his cousin must have had good genes.

Their life together got off to a pretty good start because the droving had provided sufficient funds to buy land on the Torrens River, three miles down from the settlement of Adelaide and near the township of Thebarton. The property was named Bankside and their first child, Anne Elizabeth, was born there the next year. Five more were to follow: James in 1856, Caroline in 1857, Thomas Nathaniel in 1862, Robert Burrough in 1864 and finally Eliza in 1868. Thomas Nathaniel was my grandfather.

While Johanna was preparing for the birth of their first child, Thomas worked hard clearing the land and in 1854 planted three-quarters of an acre of vines and two acres of fruit trees. Three years later he produced the first Bankside vintage and made history by exporting the first large quantity of South Australian wine to England. Things went very well for him from the outset and in 1859, just nine years after he had arrived in Australia as a very young and enthusiastic new settler, he and Johanna were able to travel to England to see the family and deliver samples of the 1858 vintage to potential buyers.

In the ensuing five years the wine industry in South Australia was to go into turmoil through over-production of poor quality grapes and subsequently poor and cheap vintages. Thomas Hardy resisted the temptation to try to cash in on a quick earn, instead choosing to maintain the price and quality of his wine in the belief that this was the only formula for long-term success. How right he was. In 1863 he had 35 acres of vineyards producing mainly Shiraz grapes. His orchards were made up of four acres of oranges for marmalade as well as citrons and lemons, which were used for candied peel, all of which were bringing a nice financial return.

Money wasn't the only thing on his mind. He wanted to see a strong local community established and took an active interest in the operation of the local school. On more than one of his many overseas trips by sailing ship last century he researched the latest in educational techniques as well as developments in the wine industry. The man was also recognised for his wonderful relationship with his employees. His attitude was described as almost paternal. Each year Bankside would stage a vintage festival where 200 employees, their families and guests would gather for a day of merriment.

Thomas Hardy could also lay claim to being one of Australia's first "greenies". Memories of him that have been recorded include

41

his planting of trees on the roadside to replace the massive eucalypts that had been felled in the name of progress and farming. He would carry a bucket of water on his buggy and water these trees each time he passed. He even made an offer to buy the city of Adelaide's sewage for use as fertiliser and the waste water from the wool washings for irrigation. He thought these two things would be beneficial to his property and stop them from being washed down the Torrens River.

Johanna Hardy died aged 43, not long after the birth of their daughter Eliza in 1868. This left Thomas Hardy with the burden of six children, the eldest being just fourteen. Many of Johanna's family had followed her to Adelaide and it was her younger sister Eliza who moved into the Hardy home to look after the children. Old Thomas Hardy must have been suitably impressed because he married her soon after—another cousin. She died in 1882.

Over the years Bankside produced excellent quality grapes, olives, lemons and oranges. In 1873 Thomas Hardy was presented with his first opportunity to expand. Dr Alexander Charles Kelly, whose name was the twelfth to appear on the Medical Register of South Australia, persuaded seven of Adelaide's well-heeled businessmen to invest in a vineyard. Dr Kelly wasn't the only medico to enter the wine business in Australia. Two other names synonymous with the wine industry came from the same field, Dr Lindeman and Dr Penfold. They undoubtedly saw wine as a wonderful medicine. Dr Kelly's operation was established in the early 1860s, with the vineyard and its products carrying the name Tintara. The shareholders selected this name after deciding their products should carry a native title. Tintinara was the original recommendation, and while it had an appeal it was considered to be too long. It was then abbreviated to Tintara. Things went well for this group in the early years, but turned sour in 1873 when some of the large quantity of wine they exported to England was returned after being declared unsuitable for drinking. That brought the final crunch to an already tight cash flow and as a result the Tintara Vineyard Company went into liquidation. Thomas Hardy sensed an opportunity there so he went down to McLaren Vale, where Tintara was located, and looked around. He decided that, even with the local and international market being depressed, the vineyard was worth buying. He made an offer for it lock, stock and barrel. The offer was accepted and the "barrels", literally, were very much in his favour. Old great grandfather Thomas, using his excellent knowledge of the industry and his skills as a wine merchant, was able to sell all the wine stocked in the cellars at Tintara. It turned into a dream deal because the cash from those sales more than covered the price he paid for the entire vineyard.

Throughout the 1870s and 80s Thomas played an ever more prominent role in the industry. He developed other vineyards in McLaren Vale and bought the old Bellevue Hotel, which was nearby, and turned it into a refreshment and wine establishment. He was also actively involved in wine exhibitions throughout the colony and overseas.

The company really started being a family affair in the mid 1880s when his cousin's son, Thomas Hardy Nottage, joined the McLaren Vale operation as a boy of fifteen . . . and spent the next 66 years there. Then in 1887, when he was 57, Thomas Hardy officially recognised the role of his sons in the business by naming the company Thomas Hardy and Sons Limited. James, aged 32, was involved with sales and distribution, Thomas Nathaniel with the mechanical side of things while Robert became a winemaker and cellarman. The vineyard operations were leaving some strong impressions on visitors, one writing: "Beginning in a small way, Mr Hardy, by his industry and pluck, has become probably the largest and most prosperous cultivator of the soil in South Australia. He gets better profit from each acre of land he cultivates than any farmer in the colony." And in 1892 a South Australian MP, Mr Blacker, announced: " . . . due to Mr Hardy's enterprise, McLaren Vale was changing from a district of deserted farms into one of great activity and increasing prosperity."

By 1894 Thomas Hardy and Sons was the colony's largest wine-maker and was winning a lion's share of the awards at major exhibitions. In the final two decades of last century Thomas Hardy travelled regularly to England, the Continent and America, studying the wine-making industry then passing on his learning to an eager industry back home. His dedication to the community was apparent through some of the positions he held, like Chairman of West Torrens school, a member of West Torrens district council, chairman of the state's first bottle-making and glass works and chairman of a jam, pickle and preserves company. When Federation came at the turn of the century Thomas Hardy seized on the opportunity. Trade barriers between the states had fallen so he immediately sent son James, after whom I was named, to Sydney to establish a branch office and cellar. In 1909 Thomas Hardy's Sydney operation made history, installing Australia's first electric bulb sign.

One event in the company history that sticks in my mind and shows the inherent resilience of the family came in 1905 when there was a disastrous fire at the Bankside cellar. Jack Stoward, who was Thomas Hardy's nephew, had come to Australia in 1892 and been employed by the company. He kept a near meticulous journal and his report on the fire best describes what happened: "It was a Saturday afternoon. Work had been carried on as usual, the whistle blew at one o'clock (closing time) and everyone had vacated the premises. Half an hour later one of the men who had lived on the property a short distance from the cellar noticed smoke issuing from the roof. Immediately he ran to the boiler room and pulled the whistle cord and tied it down. I had just reached home, about half a mile away, when I heard the whistle. I observed the smoke and returned as quickly as possible. The fire had a big hold. I started the steam pump in the well to fill the tanks in the roof of the cellar, hoping to overflow them and thus flood the floors below. It was soon realised that this was hopeless. There was nothing available to fight the fire, no water, nothing we could do. A hot north wind was blowing and the wooden floors and other woodwork were old and dry. The heat was intense and caused the staves of the vats to open and from these thin streams of wine spurted. Spirit vapours from the heated wine caught fire and burnt with blue flames. All the afternoon the fire raged, the top floors and burning casks crashed into the lower cellars, which were three feet to four feet deep with wine. Wine was also running down the roadways in streams. As there were no means of communication, a messenger had to be sent to Adelaide Fire Brigade which arrived about an hour after the fire had started. The Brigade could do very little, for there were no water mains. The nearest main was on Holbrook's Road, but the brigade hose was too short. Subsequently the Hindmarsh Volunteer Brigade arrived, but met with little success. By using its hose (from the Torrens River) it was able to get one pipe line through but it was not of much use [. . .] it was too far through the canvas hose and there was no pressure. The City Fire Brigade had brought down its fire engine, driven by steam, and put hoses from this into the cellar and pumped out the burnt wine onto the fire to try to check it. By 5 p.m. there was very little left."

44

Damage caused by the fire was estimated to have cost £25,000, a lot of money in those days. However, Thomas Hardy and his family ignored the down side of the fire and converted the disaster into an opportunity to upgrade the winemaking facilities. But the fire did bring an end to an era, the decision being to discontinue winemaking at Bankside and concentrate production at the Mile End cellars.

My grandfather, Thomas Nathaniel Hardy, began to play an increasingly important role in the business and the industry about then. He became president of the Vignerons' Association and was recognised for his efforts in campaigning for action against the damage caused by sparrows and starlings at vineyards. But he died a premature death; he was just 49 years old. Sadly, over the years, the Thomas Hardy side of the family has had a pretty tough trot. The men haven't lived long enough to achieve the appropriate financial rewards and enjoy life to the fullest. There's been a thread of death and disappointment all along, first with Thomas Nathaniel going at such a young age, then my father Tom being killed in a plane crash and, more recently, my brother Tom dying from cancer when he was only 56. But old great grandfather Thomas had a pretty good innings. He died in 1912 at the age of 82. I think the obituary in *The Register* newspaper said it all: "Generally regarded as the father of the wine industry in South Australia, he was a grand pioneer who came to South Australia as a young man and by his unbounded energy built up a business which is known in both hemispheres and which has played an important part in winning for the central State such pre-eminence as the producer of wine." When he died he had only one son living and three grandsons to carry on with the business. One of those grandsons was my father, Tom Mayfield Hardy. It's interesting to note that while the company founder was Thomas Hardy and he had a son named Thomas, my father was christened just plain Tom. His mother didn't like the name Thomas, so that was it. Regardless of that break with tradition, Tom Mayfield Hardy named one of my brothers Thomas and he in turn has had a son named Thomas.

My father was Thomas Nathaniel's only son and he entered the business in 1912 after taking a science degree at Adelaide University. He was also quite an athlete and rowed for the university. Actually the two oars he used are still mounted on the wall at our family home in Adelaide. I remember drooling over them as a child. I mightn't have known my father because he died when I was so young, but I was sure proud of his rowing skills. On 4 August 1914, the day World War I broke out, my father was in Montpellier, France, studying oenology at one of the wine colleges there. He rushed home, enlisted with the Ninth Light Horse Regiment and went on to achieve commissioned rank during the early part of the war. He then joined the 3rd Machine Gun Regiment of the Ninth Light Horse. I remember hearing stories as a child about how my father was responsible for one of the better ideas to come out of the war. He was apparently in a battle with the Turks in Palestine when he came up with a theory that the trajectory of machine gun bullets could be calculated. If this was the case then indirect fire could be used. His theory was that if you could tell him where the target was and the lie of the land in between he could work out the arc the machine gun bullets needed to take to hit that target. His superiors were sufficiently impressed to send him back to England to investigate the theory. There he teamed up with a professor and between them they developed a trajectory plotter. It was very successful and was said to have saved a lot of lives, especially at Gallipoli. It was called the Wingham-Hardy Plotter. It was a proud moment for me when I was in the school Cadet Corp to be using machine guns with the plotter fitted.

My father returned home from the war in 1919 and went back into the business. Thomas Hardy and Sons had endured the years he was absent reasonably well and by 1921 the company was recognised as one of the most diversified winemakers in the Commonwealth. However, there were tough times ahead with the Great Depression, and it was my father's job, as Managing Director, to lead the company through that period.

Sailing had become my father's sporting passion in the years after he returned from the war. He raced and cruised extensively on his own yachts and those of friends on the waters around Adelaide and across the Gulf of St. Vincent. He was a founder of the Brighton and Seacliff Yacht Club and was the very proud holder of the first Master Yachtsman's Certificate in Australia, issued on 28 September 1925. His greatest pride and joy was to be the magnificent yacht *Nerida*, built in 1933. One of the greatest moments in my life was to be able to organise for *Nerida* to be brought back into our family in 1971, restored to the beautiful, gaff-rigged configuration that it had when my father owned it, then sail on Sydney Harbour. *Nerida* is our family yacht to this day.

It was through sailing that my father was to meet my mother, Eileen Clara Ponder, an Adelaide girl who had been educated at the Wilderness School, a ladies' college in Adelaide. I know little of Mother's childhood apart from the fact that she was interested in public speaking when she left school—because I remember when I was a child that my Aunt Stella told me sometimes she would get quite fed up with Mum over her public speaking antics. Aunty Stel, being the younger sister, was often forced by my mother to be her audience while she practised for a public speaking competition. One conversation with Aunty Stel on this subject that I remember vividly came while Mum was doing some hostess and promotional work for the winery to get income for our family. On this particular day I thought my mother was going to break into tears while talking to a group of special guests about the history of the winery. But Aunty Stel assured me the emotion was all part of the act. She had seen it all when Mum practised on her.

I think Mum worked as a hairdresser after leaving school before meeting Father. I have a feeling there was another man, a boyfriend, in Mum's life before she met Father because after she died I found a photograph of a young man who lost his life in World War I. The photograph and an incident some years before she died led me to that belief. Mother didn't speak ill of anybody, except one day when I brought up Winston Churchill's name, saying I thought he did a good job in World War II, or Hitler's war as I call it. "And well he might, Jim," Mum fired back at me in the strongest of tones, "because I believe he was responsible for sending the bloom of Australia's and New Zealand's youth to their deaths in Gallipoli. It was awful, just awful." "Oops," I thought. "I'll leave that subject right there."

I never did get to learn a lot about Mother and Father's life together, probably because after Father's death there were other priorities in life for Mum while we were growing up. I know Mum became friends with the Haselgrove family, who had homes on either side of the home my father had built on the hill above the water's edge at Seacliff. Colin Haselgrove, in particular, had been a close friend of my father's, being a senior member of management at Thomas Hardy and Sons for a lot of years and a sailing companion. Apparently it was Easter in the early 1920s when Eileen and Tom met while on a sailing holiday at Port Vincent. Mum spent a lot of holiday time there with her family and actually worked with relatives in the pub during busy times. Mum loved sailing and was invited to go out for a day on the water with my father and friends. I remember Mum telling me about how she persuaded my father to let her steer the yacht. He subsequently let her take the helm, somewhat reluctantly, only to suddenly realise that this woman really knew what she was doing. That was it. My father's life as a confirmed bachelor was rapidly coming to an end. He had found the woman of his dreams.

One of the best stories to come out of their courtship at Port Vincent happened on the beach. In those days there was no such thing as mixed bathing. The men wore neck to knees at one end of the beach and the ladies were in similar costumes at the other end of the sand. Well, I guess things were moving towards a more liberated life in those days because on this day it was a case of boys will be boys and girls will be interested. The gap between the two groups became smaller and smaller until, horror upon horrors, the young men and women were actually swimming together in the middle of the beach. That happened on a Saturday and the next morning my mother, as always when she was in Port Vincent, went to church to take the Sunday School class. The time for Sunday School came and passed with not one child arriving. After a while she became concerned so went down the road to the first of the many homes of the children who normally attended her class. She went up, knocked on the door and was greeted by a woman with a distinct look of disdain on her face. "Where's little 'Johnny'," my mother asked. "Is he coming to Sunday School?" It was all too much for the woman. "We're not sending our son to a Sunday School that has a teacher who goes mixed bathing," she bellowed as she slammed the door in my mother's face. There ended Mother's time as a Sunday School teacher.

CHAPTER FOUR

The Making of a Man

AH, MY TEENAGE years—life's launching pad for an incredibly fascinating voyage of discovery. Adrenalin, the "in" drug of the time, was forever rushing through my body, giving me wonderful highs as I discovered more about sports, sorts and good times. School was thrown in there somewhere as well.

When I got back from Correll's farm it was high summer and my interest in sailing had been fired up enough for me to start hanging around the yacht club at weekends, making a nuisance of myself as only eleven year olds can, offering my services as a budding bailer boy then waiting until someone would give me a ride. Jim Freeman, who still sails with me on *Nerida* in Sydney, gave me one of my first breaks. He was one of the older blokes, one of the stars, at the club and I crewed for him on his cadet dinghy *Mystery*. He was a pretty hard taskmaster who kept bellowing at me every time I stopped bailing. Later I graduated to the fourteen footer *Miss Johnnie*, and it was worse than sailing with Jim. Even on the calmest of days I'd have to bail like buggery to keep the boat afloat—the cracks in the planks were so big I could look through them and see the seaweed on the bottom of the bay. But I couldn't really complain because all the bellowing and the occasional boot in the bum was a fact of life for a young kid who was getting the sailing bug.

It was February 1943 when I became Jim Hardy the young man. I was off to St Peter's College to start in the junior high school, called the Preparatory School. The first morning I marched out of our home very proudly, in full regalia. There I was in my brand new uniform of grey shorts and jacket, grey long socks with blue bands at the top, black leather shoes and the pièce de résistance, a little blue cap jammed down on my head. My brother David, who was in Senior School, was commissioned by Mother to show me how to get to school. He took on the task somewhat reluctantly—it wasn't the "in" thing in those days to be seen with your kid brother hanging around. We set off on the train to Adelaide, where he showed me all the trams I could catch—St Peter's, Tranmere, Payneham and so on—to get me to the school gate. When we arrived at the school David pointed me in the right direction, told me to meet him there after school so he could show me the way home, then disappeared towards the Senior School. He was gone before I could say OK. I just shrugged my shoulders and wandered on into a mass of kids milling around in the playground. At the end of the day, when David delivered me home, he had, as far as he was concerned, fulfilled his obligations. From then on I was travelling solo.

I was to find a considerable difference in the effort required to get to school when it was just behind home and school when it was on the other side of Adelaide. My tardiness around the house, or my interest in my latest project, saw me running late more often than not for the train out of Seacliff station. I'd check the clock, realise that as well as being late for the train I had no time for breakfast, so grab a piece of fried bread with plum jam on it and rush out the door.

The train I caught into Adelaide was an express. It was hauled by a very efficient steam locomotive, the RX class engine. One morning a school mate went close to making Seacliff a no-stop for the RX. As we left home he wiped some grease onto the insteps of his shoes, then when we walked across the railway line near the station he casually wiped his shoes on the railway tracks. The RX came whistling along, hit the grease and shot clean through the station that morning. When it finally stopped only the last half of the last carriage was on the platform. We were amazed how little grease it took to get that result.

I found considerable comfort in going to the same school as my brothers and my cousin, Bob Hardy. The atmosphere at St Peter's was warm and there was an air of confidence around the place. The lovely old red brick buildings of the Preparatory School seemed to emit an inviting aura. There was nothing too inviting though about the cold showers we had to take after PT—physical training—which happened every morning at 11 o'clock. I was among the fittest and the fastest during PT—the fittest when it came to the exercises and the fastest when it came to getting in and out of those freezing showers. I hated it so much that they left a lasting memory. To this day I can't stand cold showers.

The cold looks I got from Mum when my first report cards came home from my teacher, Mrs Shepley, weren't too good either. They said things like: "Jim would do better if he concentrated more," and "If Jim would do this or Jim would do that his results would improve." Bah!

The start of the following summer was just the greatest. That was when Mum came up to me one memorable day and said: "Oh Jim, you look like you're getting interested in sailing. Why don't you take on the old Cadet dinghy *Mermaid* for the season." I was dumbfounded. The excitement inside me was going crazy and I could hardly speak. "Me," I thought. "Take on the family dinghy. By myself. Wow." Right there and then all my dreams expanded into a myriad of new colours. A new and even more exciting world was before me. No more going down to the yacht club and trying to bludge a ride; no more hanging around just waiting and hoping. I had my own boat, and I was the skipper.

The moment Mum said *Mermaid* was mine I was off to the yacht club like a scalded cat. I couldn't get there quick enough to look it over and make my plans. *Mermaid* had been in the family for a lot of years but in more recent times it had been neglected because brother Tom, who had been sailing it, decided building a 24 foot auxiliary yacht and racing on big boats was far more important. There it was, my dream boat, all twelve feet of it, sitting in the back corner of the club looking, until that moment, very unloved and unwanted. To see *Mermaid's* old rudder propped up against the wall, scarred with a crack from top to bottom, reminded me of a secret I'd kept for a lot of years. The rudder had once broken into two pieces. It happened when my father came home one night and drove the car into the garage to the sound of splintering timber. He hadn't noticed the rudder lying on the garage floor and drove right over it. He and my brothers assumed the rudder, which had been stored against the wall, had fallen over. Father, I was told, had taken full responsibility and made the repair. What no one else but Jim Hardy knew was how the rudder really came to be lying on the garage floor. Some little boy had been playing with it that day and left it there. To see the rudder again reminded me of how I had kept my secret for so long and not admitted responsibility. It also reminded me yet again of how I could remember incidents involving my father but still couldn't focus on a picture of him in my mind.

Battle scarred as it was, Mermaid was a beautiful boat. Who cared if you could see daylight through the cracks in the planks and that the varnish was peeling off, and who cared if it was grossly overweight for a racing boat? To me it was just like Christmas. This wreck of an old boat was the greatest thing of all time. My first thought was to patch her and the logical solution for a kid my age was to use plasticine. So there I was resurrecting Mermaid, pressing plasticine of all colours into the cracks, when old Commodore Bob Freeman, my friend Jim Freeman's father, came up to me and told me I was fighting a losing battle. "That'll just wash out," he said to me. "The boat will float like a brick. You've got to forget that idea, Jim. You go home to bed and I'll leave some proper putty on the boat for you later tonight." And as if that wasn't enough of a great offer, he told me that if I did get the boat floating by mid-morning the next day I could row him, the Commodore, out to the official boat so he could take the salute for the season's opening day. Wow!

I found it hard to sleep that night. I kept waking up, checking the time and waiting for the slightest sign of first light. This was even more exciting than getting up at daybreak and going out with the milkman on his horse and cart years earlier. I arrived down at the club when it was still dark, excited, really excited, and sure enough old man Freeman had honoured his word. The boat was there upside down and on top of it was this brown paper parcel stained with the linseed oil from the putty that was inside. I puttied and puttied and puttied for more than five hours, frantically searching across every plank in the hull looking for the tiniest of cracks to be filled. My timing was perfect because just as I declared the job complete Commodore Freeman was standing at the water's edge, resplendent in his crisp white regalia which was topped off with gold braid on his cap and gold on his epaulettes, looking something like scrambled egg. My moment of glory had arrived. I, eleven-year-old Jim Hardy, was not only about to launch my own sailboat, but would row the Commodore out to the official boat for opening day. Some of the older guys helped me carry the boat out of the shed and down the launching ramp. As the water kissed Mermaid's hull for the first time in her new life I watched, wide-eyed, looking for signs of seepage. Bloody hell, there it was, water rushing in through the bottom of the centreboard case in the middle of the boat. I'd missed a crack in a joint. My calculations, grossly affected by pride, were that if I rowed fast enough we would reach our destination with only our feet getting wet. How wrong I was. As we drew alongside the official boat Mermaid submerged and sent a very embarrassed young man and the Commodore for a swim.

It was a somewhat ignominious start to my sailboat racing career. But the following week, after I had patched the leak using hot pitch and assembled my mates David Walker and Pat Malone as crew, we went out for our first race. It was like lambs to the slaughter, but in the ensuing months we were to learn a lot about sailing simply by making mistakes. Our performance on the water was always far from spectacular, especially when we started racing because we didn't have a jib, just a mainsail. Eventually we did find an old, worn-out jib that was next to useless, but at least it gave us two sails. Both sails were so rotten we spent as much time patching them as we did racing the boat. We were forever patching, once because we foolishly copied the big boys, who had left their boats anchored off the beach one night. They were too lazy to put them ashore over night and re-rig them the next day for another race so we followed suit. A storm came up that night; Mermaid broke loose from her mooring and was unceremoniously dumped onto the beach almost at the front door of the yacht club. That incident alone taught us a lot about weather forecasting.

Before going sailing each weekend I had to get the line marker out and prepare the court for Mum's tennis parties, which were a local social highlight for her friends. While she played tennis, she would watch me race Mermaid. We were very easy to see because Mermaid was always at the back of the fleet. Over the years some amazing people would be at home for the tennis, including a very young Rupert Murdoch. His father, Sir Keith Murdoch, owned the Adelaide News newspaper and Rupert was working there as a junior executive after returning from studies in England. He was at our place most Sundays and quite often went sailing with brother Tom. Rupert started to really enjoy sailing and one day he asked Tom which was the best yacht in Adelaide. Tom replied without hesitation that the best boat was the 58 foot Alden-designed ketch *Ilina*. Rupert's immediate response was: "OK. I'll buy it." And he did.

The one person who really stands out in my mind from that era is Sir Douglas Mawson, the Antarctic explorer and one of the greatest Australians of all time. Sir Douglas and his wife Bequita would come around not only for tennis but for bridge nights as well. It was spellbinding for a thirteen year old to sit there and talk to him about his trips to Antarctica. My imagination would run wild as he told me stories of his exploits, especially about the trip south with Shackleton. He was acting as a lieutenant to Shackleton and was in charge of the loading of the stores on the ship in Sydney in preparation for the expedition. One of the big breweries in Sydney was more than enthusiastic about the trip and kept insisting on the team accepting a donation of beer to take to the base in Antarctica. Sir Douglas was equally insistent they didn't have room for the beer. He finally softened his line to a wait-and-see attitude—if there was room on the ship after everything was loaded, then he'd consider the offer. Needless to say, other members of the expedition, knowing the beer was there for the taking, made sure they loaded the ship to leave enough room for the eighteen gallon kegs. On went the beer and off went the explorers. But any thoughts the junior members of the team had about relaxing with a perfectly chilled beer at night were quickly dashed. Sir Douglas saw the kegs as perfect ballast on the sleds when training the huskies—the dogs would rocket around the base dragging kegs of beer behind them. The pressure was on Sir Douglas for some time to tap a keg, but it wasn't until the following summer, when the temperature was around –10°C, that the nod came. The bung was removed, then shock, horror, they weren't greeted by a fabulous gush of foaming brew, just ice. That didn't deter these blokes. They knew you couldn't freeze alcohol. So they drilled into the centre of the big, wood-encased ice block and found the still liquid alcohol. They said it was like liquid gold, the sweetest liqueur they had ever tasted, so much so that some members of the team vowed to return to Sydney to market beer liqueur.

Sir Douglas also related the story of what is still regarded as one of the world's greatest feats of endurance, his trek across the ice to locate the magnetic South Pole. He was the only survivor of the trek, and that came as a miracle. My mind was painting amazing images as he told me how, in the final stages, he had fallen down a crevasse. "But you got out," I said with a look of amazement. "I had to, Jim," he said. "I don't know how I got out and I don't know where I got the strength to get out. All I knew at the time was that I had to get out and get back to the base because if I didn't, no one would have known what had happened to the expedition." Apparently when he did get back to the base he was in such terrible condition with frostbite and exposure they couldn't recognise who he was. On the lighter side, when I asked about searching for the magnetic South Pole, he said they had a compass rigged in such a way that when they were right on the spot the compass needle would actually stand on its end, vertically. "We all thought this was terrific when we found it," Sir Douglas said. "And to celebrate we had a bit of rum and a great night. In the morning, when we woke up, the South Pole had gone—disappeared." They were about to realise just how much the magnetic South Pole moved each day. They had to then go out and find it once more.

I would relate these stories to my mates at school and they would listen with intense interest. It was a real-life adventure coming first hand. For me school was providing other adventures in the form of Australian Rules football during the winter months and cricket in summer. The entire school was divided up into houses and I was nominated to Wall House, which took its name from a famous Australian cricketer. Gold was our colour for the intra-school cricket and football we played. Scholastically things were going OK. I found my level of success was proportionate to my attitude towards the teacher, and the teacher's attitude towards me. If we liked each other then I did well. One thing that I didn't enjoy was learning German. Mrs Gruendberg persevered with me for a couple of years, but I couldn't handle it. Having three genders on a table at the same time was a bit much for me—the table was masculine or something, and the cup was feminine or something, and the water was neuter. I was lost.

Discipline was always very strict at school and came in its worst form as after-school and weekend detention. An error in one's ways during the week would bring a one hour detention after school on Friday and, worse still, an additional hour on Saturday morning. That meant putting on your school uniform and heading off to school on Saturday morning for just 60 minutes. In a way it was a double dose of punishment because everyone who saw you in uniform on Saturday knew you had been a bad boy and were heading off to pay your penance. My worst experience with detention, one that I regretted, came as a result of my being late for a music class. The music lessons were conducted across in the Senior School and I calculated that the quickest way to get there and make up for my tardiness would be to pinch a guy's bike, which was in the school bike rack. He wouldn't notice the bike missing for the duration of just one music lesson, I thought. I'd have it back in the bike rack before he knew it.

Wouldn't you know it—he or someone else saw me hurtling across the school grounds on the "borrowed" bike because I was reported to the Prep School Headmaster, Mr "Cricketer" Clayton. I was duly summoned to the Headmaster's office, where I was told I was in for a two hour detention. A detention was bad at the worst of times, but this one came in the week leading up to Easter and I was scheduled to sail over to Port Vincent with our neighbour, Colin Haselgrove, on his lovely old yacht *Vamp* for the Easter holiday. The first detention was on the eve of Good Friday at a time when I was supposed to be catching a train down to Outer Harbour to join the yacht. I have never pleaded and grovelled so much in my life, all in a desperate bid to get out of coming back to detention on Easter Saturday. Finally Mr Clayton agreed, but to make his mark he kept me at school that night until just before the departure of the very last train to Outer Harbour. I rushed out to a tram, ran to the train station and made it to Outer Harbour, vowing all along to never again touch another kid's bike.

During all my younger years I was always an independent person. I could make my own fun and have a great time doing it. Such was the case when I decided I should borrow brother Tom's .22 calibre rifle and a couple of packets of bullets and head off up to a part of the vacant gully about a mile from home where we had a bitser track for racing. I thought it would be fun to shoot a few rabbits, something I had done while over at the Correll's farm a few years earlier. The fact that I was back in suburbia didn't matter to me; there were rabbits out there to be had. So there I was firing a few shots and next thing this bloke came rushing over the hill calling out what sounded like "Stop, stop." My only thought was: "Jeez, I've got to get out of here," so I started running. I kept looking over my shoulder to see this big bloke gaining on me rapidly. My first thought was to get rid of the evidence, the bullets, so I heaved them under one bush and kept running like blazes towards home, still clutching the rifle. Finally this bloke caught me—it was the local policeman in plain clothes. He grabbed me, shook me and said: "What's your name?" "Jim Hardy," I stammered, absolutely terrified. "How old are you?" "Fifteen," I replied, trying to sound every inch the man. Out came his notebook and he started writing—it gave me time to try to regain my composure and work my way out of a very awkward situation. It was time to be honest. "Actually, I'm only thirteen," I said sheepishly. Lying about my age had only lasted about three minutes. It was better to come clean and hope the cop would show more sympathy and understanding towards a younger man. Boy, was I frightened. It was as close as one could come to having "it" running down my legs. He confiscated the rifle, then took me back to the police station at Seacliff and gave me the biggest dressing down you could ever imagine. As far as I was concerned I was in deep, deep trouble. I was going off to gaol. I was gone. I've never been so scared in my life. And as if that wasn't enough I had to go home at some stage and face the music with Mum. Finally, I was allowed to leave the police station and head for home. When I arrived the policeman had already been around and told Mum what had happened. It was a very cool night in the house that evening. It was an experience that really steadied me; no more rabbit hunting in the suburbs of Adelaide.

From then on my only experience with guns was to come through school Cadets. When I started at St Peter's the choice was either Scouts, Sea Scouts or Army Cadets. In Preparatory School I went for Scouts, but once I entered Senior School the Cadets were the go, due in part to the pride I felt in my father and his military service. Every Monday, right through to the end of Senior School, it was on with my army Cadet uniform and off to school. The one disadvantage of Cadets over Scouts, especially when I was younger, was having to lug big 303 rifles around on parade. The things seemed to be as tall as I was and felt just as heavy. One week of our May holidays each year was spent at Woodside Army camp, and that was a lot of fun. I look back on it as very good training for a young man—an excellent form of discipline. There was another advantage of course. Being in uniform every Monday meant I didn't have to do PT. It was considered to be too difficult to get out of and back into the uniform in time. Even better was the fact that I faced one less cold shower each week.

A high water mark in my sailing career came in my second winter back home after the stint at Correll's farm. Our first season of racing *Mermaid* had been the apprenticeship as far as I was concerned and now it was time to get serious, using whatever I could find to make her a better boat. I had the good ship at home so I could work on her at night and weekends. The hull was still very much the worse for wear, with cracked planks being the biggest bugbear. My crew was just as enthusiastic for the old girl and would come around and work with me putting patches on the hull. If I couldn't make new fittings for the boat from what material was lying around home then I would have to work to save and buy it. However, we did have a sponsor, in the loosest sense of the word, in the form of the state's railway. While travelling to and from school on the train each day my keen eyes noticed the wonderful woodwork in the carriage, and how it was held in place with brass screws, the perfect fastenings for boat building. Brass screws were not available for purchase because of the war, but *Mermaid* was a lady in need. I, Jim Hardy, couldn't steal them so I thought the best thing I could do was to replace them. I went down to where brother Tom was building his yacht and found steel screws that were nearly identical to the ones used on the trains. I took a pocket full of them, found a suitable screwdriver and was then fully prepared for my trips to school. For every four brass screws I removed I used two steel ones to hold the panels in place. I thought that was a fair exchange, and the carriage remained intact. How very considerate of me. At one stage I found I had been cheated—one of the screws I used on *Mermaid* began rusting. It was a brass-plated steel screw. I overcame that problem by removing a magnet from a radio speaker brother David had built and used it to check every screw before I removed it.

One night I was toiling away on *Mermaid* while Mother was entertaining guests from our interstate branch offices with a barbecue at home. During dinner Ralph Kelly—his nickname was "Ned Kelly"—came out to the garage to watch the budding boat builder at work. He was a great friend of my father's, a tough Gallipoli veteran and great salesman who became New South Wales Manager of Thomas Hardy's after my dad died. "What are you doing, young fellow?" he inquired, standing at the garage door. I explained the patching and the circumstances surrounding *Mermaid*. I told him how we'd had a lot of fun with her in our first season but were far from competitive, even though we'd finally found an old jib. "Our real problem is sails," I said. "They're rotten and I'm forever repairing them." He asked why I couldn't get new ones. "New sails . . . we can't afford new sails," I said. "Besides, there aren't any new sails available here in Adelaide. The only bloke making sails for these boats is a guy named Salton in Sydney." So much for that conversation, until some months later when my mother came out to me and said, with what I now know was a mock look of surprise: "Oh Jim, there's a parcel here for you from Sydney."

"A parcel," I said, completely puzzled, "from Sydney?" Mother just turned and walked away as if not interested—not much she wasn't. She knew what was going on. I opened this parcel and blow me down, it's a brand new jib and mainsail for *Mermaid* made by W. Salton of Drummoyne, Sydney. On top of the sails was this card from Ralph Kelly wishing me all the luck in the world. Jeezus, you would have thought I'd won the bloody lottery. I was whooping and hollering, wanting to let the world know my good fortune. There was new enthusiasm for the patching and painting of the hull over the rest of winter. How fantastic it was to get *Mermaid* down to the club for the first race of the new season and pull out the new sails for all to see. The old girl had a new lease of life and instead of coming last, last and last in every race, we kids were starting to beat some of the older blokes by coming second last and third last. We were on our way up the ladder.

Frustration with the seemingly endless amount of maintenance required for *Mermaid*, and our lack of competitiveness with the new sails, led me to decide to build the new Cadet dinghy. The only way I could get that new hull and do the sails justice was to build it myself. I had watched brother David build telephones and Tom build yachts and decided all that was needed to build a new boat was desire and determination. Tom's girlfriend, whom he later married, was Barbara Begg, daughter of Keith "Doc" Begg, an Adelaide customs agent who built boats in his spare time. Hearing that I wanted to build a Cadet, Doc offered to introduce me to George Ross, the doyen of Adelaide's boat builders, who lived out at Woodville. Doc took me out there and I met this wonderful old man who reminded me of a philosopher who knew just everything about building sailing boats, and life in general. To me the old iron shed where he had worked was like a miniature maritime museum. He was too old to build boats any more but he proudly took time to walk me through his shed full of memories, showing me all his tools, all the different types of timber, the moulds he used to build different boats and at the same time explaining some of the techniques he used. I was like a kid in a candy store. As if that wasn't enough he offered me the use of his Cadet dinghy moulds and patterns and then, to my amazement, said he would sell me all the western red cedar I would need for planking the hull. That timber was like gold in those days. It was perfect for planking but was almost impossible to find. However, old George just happened to have some of the very finest tucked away under his house.

I had everything I needed to build my boat—except the money. There was only one answer—off to work in Dave Walker's father's market garden. Every weekend and often after school I'd be down there working. Cucumbers were the big thing, along with tomatoes, peas and beans. The beans were far from my favourite; I didn't like bending over all day picking string beans. Seeing the cash tin starting to fill up did help though and eventually, with a little push along from Mum's purse, I found I had enough to buy the timber and start building. My crew was as keen as ever so weekends and nights were devoted to the project. After putting the timber frames of the mould in place, our first part of the building job was to attach the two planks called the garboards, which ran the full length of the hull, on either side of the keel. After some pushing and shoving we three junior boat builders got the garboard for the starboard side located, then split six planks trying to get the port side plank attached. Finally, with all the planks in place, it was time to fit the ribs inside the hull so it would hold its shape and have strength. I'd seen my brother steaming the ribs for his yacht to make them bend into shape without any effort so I set up a similar system with a long, six inch diameter steam pipe stuck out of the garage window and down to a fireplace. To fuel the fire we walked along the nearby railway line and collected coal that had fallen from the steam train tenders. We lit the fire, put water in the pipe and boiled it before inserting the karri timber ribs. After steaming for a while the ribs would go really soft, then we would take them out, bend them across the inside of the hull and finally attach them to the planking. My woodwork classes at school with Mr Bob Matthews, George Ross's good tips and Doc Begg's encouragement made all this seem a relatively simple task. Even when we did strike a problem there was always someone there to help. The only person not really interested was brother Tom, who had discovered love and university were far more important things than his kid brother's boat. We improvised where we could, even to the extent of going into the mangrove swamps near Port Adelaide at low tide to find the perfectly angled piece of mangrove branch to shape into a corner piece to strengthen the hull or support the seats. The state railway once again contributed with, you could say, the supply of brass screws.

It took us all winter to build the boat and it turned out beautifully. Incredibly, it seemed naming the boat was far more difficult than building it. All I knew was that I wanted an Aboriginal word. I searched through books for weeks but it wasn't until a friend of Mum's in Sydney sent down a handwritten list of Aboriginal words and their meanings that I found nocroo, meaning speed. I thought: "That's me. Speed. That's the way to go." So *Nocroo* it was. My crew had great fun with the name, continually reminding me it should be "no crew". Oddly enough it turned out that the "c" in the name should have been an "o"—the woman's handwriting hadn't joined it properly. So I read it as "nocroo" instead of "nooroo". But *Nocroo* it was named and *Nocroo* it remained.

I find it interesting to compare what we were achieving as thirteen and fourteen year olds back then with what similar aged kids are doing today. Sure it's a generalisation, but our fun involved things we made—rafts and billycarts and bits for the boat. I know that when my son David and his mates were thirteen or fourteen I thought back to what I was doing at that age: I was building my own twelve foot Cadet dinghy to race. If I had given these young guys a plan and some wood at that age and said "go to it", they would have looked at me blankly and asked "how" and "why". In many ways I think we were more fortunate as children when compared with those of today's society. Our fun was self generated and essentially self funded. And with no television or computers it was a very different life. Some evenings there would be homework to be completed, on other nights I would work on the boat or the sails. Often I would spend an evening after supper glued to the radio listening to exciting serials like "The Shadow" and "The Search for the Golden Boomerang".

The highlight of each season was the trip to Kangaroo Island for a regatta. It was a big deal, especially for a kid my age, loading the boats onto a big sailing ketch down at Port Adelaide. The first year I took *Mermaid* and the next year was with *Nocroo*. On the trip with *Mermaid* we sailed across on the *Reginald M*, a huge trading ketch about 100 feet long which today is on display at Warrnambool. The other ketch accompanying us was called *Adonis*. Off we went down to the island under full sail on this ketch, our Cadet dinghies tied to the deck. How fantastic it was to be going away with the older blokes from the yacht club for a week of sailing. Of course, being men, we drank grog and had a wow of a time on the trip. It all came to an end for me after just three days. Down I went with a dose of the mumps and spent the rest of the week in the hospital on the island. My brother Tom was down there with his beautiful 24 foot yacht *Lialeeta*, so it was decided that the best way for me to get back at the end of the week was with him on his yacht. I could stay warm and be well looked after, as the doctor requested. The doc told Tom I had to keep my neck and face warm and wasn't to be out in the cold air. Tom had other ideas. He and his crew had their girlfriends on board for the trip back to Adelaide's Outer Harbour, so the last place they wanted to be was up on deck. And the last place they wanted me was below deck. There I was, all rugged up but out in the cold air, sailing *Lialeeta* home by myself, wondering just what on earth was going on down below.

The next year we took *Nocroo* down to the island aboard *Adonis* and, being a year older, my crew and I were then real men. We were going to really drink with the older blokes. We had a flagon of port that had found its way out of my mother's cellar, unbeknown to her. When we pitched our tent on the beach I buried the flagon for safekeeping. Unwisely, I didn't tell one of my crew, Dave Walker, where I'd buried it. The next scene was Dave going around dropping big rocks on the fly of the tent to keep the draught out. There was a dull thud as one rock hit the ground. The sand started changing colour to a deep red. The flagon was broken and all the Gold Label port started seeping to the surface. We were obviously determined to have a drink on that trip so made some alternative arrangements. It was to be the first time in my life I had over-indulged. I don't remember it, but Dave Walker tells me that at around 3 am, after a big party, I was down on the beach sitting in about three inches of water, fully clothed, trying to clean myself up. I was a sick boy. The demon drink had struck.

Having achieved my Qualifying Certificate through a pretty good exam result I was then out of Preparatory School, into long pants and off to Senior School. My results remained commensurate with my attitude towards the master. Part of the problem with the teachers was that Hitler's war led to the school recycling some old timers. One or two who were brought back, like Crusty Gillam, were wonderful, but it seemed others were there just for our entertainment. One we called Socrates was just off the planet—an absent-minded professor—highly qualified scholastically, but as far as teaching me was concerned he was a dead loss. One of the disappointing turning points for me came when I was transferred—put up a class because I'd topped my grade. After that I just couldn't get going, hating the new environment and not liking the new master. I didn't start doing well again until I returned to my original master, the guy I liked, Mr Horace Matters. I guess I was king of the kids in the original class, then became a smaller fish in a bigger bowl when they moved me up.

I had my moments of madness at school and, just like the incident with the bike in Preparatory School, I seemed always to be on the receiving end of my own stupidity. There was a rowing machine at school, a unit that was fixed in one position over a pool so the school crews could train. While I was watching these older guys go through a session one day I saw the opportunity to level a score with a guy, Bill Hollis, who had been giving me a hard time. I didn't like him at all so, with a hatpin at the ready, I waited for my chance then gave him a not-so-subtle prod. He howled and I took off around the swimming pool with him chasing me. I tripped, went hurtling through the air and crashed headlong into the edge of the pool, knocking myself out. I woke up in the school infirmary hours after the incident. Concussion was my reward.

Hollis was to level the score with me a while later. One day I was watching through the keyhole into the prefect's room while this guy, Bungey, was caning a mate of mine. Bill Hollis came up from behind and gave me one almighty shove. Crash! I hit the door, it burst open, and I executed a spectacular somersault into the room, stopping right at the prefect's feet. "OK, Hardy, you're next," the prefect bellowed. I got six of the best, one for gate-crashing and the others for good measure.

There was always keen competition in the sporting activities at the school. It seemed that every afternoon we had some type of competition. Standard sports it was called where you scored points each day for your level of success in whatever was going. We were down the back of the school on one of the ovals one day where I was competing in the long jump. We were allowed three jumps, and after completing my first I returned to the group waiting for their second attempt. While I was standing there I noticed a group of guys running around the track doing an 880 yard race. Well, by the time they got to where I was they had almost completed the first of two laps and I thought: "Here's a chance to really get some points." So I eased myself into this group as they ran past. I picked up the pace and thought: "Hell, if I go hard enough I could win this race and get maximum points." We came around the final turn and I ran as hard and as fast as I could and finished sixth. That was great for me because I hated running. They logged my time and I was as pleased as punch, knowing I'd taken a lot of points. Two days later one of my school mates, Gerry Hargrave, came up to me and said: "Oh, congratulations, Jim. I see you've made the athletics squad." I said: "What do you mean?" "Jim, you're in the long distance running squad—the 880 squad." He didn't need to say any more. The next scene was Mr Vollugi, the athletics coach, lining up his squad, about ten of us, for an 880. After I staggered home a distant last Mr Vollugi came up to me and asked: "Are you all right, Hardy?" "I am sir. I'm just a little puffed." He then asked if I was ill, to which I responded that extreme fatigue at that time was my only problem. "Is that as good as you can run, Hardy?" "That's—puff— the best—puff—I can—puff—possibly run," I gasped. "Oh dear," he said. "Then I'm afraid you'll have to be excused from the squad." "Oh, don't worry about it," I said with a feigned look of distinct disappointment.

Guy Fawkes Night was an adventure each year. It seemed that the blast you got was proportionate to your age. Whereas when you were young things like throwdowns, Tom Thumbs and sparklers were the go, in your teenage years it was penny bungers, twopenny bungers, yankee boys and anything else that would cause a big bang. Like everywhere else in Australia bonfires burned on Guy Fawkes Night, nowhere more so than down at the yacht club. The guys collected trees and timber from all over the district to create a very impressive inferno. It was a perfect opportunity for some fun. My mates and I had learned at St Peter's College that if you mixed sulphur, saltpetre and carbon you could make a bang that would make a twopenny bunger a mere pop in comparison. This year we made a perfect brew, sealed it in a piece of copper pipe and slipped it into the base of the yacht club bonfire while no one was looking. Talk about the night going off with a bang. Everyone was standing around having a wonderful time, letting off skyrockets, bungers and these sparkling things while watching the bonfire burn down to a pile of red embers when suddenly there was an almighty explosion. Everyone got a great laugh out of it after the initial shock, so the following year we decided we'd make it a tradition. Unfortunately, youthful exuberance outweighed common sense. When we couldn't get saltpetre from the school we started using potassium chlorate in our pipe bombs. We knew how dangerous it was, how it would explode if you hammered it or put it under excessive pressure, because we used to put small mounds of it on the train line. The old steam train would come rattling along, hit the little mounds and there would be a very impressive bang, so much so the poor old train driver would stop the train then get out to see if he still had all his wheels. One night we were out in the garage at home—Pat Malone, Dave Walker and me—foolishly making pipe bombs using potassium chlorate. Pat and I were standing over these tubes being, we thought, ever so careful, gently tapping them shut with a hammer. We obviously weren't gentle enough because next there was an incredible explosion. We were blown out through the garage door and Dave, seeing the blood everywhere, shouted: "Jim, are you OK? I think you've blown your hand off."

I looked down and saw everything was in one piece. "My hands are OK. It must be Pat," And sure enough, there was Pat with a finger and the lower part of his hand blown apart. Mum was having a dinner party in the house and Walker, as only he could do, walked into the house and said casually: "Sorry to interrupt but we've had an accident outside. I think you should come out." Thankfully my cousin from New Zealand, a trained nurse, and her husband, a doctor, were there. They put a tourniquet on Pat's arm while someone called an ambulance. It was a horrible sight all round with the garage, which was swimming in blood. This all happened not long before we were to sit for the Intermediate Certificate at school. Pat finished up doing most of his exams from a hospital bed and, wouldn't you know it, he passed with ease while Dave scraped through and I fell by the wayside. I passed only three of the necessary five subjects.

Life's education was very broad based at this stage. Through Mum's involvement in the church I became interested in religion and for a time assisted the minister with communion at the local All Saints Church. Of course it was Hardy's port we used to mix with water to prepare for the service. In what became a regular ritual, Reverend Lloyd would hold the chalice with the port in it and I'd start pouring in the water. "Not too much water, Jim. Not too much water," he'd say anxiously. Then he would take an impressive swig, checking that the formula was acceptable.

Around this time horses also played a part in my life. It was an experience that didn't come through desire, but necessity—to keep the damn things alive. With so much vacant land around us there was plenty of room for riding, and both sister Pam and brother David had horses. Pam had things worked out very nicely for her horse, Judy. She was at The Wilderness School as a weekly boarder, but that didn't matter because young brother Jim could look after the horse and she'd graciously let me ride it. There I was out the back of home every day feeding bloody Judy. David, without consultation with me, decided on a similar arrangement for his horse, named Bracelet, a retired racehorse. Boy, it must have been great having a kid brother to fill in the gaps in one's life. I wasn't overly excited about riding these things, but one day I did rig Bracelet and head off down Brighton Road from the cement works. Things were going just fine, tentative as I was, until a big blue cement truck roared past, stirring up dust and gravel. That was all too much for Bracelet and she took off at a million miles an hour, bolting into an open paddock with me still attached. A jockey I am not, so when this thing started hurdling hollows and fallen trees I was in a lot of bother. One foot came out of the stirrup and the big slide was on, right around, underneath its stomach until I was being dragged along the ground. Finally my foot came free from the other stirrup

66

and I went out the back of the horse, under its hooves, like a skittled dog. I was pretty dusted up, cut and bruised, but nothing was broken. I walked home, determined to give Bracelet a kick in the bum and even more determined to tell Pam and David what they could do with their hayburners.

Rough times weren't the only thing to be had. There were some really beautiful experiences in the form of girls, beautiful girls. No one had to teach me anything about them—it was all coming very naturally. Social activities were generally restricted to weekends because school hours were long and demanding, especially when I was rowing. They were long days, leaving home before eight in the morning and not getting back until eight at night. The hub of our social activities at weekends was the Argosy on the foreshore at Seacliff. There was a milkbar at one end, a fish and chip shop at the other and in between you had all the action—theatre, dance hall, roller skating, badminton. Most Saturday nights our entertainment was found in the theatre. If you had struck it lucky you would take a girl, show her off to your mates, then go and sit up the back of the theatre to discover how receptive she was to your advances. If you weren't with a girl, as was more often the case for me, you would spend the night on the prowl, trying to woo one away from a flock—we were at an age when most girls thought there was safety in numbers. The local dances held at the Argosy also provided opportunities to extend the hand of friendship to the opposite sex and many a good time was had at these functions. Sometimes the action was down at Glenelg, so the big deal was to sail there in the afternoon and spend the night. It was one big, happy fraternity with everyone having a good time. There were a few rogues and hooligans, but they were kept in check. Just as is the case today, a few people broke the law by drinking before they were 21. Now and again there were brawls, and now and again there were people in trouble. One night one of the guys who was out to impress stole his father's car, drove it too fast, hit a drain on the side of the road and did a loop the loop, badly injuring one of the passengers. Sad as that was, it was a chilling reminder to all of us growing up in that community how egos and ignorance could cause accidents.

Occasionally there would be parties at the yacht club, but Seacliff and Brighton girls weren't allowed to go to those functions, their parents being certain they knew what happened in the sandhills behind the clubhouse. They were probably right. The only girls you'd find at the yacht club were from outside the district, but that was OK by us. One of the better parties each sailing season was down at the Outer Harbour. We'd sail our Cadet dinghies down for a fantastic night and a big race the next day. The first year I sailed my boat down there saw me with plans for plenty of action at the party. There were going to be some very nice girls present. After sailing in and unrigging the boat, Dave Walker decided to jump aboard. He did so by leaping onto the beautiful plywood bowsprit I had made; it promptly snapped in half because it was unsupported. So that night there I was with brother Tom's father-in-law to be, Keith Begg, making a new bowsprit while my crew and all the girls had a wow of a night at the party. And, as if that wasn't enough, I was told Dave Walker achieved everything I was planning.

One other social spot in our district was the Grundy Hall at St Judes Church near Brighton Public School. That was where I thought I had discovered my role in life, my career. I genuinely believed I would become a magician. It all started when I was in junior school. Brother David had some magician books and he used to do some sleight of hand. I was very impressed with that and then became even more inspired when I saw one of Australia's leading magicians, The Great Levant, do his show at the Theatre Royal in Adelaide. That was enough for me—conjuring was the way to go. I got right into it and in the winter months, when I wasn't sailing in the Cadet dinghies, I'd do this bit of a show at Grundy Hall. Dave Walker was my assistant—until the day he almost destroyed my act. One of my tricks involved a padded trough I made on the side of a card table I used. Aunt Madeline's alarm clock was a prop I had on the table, which was set to go off halfway through the act. When this thing started clanging away I'd make some patter about the so-and-so alarm clock going off before I'd finished. At one end of the trough I'd built a small container for confetti so that when the alarm went off, and while I was talking to the audience, I could pick up a handful of the stuff. I'd grab the clock, press the stop button on top and in one action swing my arm down, dropping the clock in the padded trough, then come up on the end of the swing with confetti thrown in the air. It was a great little trick until one night I came out to great applause, only to realise Walker had set up the table with the trough facing the crowd. All I could do was, while talking with the audience, very casually turn the table around and get on with the show.

My proficiency as a magician got to the stage where I actually bred rabbits for my own version of the rabbit-out-of-the-hat trick. I thought that was always a good act, seeing the way magicians used to take their top hat off then pull out a pigeon or a rabbit. The trick with it was to wear black tails, so I wore my father's tails which were so old they had a green stripe across the back where the sun had got at them. In behind the front flap of the coat I fitted a large pocket so I could put into it whatever I wanted to take out of the hat. The trick for the magician is to hold the hat in front of you so people looking at you see a black hat and a black jacket. That way when you make your move it looks like your hand is going into the hat, but it's going just behind the hat and into the big pocket to take out your rabbit or your pigeon. I wasn't big enough to have a full size rabbit so I started breeding my own little white ones. Well, you wouldn't want to know my luck. I'm at home one day on our tennis court bowling a cricket ball at a wine crate against the side wall of the house, which backed on to the court. I bowled the ball just as my baby white rabbit was running across the court to its hutch in the corner, and I hit it, fair on the back of the head. It just stopped in its tracks and rolled over. I ran across, picked it up and took it inside where, with the help of our old maid, Mrs Walker, I gave it a teaspoon of brandy. The rabbit was shivering until I forced this little bit of brandy into its tiny mouth, then it just got stiffer and stiffer and stiffer. It was curtains for the rabbit before it had even had a chance to be a star. That fatal blow and a growing interest in girls led me to decide that there were a lot better things in life than being a magician.

When it came to girls there was one disadvantage associated with living in Brighton and Seacliff—an inability to dance. My school mates who lived in the city all went to Norah Stewart's dancing school, but we were a bit isolated living where we did. It was frustrating when you went to a dance because the city blokes could score with the good-looking toffy girls while we non-dancers from the coast could only look on. It was typical of any dance for young people in those days—blokes up one end, girls down the other, all pretending they're not scanning the scene for a suitable contact for the evening. Every now and then I'd spot a young lady who was too hard to resist and pluck up enough courage to go and ask her to dance. I'd ask, she'd accept, I would apologise for my inability to dance then plait my feet and stumble around trying to be really cool. Half-way through the dance she'd politely thank me, then return to her flock and I would retire hurt. Next thing you'd see a city guy wheeling her around the room having a wonderful time. This coastal outcast would then return home and convince himself that the yacht club girls were much nicer and more welcoming than the toffy city girls.

Dancer I may not have been, but I did become the proud holder of a driver's licence the day I was eligible. I already knew how to drive because David Walker's father, Stan, who had essentially become my foster father, let me drive his car on country roads when we were away on hunting trips. My sixteenth birthday, 20 November 1948, was the day for the licence and boy, did I have to do some scheming. There was no driving test required, only evidence of your age and, a written test to answer a few simple questions you had swatted up on. My big problem was that I was at school that day—at least it seemed a big problem. After much thought I worked out that if I ducked out after the first class in the morning and missed the next two periods, which were practical chemistry and a free period in the school library, there was probably enough time to get uptown and back without being missed. I would just slide into the morning tea break or, even if I was late, I could slide back into the PT class without being seen. It all went according to plan. I crept out through the back of the school, went up town, got my licence then got back in time to casually move into the PT class. Perfect—until the end of the day when we were all assembled for what we called a muster. At the end of the muster our house master, Mr Symonds, announced: "Hardy, stay behind. I want to speak with you." I thought: "Bloody hell. What's gone wrong. Somebody's spotted me going out of the school." He came up to me and asked very sternly: "Where were you this morning, Hardy?" "Play dumb," was the message from my brain. "When, Sir? Where? Why?" I stammered. "We took a roll call during the library period before morning recess and you weren't there," he stated. "Hell," I thought. "They've never taken a roll call throughout this entire year and they take one today. Think fast." "I must have been in the white city," I said, the white city being our polite reference to the water closet, the toilet. I was on the verge of deep, deep trouble but my act must have been convincing.

He swallowed my excuse. I had skirted disaster with great skill and had my driver's licence in my pocket.

Just as it is today, sport, or being in a sporting team, did provide some magnetic attraction for the opposite sex. I was heavily into football and rowing within the school and that provided some distinct advantages over non-sporting types. With my father and brother David both having rowed for the school I was dead set determined to get involved. The school had a lovely rowing house nearby on the banks of the Torrens River, and soon after I entered Senior School I found myself rowing in tub slides. My ultimate goal was to get into the school eight and have a crack at the Head of the River, and fortunately I achieved that in my final year. I rowed Number Three in the eight, just as my father did in the Inter Varsity crew, and on the big day we knew the crew to beat came from Prince Alfred College. Well, we rowed our hearts out and sure enough St Peter's College won the Head of the River. What a celebration that was, all eight of us walking around in beautiful cream sweaters with crossed oars on the front, which identified us as the winning crew. What was even better was that you could take your pick of the supporters. There was a beautiful little lady I fancied standing on the banks of the Torrens who had no hesitation in coming to dinner and the Theatre Royal with me that night. What a score that was. Suddenly every minute of training was worthwhile.

Equally satisfying was my first interstate trip, by train to Melbourne to represent the school in football matches against Geelong Grammar and Melbourne Grammar. We had won every match played against other schools in Adelaide, the ultimate win being against Prince Alfred College at Adelaide Oval when fullback Jim Hardy took out a best player award. We beat Geelong Grammar then went on to meet Melbourne Grammar in what I believe was the last schoolboy match to be played on the Melbourne Cricket Ground. It was in September 1950. What a disaster. I had more goals scored against me from free kicks in that game than I had seen all season. At three-quarter time I went up to our coach, Mr Vollugi, and asked: "Sir, what am I doing wrong? Why am I giving away all these free kicks?"

"I don't know, Hardy. All I know is that the umpire, Bully Taylor, is the uncle of the captain of Melbourne Grammar."

Back out I went for the last quarter and bugger me, there's a skirmish and I'm knocked out. They brought me around, but not before my mate Gerry Hargrave had three kick outs in my stead. I continued on with the game in a dazed state, then saw Vollugi standing on the sideline calling out. I thought he was calling to me, calling me off the field, so I started to head for the sideline. Then, as I got close to him, he shouted: "Get back there, Hardy. You're bad enough, but Moffatt's hopeless." John Moffatt, a half-back flank and a good friend, must have been playing really badly because he was taken off while I continued on in a daze.

All the memories of that match came back twenty years later, in September 1970 while I was steering *Gretel II* in the America's Cup. We were tossed out of race after that historic and very controversial protest where we collided with the American defender, *Intrepid*. I received a huge number of telegrams from around the world, and one I got from Australia was simply addressed: "Jim Hardy. Yacht *Gretel II*. Newport. Rhode Island." It read: "Bad luck Hardy. It looks like they've got Bully Taylor umpiring again." It was signed "Trunk", Mr Vollugi's nickname. That reinforced in my mind what a great school St Peter's was. Twenty years after that game in Melbourne Vollugi could take the time to send me such a poignant telegram. St Peter's was a real family.

I probably would not have been able to stay at St Peter's for my entire schooling if Sir James Gosse had not stood by the promise he made to my mother all those years earlier and paid for my schooling. He followed my progress with keen interest, in fact to such a degree that at the start of each term my mother would arrange for me to go into his office to meet with him and talk about what I was doing. Often he would give me a book on some special subject. He would write words of encouragement inside the cover and sign it: "Jimmy Gosse".

When I completed my final year exams I went along to see him and he did everything he could to encourage me to stay one more year for my Leaving Honours Certificate. But all my mates had decided to leave school that year and I thought it was time for Jim Hardy to head out into the big, wide world as well.

Chapter Five

Guns 'n' Grapes 'n' Roses

COMMON SENSE TOLD ME there wasn't a career opportunity for Jim Hardy in the family wine business. All the bases had been well covered by other family members. The winemaking side didn't really interest me, primarily because both my cousin Bob and brother David were qualified winemakers. On top of that brother Tom held a Bachelor of Science and Engineering—a war-time degree—so had the mechanical and laboratory sides of the business under his wing. Above all this was the fact that I was being a bit pig headed. I had decided I wanted to prove myself somewhere else. I certainly didn't want people to say "Oh, he's only come into this because he's in the family. He's got the silver spoon. He's the boss's son." That really did play on my mind. But while I knew what I didn't want to do as far as my career was concerned, I was an even greater distance from knowing what I did want to do.

The only solution when I left St Peter's College was to have a holiday, go sailing and hope things would sort themselves out. At Christmas I headed for Perth with *Nocroo* and crew to race for the Stonehaven Cup, the big one. No South Australian had ever won it so you can imagine the jubilation on the Swan River when we took out the final heat and secured the points needed to claim the trophy. But our jubilation lasted only a matter of minutes. We sailed back to the beach at Crawley Bay to a great reception and watched the next two boats finish. The boat coming in second was *Victor*, from Victoria, and behind it was the Tasmanian boat *Koala*. About

50 yards from the finish line a stainless steel weld on *Victor*'s masthead fitting broke and the entire rig went crashing over the side. That let *Koala* sail through to second place and give her the additional points needed to win the Stonehaven Cup. We lost by one point. The Stonehaven Cup had been ours for five minutes. It was all too much for one of my crew, Tom Philipson. He was absolutely pissed off, so much so that he went on a bender and we didn't see him for 24 hours. Mum was in Perth and that was one of the few times in my life she actually chastised me. When the trophy presentation came up Tom was, as we say in the wine industry, suffering industrial fatigue, and didn't turn up. I arrived about half an hour late and Mum let me know very definitely that as far as she was concerned we were displaying bad sportsmanship. It was no way to react. Some consolation for our loss came in a telegram from brother David in Adelaide. It was to tell David Walker and myself that we had passed our Leaving Certificate exams in six subjects. You beauty—no more school!

The Stonehaven Cup, was considered to be the Australian Championship, and restricted to competitors under nineteen years of age, so Perth was the end of my years in Cadets. It was time to move into a senior class so I decided to build a 12 Square Metre Sharpie, the Sharpies being a well established dinghy class at Brighton and Seacliff Yacht Club.

Mum had a surprise for me when I returned to Adelaide, one I wasn't too excited about. She had decided my career was in the wine industry so took it upon herself to enrol me in Roseworthy College, near Gawler in the Barossa Valley, to do the oenology course. I did not agree so my only option was to go to see the chairman of Thomas Hardy and Sons, Uncle Ken Hardy, and convince myself once and for all that there were no opportunities available. Uncle Ken agreed with me then suggested I consider joining Elders Smith, a very diversified company that would give me good training in many aspects of commercial life. I took his advice, went for an interview and started work in February 1951.

I started in the Correspondence Department then moved to a position where they called me the Number 3 Teller. My daily routine involved two tasks, to do all the banking then scour Adelaide for good quality cigarettes for the senior teller, Bob Gunn. There can't have been too many intelligent criminals in Adelaide those days because each day, at the same time, I would set off from Elders Smith in Currie Street and walk all the way down to the Bank of New South Wales on North Terrace carrying this little brown leather case crammed with huge amounts of cash and cheques. It was my job to go into every tobacconist on the return trip and try to secure the decent brands, like Craven A's, Turf and Capstans. My age usually went against me in the negotiations with the tobacconists, so I finished up with the cheaper brands, like State Express and Black and White. When I did return with the good brands I was the office hero.

Not long after I started at Elders talk of compulsory military service via conscription started to surface. I had enrolled at the School of Mines in Adelaide, which is now part of the University of South Australia, to do the Preparatory Bookkeeping course so decided to join the Citizen Military Force's University Regiment at the school with the hope I could avoid being called up. The thought of conscription didn't appeal to me. I had been happy in the school cadets and was happy in the CMF because it seemed that in each group I could dictate a little as to what I did and where I went. But with conscription I would be told what to do, and I didn't like that. It was in the regiment that my size 13 feet first became an embarrassment. The army couldn't supply boots big enough for me, so while everyone else marched around in army boots I was wearing my black leather street shoes. My CMF plot wasn't to matter because soon after I joined any scheme to avoid call-up by being in the CMF didn't hold water. Prime Minister Menzies was quick to announce it was conscription for every able-bodied young man of my age in Australia—and on top of that the army had boots to fit me.

After working for Elders for just nine months I was off to Keswick Barracks with Dave Walker, Jim Macpherson and Jim Dickson for our military medical. We took it in turns to go in to see the doctor. Dave Walker came out smiling—he wasn't accepted because he had flat feet. Jim Macpherson came out smiling—he wasn't accepted because of impaired vision in one eye. Jim Dickson came out smiling—he wasn't accepted because he had a hernia. Jim Hardy came out with a clean bill of health—I was conscripted for the first intake of national service in 1951.

On the allotted day I reported to the Torrens Parade Ground in Adelaide from where I, and everyone else, was shipped off to Woodside for uniform issue. I was quite comfortable because I was with a whole bunch of blokes my age who all felt exactly as I did—we were in there for three months, there was nothing we could do about it, so we may as well enjoy it. From the outset there was mumbling among the group about the Broken Hill guys. They had apparently decided they didn't like some bloke, because he annoyed them when they travelled down to Adelaide, so they literally threw him off the train. The rumour was the guy on the receiving end of their hospitality was in Daws Road Military Hospital with a couple of broken limbs. That night, the very first night of conscription, it became apparent I was the Broken Hill mob's next target. We had finished learning some parade duties and were all lined up for dinner. Each one of us had a dixie, a metal dish with a handle on the side, and the cooks were slopping mashed potatoes, peas and sausages onto them. From out of nowhere a big Broken Hill bloke loomed up alongside me and said rather gruffly: "College boy, eh?"

"Yes. What's your problem?"

"Come down the back. Come on, down the back and we'll straighten you out," was his curt reply.

I knew exactly what he meant. I thought: "This doesn't sound too good. I'm here just one day and some bloke's trying to pick me." Being the complete diplomat I politely ignored him, sat down and went about trying to swallow my dinner. The next night was a repeat performance. This fellow came up to me and said: "Hey, yellow belly. Come on down the back. We want to see you." Doing everything I could to appear perfectly composed, and knowing I was a better talker than a fighter, I asked: "Look, mate, what's your problem?" Barbs were flying at me all night but somehow I managed to avoid the confrontation.

On day three I was walking back through a line of tents towards the one I shared with a bunch of other guys and lo and behold the Broken Hill boys had roped off an area and two blokes, one a very dark Aborigine, were in there dancing around, boxing. I'd walked slap bang into it and there was no way out. The fellow who seemed to be the organiser spotted me and shouted: "Hey, yellow belly. Put the gloves on." My mind raced, not to mention my pulse—and there was another part of my anatomy that wasn't feeling too comfortable at the time either. I thought: "I have to put up with this for three months. Three months of intimidation. I'd be better off in Daws Road hospital with a broken nose than put up with this." It was a case of fight for freedom.

As they put the gloves on me my thoughts rushed back to brother David and when he boxed. I was trying to remember everything he did, everything he told me. I played as dumb as I could, saying things like: "Hell, these gloves are big, aren't they?" They put me in against the Aboriginal guy. Within seconds he'd whacked me around the ears a couple of times and they were burning. I wasn't enjoying it at all. I just kept reaching out with my left arm, dancing around and reaching out all the time trying to fend this guy off. Well, I guess in sport there's a lot in confidence because as we danced around towards one side of the ring I could hear the guys outside the ring talking to each other. It was possibly because my ears were burning so much that they were super sensitive when it came to hearing. I could hear one of the guys say with some amazement: "Reckons he's never boxed. Look at his left." That was all I needed to hear. I used my left more and more and quickly realised that if I stood side on and used my left this guy didn't have the reach he needed to hit me. He started missing me, then I landed a couple of good ones and the guy shook his head. I started to get on top of him. My adrenalin was pumping. Suddenly I was mad with zeal. I was going to kill the bloke—I was getting into him at 100 miles an hour. Finally they had to drag us apart. A big guy, the leader of the Broken Hill mob whose nickname was "God," came over and congratulated me somewhat reluctantly.

"Do you drink at all?" he asked.

"Why?"

"Well, we're having a bit of grog in our tent tonight and you'd be very welcome to join us."

I thought that sounded pretty good, an offer made even more appealing because it was illegal to have grog in the place.

After dark I went across to their tent and was amazed how much grog they had smuggled in. I can still see the flagons, half gallon flagons of Hamilton's Muscatel and Sweet Sherry. They were drinking it out of army pannikins, big mugs, and I thought: "I'm going to last five minutes drinking that stuff." I spotted a flagon of burgundy, played dumb once more and asked: "Oh, what's this like?"

"Don't touch that," was the immediate advice from God. "It'll kill you, I've tried it."

But I knew it was about half the strength of the sherry and

muscat so announced after one muscat that I would drink the burgundy. I poured a decent amount into a pannikin and started drinking.

"Can you really drink that stuff?" "God" asked with a look of amazement that had a liberal dose of respect mixed with it.

"I'll put up with it."

We told jokes and yarned a lot until the muscatel and sweet sherry started taking its toll. Some guys just faded away while others went outside to spew their hearts up. The closing scene was me helping "God", who was in an alcoholic daze, find his way into his bed, then I headed back to my tent feeling only a fraction the worse for wear. From that day on the college boy was a great mate of the blokes from Broken Hill. And I can say that if ever I had been in a position where I had to choose a team to be with in a trench during a war it would be them. As it was they requested I be part of their group when they went to the Murray River to fill sand bags and fight the floods.

The three months of full-time service were pretty uneventful. It was mainly infantry-type activities with 303 rifles, Bren guns and the like. We did have two guys carted off to hospital when our tear gas training went very wrong. The army issued us with vintage gas masks. I remember being a little concerned about what lay ahead when I pulled my mask out of the canister to see that the date on it was 1943. When I put mine on I was relieved to discover it leaked only a small amount around the edges. But some of the guys were using masks that, it was discovered later, were so badly perished they leaked something awful. We had to run through a gas chamber, stop, do some exercises until we were puffing, then run out. The guys wearing the perished masks collapsed and had to be dragged out.

By the end of my three months service I had risen to the dizzy heights of Corporal, and our Number Five platoon won the regiment drill competition. That led to us being at the head of the march through the streets of Adelaide to celebrate the completion of the initial training for the intake of national servicemen.

Following our full-time commitment we had to choose what section of the army we wanted to go into for the remaining three years of service. It was compulsory we attend training one night a week over that period as well as a two week camp each year. I elected to go into the artillery because the thought of dragging guns around and being three to four miles behind the infantry, who were at the front line with bayonets on their rifles, sounded pretty good.

My career path in life remained as a wide and winding road to an unknown destination. Elders Smith was just a job and the bookkeeping course did nothing to inspire or enthuse me. Little did I know that over at Port Vincent Jack Correll was formulating his own plans for me. Age was starting to slow him and the task of working and maintaining his property was becoming more arduous. He and Glad had no children to take over the reins and share farmers were proving to be more trouble than they were worth. Jack's solution was to try to get me, their next best thing to a son, to go and work as a share farmer. He called me, made the offer and I jumped at it. I had retained all the great memories of the two years I spent there as a lad so in a way it was like going home. The additional bonus was that it would get me out of my weekly obligations to National Service. The army agreed to let me go on the understanding that I attend more weekend bivouacs and serve additional time at the annual camp.

It was a good arrangement I had with Jack. I had to pay for my own grain and corn sacks for a one-third share of the profit while he provided all the machinery and the fertiliser. As an additional incentive Jack offered me a share of his wool profits—a good deal considering it was selling for around one pound per pound. Shearing was to become one of my favourite jobs. I actually enjoyed seeing the sheep come into the shed looking like four-legged sumo wrestlers then going out minutes later resembling Twiggy. The shearing troupe of Leo Travis and Owen Baker worked the district, including Corrells' farm. They were great blokes and we hit it off well. At one stage I left the farm for a two week period and travelled with them as a shearer. Jack came and told me they had asked if I could join them and that he had agreed. "May as well go and chaff-up someone else's wool as well as mine," he said dryly. "Chaff" was a reference to wool that had been hacked at by a shearer instead of removed with long, sweeping blows. Chaffing or not, I got up to 50 sheep a day, which earned me three pounds ten shillings a day—bloody good money for a twenty year old. It was a tough two weeks but well worth it, both financially and in giving me a greater appreciation for just how hard shearers worked to earn a quid. When the troupe was on the farm Aunt Glad would provide lunch. In those days blue swimmer crabs were a dime a dozen at Port Vincent and rabbits were even more plentiful, so lunch was always sandwiches groaning under the weight of crab or rabbit. Today they would be a delicacy but the shearers would bite into them, go "bah", chuck them away and complain about not getting decent food. Even the dogs turned their noses up at them.

The Corrells were tough but honest and because of that I really enjoyed being a part of their life. The property was around 5000 acres and the house, named St Neots, was a lovely Australian country bungalow with a bull-nose verandah all the way around it. As a home it was very comfortable and for me, being made to feel as though I was their son made for pleasant times. The three of us would be up at around six every day, enjoy the best country-style breakfast you could imagine—bacon, eggs, lamb chops, steak—then get into a busy day which, for Jack and me, usually involved working the fields, fixing fences, crutching sheep or repairing equipment. The two years I had spent there a decade earlier certainly helped because I knew all the paddocks and their features. Jack gave me the Racecourse Paddock to sow with barley, something I had to do in my own time. I was late seeding it so just lived with the hope that it would rain and give the stuff a start. One day soon after sowing I was in the shearing shed with old Leo Travis, and we heard these heavy rain drops starting to hit the tin roof like small pebbles.

"Jim. Listen to that on the roof."

"What about it, Leo?"

"They're threepenny bits for you Jim. Every one of them is helping your grain." Unfortunately though the grain didn't come up quite as well as I'd hoped and when the barley inspector came around to check on the quality of the crop prior to harvest he said it was only good for feed. You got top price for malting barley, which could be used for beer; milling barley brought the second best price and feed barley was the lowest quality. On having the inspector's report old Jack showed his true colours once again. He took the inspector deeper into the field, showed him some more of the crop and probably whispered a few words about this twenty-year-old kid trying to get a start with farming. By the time the inspector and Jack emerged from the middle of the paddock it had been decided I had a crop of milling barley. The harvest was completed and the ensuing weekend saw me out in the paddock from daylight until dark sewing up bags full of barley.

One thing I did learn that year was the difference between youth and experience, courtesy of the fat lamb season. Jack had one Merino ram and quite a few young Dorset Horn rams, his plan being to put the Dorset's over Merino ewes to produce fat lambs. The old merino ram had battle scars all over him and looked about 100 years old. Come mating time there would be a couple of ewes just standing there, head down, eating the grass. The next thing two Dorset Horns would get the urge and immediately begin fighting one another over winning the favours of the ewes. But while they were trying to belt each other's brains out the old Merino ram would casually walk up, do the job on the ewes, then retire. It was so funny to watch. The old bastard was so cunning. Come May, when the lambs dropped, his score card was there for all to see. Very impressive. He'd got about ten to one on the Dorsets.

On the odd occasion I would jump into old Jack's buckboard and drive over to Adelaide to see the family and do some business for the farm. One day I was walking through the city when a girl came out of the crowd and said: "Hello, Jim, I'm Anne Jackson." We chatted for a few minutes about nothing in particular, except for the fact that I had apparently dated one of her girlfriends. We said our goodbyes and I walked away thinking, "That was an interesting approach." I thought nothing more of it, mainly because I was living in Port Vincent, where I was having a great time socially anyway. When I first went back to Corrells' I was saddened to learn my school-time sweetheart, Nita Starkey, had slipped through my net and gone off with David Hill, who had worked for the Corrells' for a few years. But it wasn't long before I was into the scene over there and enjoying the company of Glenys Hogben, the daughter of Port Vincent's Post Office Manager. It was never anything serious, but we did enjoy seeing each other. We had some great times, particularly when we went across to the Minlaton dance at Yorke Peninsula. Ironically I went into a restaurant in Adelaide just a few years ago and realised the maitre d', a very charming young lady, was Glenys' daughter. I had to tell her how her mother had been equally charming.

I was always mad keen about Australian rules football so in the winter months in Port Vincent I was really enjoying playing in the top grade for the local club, which was part of the Southern Yorke

Peninsula competition. I played as a ruckman and that season we went through to play in the grand final against Curramulka. Lack of rain had the dust bowl of an oval very dry and bony. In the first quarter I went up for a ball from a boundary throw-in with the intention of tapping it over to our rover. When I crashed to the ground the opposing ruckman came down on top of my leg. Instant agony. I looked down and saw my right leg out at right angles, sideways, completely dislocated at the knee. "Shouldn't look like that," I thought. I was carried from the field for the first time since I started playing the game at school. I was never able to play football properly again. I tried everything, including a knee brace from Chicago, to get back on to the field, but nothing worked. Eventually, in 1964, I had to have the cartilage removed, then a few years ago the knee was reconstructed, complete with a couple of bolts. Not surprisingly my knee blew up like a balloon and I was forced to spend two weeks in bed at the farm. Old Jack was never keen on me playing football so there was no sympathy whatsoever then or during the following weeks while I hobbled around trying to do my job.

With there being no yacht club at Port Vincent the only way I could get out on the water in the warmer months was to bring across from Adelaide the twelve square metre Sharpie I had managed to build in the family garage, with a lot of help from Dave Phillips, while working at Elders and doing National Service. I named it *T.M. Hardy*, after my late father. The locals loved me having the boat at Port Vincent because it represented an opportunity to learn to sail. Later they were to open what became a very successful sailing club in this attractive little village.

Early in 1953 I had to go to my big National Service yearly camp. It was over a two week period, and because Gunner Hardy had escaped the Monday night classes by being in Port Vincent they called me to the camp at Caloote, on the River Murray, two weeks early to work with the advance party putting up the tents. Just before I went to the camp I felt I strained a stomach muscle while dipping sheep—I had to lift the big weathers into the dip trough—so I did what most people did in those days and took a BEX or Vincents APC to relieve the pain. They didn't work so I went along to the army doctor to get the problem checked out.

Initially at the camp I was a GPOAC—a Gun Position Officer's Assistant. My job was to work out for the Gun Position Officer what the range and bearing was for the target. We had an Observation Officer between three and four miles down range who would call back on the landline target references after we fired each live round. He'd say how many hundreds of yards to the left or right, or up or down, we needed to aim to hit the target. Using this information I could plot the aim for the next round by placing a see-through grid over the top of our map. One morning before dawn we had two batteries of four 25 pounders operating and after the first round was fired there was a frantic call from an obviously distressed Observation Officer to cease firing. We knew it was serious because the call came over the radio as well as the land line. In this type of training exercise rule one was not to use the radio for fear of interception by the supposed enemy. As it turned out rule one should have been "get your range and bearing right" because my mate Ian McWhinnie, who was the GPOAC for the other four gun battery, had used his chart grid sideways. That reversed the position of the target to the degree where the Observation Officer was in the centre of the target for the high explosive shells. There was embarrassment all around after that little mistake and there was more embarrassment to follow some weeks later because we left a surprise behind for the farmer whose property we were using for the practice. One of the shells didn't explode after we fired it, but it sure went up when the farmer dragged his plough across it. The incident brought to an end the use of live shells for National Service artillery practice.

When the medical report on my stomach problem came back from the doctor it turned out that what I thought was a pulled muscle was a hernia. On hearing this, John Minks, who was Captain of the four gun battery I was attached to, said they were short of a steward in the Officers' Mess. I had known him before going to camp because he was Sales Manager of Reynella Wines and a good friend of Colin Haselgrove, who was the boss of Chateau Reynella.

"Steward in the Officers' Mess," I said. "What does that entail?"

"You've got to look after all the grog for the officers. You have to live in a tent attached to the mess with all the liquor stored in it. You won't be required to go on parade and all you have to do is serve the liquor to the officers in their mess tent and take the wine around to them at their dining tables."

"Gosh. It's short notice, John. But I've thought about it long enough. OK, I'll accept."

What a great time that was. On a few evenings I'd invite a few of my mates, Ian McWhinney and company, to come up and we would sit in the semi dark, just with the light of a very low hurricane lamp, and enjoy a few grogs on the Officers' Mess account.

One night the Colonel of the 13th Regiment brought in the Survey Officer; they came up to me before dinner and the CO said: "I'll have my usual, Gunner Hardy." I knew that was a St Agnes Brandy and soda. He then turned to the Survey Officer and asked what he would like. "I'll have the same as you're having," was the reply. I stepped in at that stage and apologised, saying to the Survey Officer that I was running short of St Agnes Brandy.

"That's the CO's favourite. Would you mind if you have Tolley's TST brandy?" I asked.

"Gunner Hardy. I wouldn't know one brandy from another. That's fine with me."

I poured one brandy out of the St Agnes bottle for the CO and the other out of the TST bottle for the Survey Officer. Unbeknown to the CO I'd already run out of the St Agnes Brandy, so the St Agnes bottle was half full of the TST brandy. You could see it coming. They had their first mouthful and sure enough the CO turned to the Survey Officer and said: "How can you drink that stuff, that TST brandy?"

"It tastes just fine to me."

I couldn't help myself. I had to be excused. I was doubled up, trying desperately to stop myself laughing in case they could hear me.

The inevitable operation on my hernia followed the end of the camp. Off I went to Daws Road hospital for an operation. The doctor who was to operate on me, Dr. Alan F. Hobbs, was a lovely guy, an ex-Changi prisoner of war and one of those doctors you feel really comfortable with. He was a teaching doctor at the hospital and before I went in for the operation he asked if I would mind if his students watched. I felt OK about that until he said we would have to do the operation under just a local anaesthetic so the students could get a better appreciation of what was happening. He assured me that if I felt any pain he would hit me with more injections and I wouldn't feel a thing. They very kindly put this screen up from my stomach so I couldn't see what was going on, gave me injections around the hernia and got things underway. The feeling as he cut me open was a weird sensation. It was as though he was dragging a feather across my stomach, but I could feel no pain. When he got into the problem area and lifted my intestines, or whatever else, I could feel this enormous sort of relief. A pressure had come off. At that stage he called the students over, girls and blokes, and I'm lying there listening to him explain what was going on in my stomach. My stomach! I was thinking: "I'm not very keen on this," as he said things like: "Look here and you'll see how it's broken through the stomach wall." Yuk! Then he sewed me up and had the students watch once more while he asked me to put my wrist to my mouth and blow on it as hard as I could. "See all the stomach muscles tightening up," he said as he continued to sew.

I could feel the next layer being sewn up something awful and all I could think was how stupid I'd been letting myself get sucked in to becoming a human guinea pig. I must have been the only guy who had fallen for that. It was the last time I'd ever lend my body to the cause of medicine.

While lying in the hospital ward recovering I had plenty of time to think. What was I going to do? Would I or would I not go back to Corrells' farm? I realised that if I got another hernia I would be of no use to Jack Correll and also create plenty of problems for myself. So the first decision was made—no more farming. Then I started thinking about the family business and how all the bases had been covered by family members. I turned it all over and over in my mind and, bingo! The accountancy side, the commercial side, wasn't covered. It was a definite opening, an area that had never been covered by a family member. Reinforcing all these thoughts was a growing belief within myself that my father would have wanted me to follow him into the company.

I kept my thoughts to myself while I enrolled once more at the School of Mines. If I wanted to get my diploma in accountancy I would have to first pass Preparatory Bookkeeping, so that was my initial target. I had made enough money at Corrells'—more than one thousand pounds—to support myself for a while so decided I would also improve my knowledge and skills in other areas. I took on courses in ocean navigation, fitting and turning and carpentry to virtually become a full-time student.

I was more than pleased to come away from the Corrells' with such a tidy sum, especially after the locals left me¹ in no doubt I was the first person ever to leave the farm with a profit. They saw Jack and Glad as a really tough pair. For me he certainly was tough but he was also a very fair and nice man.

The money created a lot of opportunities, the most important being the chance to build a new Cadet dinghy for a younger friend, Freddie Neill, who I thought was the most promising junior in the yacht club. I just felt it would give him a chance and be a nice contribution to the club. The great reward was that he became the first South Australian to ever win the Stonehaven Cup . . . in *Noc Too*, the boat I built for him. That boat is now in the South Australian Maritime Museum and, I'm pleased to say, my old boat *Nocroo*, which has been doing community service as a salad bar in the Seacliff Hotel in more recent times, has been earmarked to join it.

By now there were four things very prominent in my life: bookkeeping, boats, football and girls. I would travel to the School of Mines by train each day, an experience that was only made pleasant by the number of beautiful girls who were travelling at the same time. There in the crowd one day was Anne Jackson, the girl who had walked up to me in Adelaide about a year earlier to simply say hello. I was intrigued by her actions then so decided it was my turn to make the approach. Anne was working in an airline's city office as a secretary and while the old train rattled its way towards downtown Adelaide we went through the usual boy meets girl small talk procedure. After a couple more of these train trip encounters I plucked up the courage to ask her to the theatre. She set me back a step or two by saying my invitation would have to be cleared by her parents. I got the distinct impression that Jim Hardy had a bit of a reputation, something most undeserved. Really! The "all clear" signal came from Anne's parents, but not before the rules for the evening had been laid out very plainly. So Anne was on the scene and, to the benefit of our relationship, she simultaneously strengthened her friendship with a girl, Jill Griffith, who lived across the road from our home at Seacliff. It was a wonderful age to be experiencing a blossoming relationship. It was all fresh, new, and full of daring. I was twenty and she was seventeen. Just marvellous. A couple of times at weekends, when I was building Fred's Cadet dinghy in the garage, Anne and Jill would come across and bang on the garage door, just to announce themselves. It was simply a "cheerio" call, just to let me know Anne was there and the interest remained.

Slowly but surely during 1953 my interest and pride in the family company gained strength. It was the centenary year, 100 years since great grandfather Thomas Hardy started growing grapes at Bankside. From the start of the year there were various functions at the wineries and in the vineyards to which I'd been invited. I met some very interesting people and found I was genuinely interested in what was happening. It was at the actual centenary celebration, a very memorable party for near 300 guests in April 1953, that things crystallised in my mind and I realised it was time I became more serious about business, rather than flitting around doing my own thing. In particular it was my mother's contribution to that fantastic day of festivities that filled me with pride and spurred me. Her efforts were such that the book detailing the company history chronicled: "One of the stars of the luncheon was Tom Mayfield's widow, the amazing Eileen Hardy. Witty, outgiving, indefatigable, over the years she had been the unpaid and indispensable unofficial hostess for the Company. At this centenary picnic she gave one of her brilliantly amusing and pungent speeches full of laughter, love and earthy good humour. From beginning to end the whole day was a magnificent success."

With the centenary celebrations still fresh in the air and my bookkeeping and accounting studies at the School of Mines progressing well, I thought it wise to make my move. I arranged to meet the General Manager, Dick Clark, or Mr Clark as everyone called him, for an interview and it was then I told him I was prepared to do the course at the school because I saw it as a benefit to the company. He agreed and much to my relief, and pleasure, I was given a job as a shipping clerk. In October 1953, just a month before I turned 21, I started work with Thomas Hardy and Sons. I was to remain as a shipping clerk for more than a year, organising for the delivery of the bulk of our wine to the east coast of Australia plus some to New Zealand and England.

While I felt I had done a great job building my Sharpie *T. M. Hardy*, I was not having a lot of success with it, due in no small way to the fact that I was then in among the big boys. I was at the bottom of the learning curve. However, the boat was good enough to get us into the six-boat South Australian team chosen to go to Sydney to compete in the regatta that was to be staged as part of the Queen's Royal Tour in 1954. What a memorable moment in life that was, my first big solo trip. My travels to Perth four years earlier for the Stonehaven Cup had been with maternal management. This time though I had been let off the leash, and to make things even better, Mum entrusted me with her wonderful two tone Daimler, a huge, lumbering thing that was eighteen years old.

With the car laden to the gunwales with gear, and the boat securely fastened to a trailer, David Phillips, Jim Macpherson and I headed east for Murray Bridge, our first stop and the point where we collected our fourth crewman, Dick Bartholomaeus, a University of South Australia dentistry student who had been at University regiment camp. With Dick and his gear now on board the combined weight of the four of us plus a 550 pound Sharpie on a trailer saw the old Daimler really struggling. We worked out we were averaging just 42 miles per hour, so it was no surprise that we took four days to get to Sydney. We saw plenty of the countryside. At Warracknabeal Dave Phillips announced he wanted to collect every Daimler of that model in Australia.

"It's an oil producer, not an oil consumer," he told us after double checking the dipstick when we pulled into a service station to satisfy the Daimler's incredible thirst for petrol. "We can make money out of this," Dave announced.

No such luck.

As one of the first cars with gear pre-selection operating through a thing called fluid drive, oil was somehow finding its way from the gearbox back to the sump.

At Benalla our urgent requirement for copious quantities of Victorian beer to settle the dust certainly didn't endear us to the locals. When we arrived the sky was thick with brown smoke. The big town gong was sounding . . . bong, bong, bong . . . calling everyone out to fight a bushfire on the outskirts. We called for a vote on bushfire or beer. The case for beer was that we weren't locals, we were very thirsty, and our purchase would support local business. It won. So we sat on the verandah of the pub drinking very chilled Victorian beer while we watched the locals fight the bushfire.

The regatta in Sydney was a really big deal, run by the very august Royal Sydney Yacht Squadron. The interstate crews were accommodated in hammocks on the *Belubra*, a Manly ferry that was docked just adjacent to the club. A little launch that resembled the *African Queen* shuttled us between the ferry and the club, where they served breakfast for four shillings, lunch for five and the evening meal for six shillings. The atmosphere and excitement around the arrival of the majestic ship *Gothic* into Sydney Harbour with the newly crowned Queen Elizabeth aboard was quite something. The harbour was packed with spectator boats and thousands of people lined the shore. We watched all the action from the deck of the *Belubra*.

The Royal Visit Regatta was a real education. We youngsters from Adelaide would learn there was a big difference between racing kids of similar age in the Cadets and racing adults in such a highly competitive class as the 12 Square Metre Sharpie. In some areas of the big league it seemed the only rule was to break the rules until you were caught. For example, at the Annual General Meeting of the class during the regatta we were shown this amazing device called a venturi. It really opened my eyes—a tube where water went in one end, was squeezed in the middle, then expanded at the back. All of this created a suction that drained water out of the boat through a tiny tube that was screwed into the bottom of the hull. Also on exhibit at the meeting was a more simple version of this venturi, just a vertical piece of tube with the back cut away on the part that protruded below the bottom of the boat. When the boat was moving through the water the reduction in pressure created behind the tube was enough to suck water from the hull. Amazing! Until then we had been using pumps, scoops, even buckets to get water out of the boat while we were racing. As excited as we were about these venturis, they were banned from the regatta. But while the ruling was good enough for me it wasn't good enough for some others. I learned later in life that the venturis had been the reason Western Australia's Rolly Tasker was able to get his boat upright and sailing again after a capsize. And in one race I sailed past Queensland's John Cuneo when his boat capsized, and there for all to see were these little black venturis sticking out of the bottom of the boat. But who was I to create a stir when I was so new to the big league? Regardless of this the regatta certainly whet my appetite for more top level competition. At 21 years of age I had met and raced against some of the legends of Australian sailing, men in their 30s and 40s who had come from all over Australia.

There was another memorable sailing excursion that year, this time to Port Vincent. Such trips happened annually at Easter, sometimes to Goolwa, at the entrance to the Murray River, other times to Lake Bonney or Port Vincent.

Many of the ocean-racing yacht fleet from the Royal South Australian Yacht Squadron in Adelaide had made the pilgrimage across the Gulf of St. Vincent to Port Vincent this particular Easter and when we arrived from Adelaide by road with our Sharpie on the trailer, there, taking pride of place in the middle of the bay right off the wharf, was Norm Howard's gleaming new 42ft yacht, *Southern Myth*. Also dominating the scene, and tied alongside the dock, was the very large trading ketch, *Reginald M*, her rugged topsides and rig leaving no doubt she had seen a hard-working life.

We had a great time sailing by day and partying by night, all the time sampling copious quantities of the Hardy product. On the Sunday morning, at around 2 a.m., what I call 'industrial fatigue' had set in and Dick Bartholomaeus, Pat Malone and I were ready for mischief. A plan unfolded and to execute it I first had to make my way from the caravan park where we were camped to Jack Correll's farm, which had been home for me a few years earlier. I knew the dogs would be around the house, so to ensure they didn't bark I called them by name as I crept towards the front gate. I headed for the workshed at the back of the house where I found a large tin of white paint and some brushes.

Minutes later I was back with the blokes and we headed down to the beach where we 'borrowed' a dinghy, paddled out into the night, around the end of the wharf and up alongside the *Reginald M*. As if our industrial fatigue didn't have us sufficiently unstable, the dinghy kept trying to capsize. It became obvious Pat's job was to steady us alongside the ship while Dick and I started the task. Using a small brush to outline the 2 feet high letters on the ship's black bulwark, Dick worked his way along the ship while I followed behind filling them in—all the time trying to be as quiet as possible. All hell would have broken loose had we woken anyone. About 40 minutes later our handiwork was complete and we ever so stealthily paddled away from the ship to admire our artistic talent, which was highlighted by the glow of the Easter full moon. There, for all to see when the sun came up were the words '*Southern Myth II*' on the side of the far from sleek ketch *Reginald M*.

We went back to our camp and collapsed, looking forward to sharing in the fun we had provided while we enjoyed breakfast.

Much to our disappointment the industrial fatigue led to total fatigue and we slept right through breakfast. In fact it was so late when we finally did surface all the yachts, and *Reginald M*, had disappeared over the horizon and were on their way back to Adelaide.

We were disappointed because everything was so quiet. I thought: "Oh well, someone must have seen it. I hope they got as much of a laugh this morning as we did last night."

Recuperation for me and my Sharpie crew that day came via a fishing trip with my brother Tom who was still there with his little yacht, *Lialeeta*. We went out to the Orontes Bank, which is a ten-fathom bank about 10 miles off Port Vincent. It's a good snapper fishing ground.

We had our lines over the side and were catching quite a few 4lb and 5lb snapper—quite big fish—when suddenly, down below the surface, I saw this monstrous grey thing and said to the guys: "I think there's a giant stingray down there." It went away then a few minutes later it came back, this time closer to the surface. I couldn't believe my eyes. It was a huge Great White Pointer shark.

Tom's boat was 24 feet long and this shark looked to be the same length. Tom said: "I've got a big shark hook and a wire trace. We'll have a go at this."

Dick Bartholomaeus couldn't believe what he was seeing, let alone what he was hearing. He stood in the companionway muttering: "You're crazy. You blokes are mad." I said to Tom: "Where is that Luger pistol you've got on board?"

I found the pistol, loaded it and positioned myself in the cockpit while Tom baited a big hook with snapper heads. The hook had a wire trace about 8 feet long attached to it which was then attached to a roll of thick manila rope. We used a small kapok fender for a float so the bait was set just below the surface. Tom threw the baited hook over the side and let it settle. Within seconds this huge grey beast just appeared out of nowhere and went straight for I cannot forget seeing the huge gills and realising just how big crooked they were—about one foot high.

The shark came around, eyed off the bait, then ignored it.

Very strange, we thought as it just kept cruising below the yacht. Tom suddenly twigged: "I know what he's after."

He had been spotlight shooting the night before on the Correll's farm and had some rabbits and a couple of hares gutted and hanging in the rigging. There was just a drop of blood occasionally dripping out of their noses and into the water. "That's what he's after. The rabbits. It's the blood attracting him." Dick continued muttering: "Forget it you blokes. You're mad."

Tom grabbed one of the rabbits, skinned it in a flash and put a hook through it. He then threw this bait out and sure enough around the side of the yacht yet again came this massive shark. We watched in awe as it rolled on its side and opened its enormous mouth. It was only 10 feet away and the water was so clear I could see a double row of huge triangular teeth lining a hole that was big enough for me to fit through.

Bang! He hit the bait and away went the rabbit, the hook, the wire, the float and the rope—screaming away from the yacht. We weren't anchored, just drifting, and Tom quickly looped the rope around a cleat on the side in the cockpit. He frantically eased the rope out while the little *Lialeeta* was being dragged through the ocean backwards. Every now and then the shark would turn and come back towards us. Tom would hastily haul in as much rope as he could while I took aim with the Luger. We had one very angry and very large shark in our presence now and we knew if it leapt out of the water and attacked us it wouldn't be a world first.

Fortunately it didn't get too close to the boat and eventually it turned and ran, taking almost the entire length of rope with it. Next thing it came out of the water, thrashed and crashed around then fell back into the water. There was one almighty bang. It had snapped the half-inch thick rope right where it joined the wire. The shark was gone.

Thinking back we realised we were lucky it didn't come up out of the water and attack the rabbits in the rigging. The Great White can go crazy at times.

With that excursion behind us it was time to head back to Adelaide and when I arrived home the first thing mother—who had also been in Port Vincent—greeted me with was: "Jim, you wouldn't believe what happened. Some vandals painted 'Southern Myth II' on the bulwark of *Reginald M*."

She said she heard the captain of the *Reginald M*, Captain Heritage, berating the Commodore of the Squadron, Henry Rymill, in the main street of Port Vincent "using language I never knew existed."

Norm Howard and others apparently thought it was a great joke and took plenty of photographs, but we had no desire to own up to the artwork. Incredibly our code of silence on the episode stayed in place for 40 years. It wasn't until I was given the honour of heading the ceremony at the Royal South Australian Yacht Squadron in 1994 for the recommissioning of *Southern Myth* in preparation for the 50th anniversary Sydney–Hobart race that I admitted to the handiwork.

While the company always encouraged my participation in sailing it still expected maximum effort from me in the office, though I'm not sure I ever reached their expectations! I progressed from shipping clerk towards the sales area of the business, where one of my major roles was to act as a sort of host to people visiting the office. They were mainly buyers and it was my job to take them for a cool drink in the cellar or sample room so they could appreciate the quality of Hardy's wines. It didn't take me long to realise that if I wasn't careful this company hospitality on my part could become an occupational hazard, because it was obvious that there was an ever-increasing number of regular buyers who wanted all the free drinks they could get for just the few bottles of wine they could buy.

If there was an occupational hazard for the company it was, and I say it in the nicest possible way, my mother. She would blow into the office from time to time and when she did I could sense some people cringing and almost hiding behind their desks. The word would go around the office—"Auntie Eileen has come in the door"— and that meant all work would stop. When she was there no one was able to work. Mother would round everyone up, starting with the assistant secretary Ray Drew, refusing to listen to anyone saying "No", and take them into the sampling room were they would have to have one or two drinks with her and shoot the breeze. Mother was such an influential woman even the general manager, old Dick Clark, would have a sweat on his brow as soon as she walked through the door. While the management might not have been too impressed, the staff really did love her. The interesting thing about Mum was that I never saw her drink on her own, even at home. She believed that wine should always be appreciated with some food and in the company of others—so she would go out and round up somebody. Of course when you are offering free drinks it is not hard to find someone to join you.

Everyone remembers buying their first car and the freedom and social status it brought. No one was more proud than me on a special day in 1955 when I bought Pat Malone's father's old "A" Model Ford buckboard, or utility as most people would call it. It cost the princely sum of 25 pounds, and was a 1929, green-grey, very rusty four-cylinder model with no canopy. You could call it an open touring model, which was ideal for dragging a boat around or putting junk in the back, but it certainly wasn't too good for my courting with Anne. This unfortunate feature came to light very early, on a night when I was unable to borrow Mum's Daimler to take Anne to the Theatre Royal in Adelaide. Off we went in the old Ford with one very special piece of equipment, an umbrella, not because of rain but because dark, rusty water would come spitting out of the top of the radiator. If it wasn't for the umbrella Anne and her theatre frock would have taken on an appearance that had distinct similarities to a dalmatian. Anne and I always enjoyed going to the theatre and occasionally I would agree to indulge in another of her favourite pastimes, dancing. I would be dragged along reluctantly, stressing two points—I couldn't dance, and there was no alcohol available. I combated the latter problem by sneaking in my own supply of brandy in a hip flask that I could add to dry ginger ale or cola. That in turn eased the pain of my first problem. It made the dancing a bit easier.

The year was made even more memorable through my participation in my first Sydney–Hobart yacht race. For a sailing enthusiast like me it was the equivalent of stepping from youth to manhood. I went with South Australia's better known offshore yachtsman Norm Howard and his famous yacht *Southern Myth*. He had done pretty well at his first attempt in the previous year's Hobart race and there were high expectations placed on him this time around. Unfortunately, like so many offshore sailors in those days, he had become trapped in the handicap game. He was forever trying to reduce the handicap rating on the yacht, not realising that at the same time he was downgrading the yacht's performance potential at an even greater rate. He had reduced the area of the mainsail dramatically, something that would have been fine if you were sailing in twenty knot winds all the time. But that wasn't to be the case in a race like the Sydney–Hobart. The yacht lacked horsepower in light winds. He invited Dick Bartholomaeus and myself to join his regular crew of old St Peter's College blokes for what I thought would be a very exciting adventure. Dick Clark continued with his support of my sailing activities by not only giving me the time off to do the race, but to do the delivery voyage to Sydney as well. By the time we got to Sydney I had wished in some ways I hadn't done the voyage because head winds turned what would normally be a seven day trip into a two week test of endurance. We did spend about 24 hours in Waterloo Bay behind Wilson's Promontory, where we tried to tamper with the cliff face. There was a great big rock perched on top of the hill and the aim was to get it over the edge and into the sea. It had become a challenge for passing yachtsmen for some time and we arrived well equipped for it. We lugged big hydraulic jacks up the hill to achieve our goal. Some hours later we sailed from Waterloo Bay with the rock still sitting on top of the hill and two broken jacks in the bilge of the yacht.

Having been to Sydney a couple of years earlier Dick and I thought we knew what was going on around town and where to find the action. It was Christmas Day and it didn't take us long to find a couple of very nice Australian girls who were to set sail the next day on the ocean liner *Stratheden* for England. We took them to dinner and in return they invited us back to the ship so they could return the hospitality. The offer was too good to refuse and greatly outweighed the fact that the Sydney–Hobart race started at midday the next day. We were on the ship until the wee hours, and when we got back to the Cruising Yacht Club at Rushcutters Bay there was just enough dawn light to work out which yacht was which. We found *Southern Myth* and decided it best to slip through the forward hatch to go below deck in consideration of those who were sleeping, and to decrease the chance of having to explain our whereabouts should we wake the owner. My bunk was in the bow so I had no trouble finding my way. I just slipped in fully clothed, collar, tie and all. Wouldn't you know it—the next thing there is this almighty crash. Dick collected something in the darkness, fell on his back on the cabin floor and woke everyone. We had blown it. From out of the darkness back aft Norm Howard inquired sarcastically from his bunk: "Have you blokes had a nice evening?" There were only a couple of hours sleep to be had before the noise on the dock and around the club left no doubt it was race day. It was a day I had dreamed about. I was going to be aboard a yacht for the Sydney–Hobart race, one of the world's three offshore racing classics and a race that until that moment I had only read about and hoped for the chance to compete in. The thrill of the start was beyond my greatest dreams. It was a glorious day: sunny, clear skies and a perfect north-east breeze. Every headland, every vantage point along the harbour shoreline was just packed with people while on the water just about anything that floated seemed to be there crammed with spectators. And there at the front of the fleet were the two big boats, *Kurrewa* and *Even*, looking absolutely sensational as they charged towards the Heads. Their new creamy white cotton sails were pristine and the crews looked equally smart, the *Kurrewa* crew wearing all white and the *Even* crew in red shirts.

The strong following winds suited *Southern Myth* with her smaller mainsail and we managed to drop our rivals astern over the first 48 hours. But off the Tasmanian coast it became another "if only" race. If only the wind had held and if only we had been closer to the Tasmanian coast we would have done very well. For 24 hours we sat becalmed well offshore, the small mainsail that had been cut down to improve our handicap being of no use in our efforts to catch the occasional puffs that found us. We just sat there and watched helplessly as other yachts that had been so far behind we couldn't see them crept up over the horizon and sailed past, right in on the rocks. Regardless of the frustration and our disappointing result I looked on the race as a wonderful experience. And of course, as with any young bloke doing his first Hobart race, there was the consolation of having a pretty exciting time when we arrived. The young ladies just seemed to be there waiting for the yachts to arrive . . . not for me of course, but for my friends. I just went along to make up the numbers!

I flew back to Adelaide to a far from warm reception from Anne. The waterfront tomtoms had been working overtime and word had reached her about Bart and me and the ladies from the *Stratheden*. I thought we were safe, especially after hearing mates say things like: "Don't worry. Word won't get back to Adelaide." Well, not only did it get back, but it was there before we returned. Anne was far from impressed and really twisted my ear. I was a good boy after that, for many, many years. Ah, another lesson.

I was becoming more competitive on the sailing scene in Adelaide but needed a better boat to have any chance of knocking off the top guys from around Australia. So when the chance came to buy one of the best Sharpies in the country, *Swan*—a beautiful Tasmanian-built boat—I jumped at it. My results improved immediately, so much so that I finished second to Rolly Tasker in the Sharpie Australian Championship in Adelaide in the 1955/56 season.

My career was also taking some interesting turns for the better. Dick Clark was sufficiently impressed with my study efforts and my work in the office that he decided it was time I went out on the road and learnt more about the business. I was finding the part-time study and work very interesting. The Diploma of Accountancy course comprised twelve subjects and I was doing the maximum allowed, two subjects each year. I was finding things like company law, mercantile law and income tax law more interesting than straight accountancy and at one stage it crossed my mind that I might switch and study law at the Adelaide University, next door to the School of Mines. Then one day the head of the school came in, Lyle Braddock, who was to later become head of the Australian Society of Accountants, and hit me right between the eyes with the most logical piece of thinking on accountancy. "There is only one thing to remember on this course," this old codger said, then moved over to the chalk board and wrote in bold letters: "Sales less cost of sales equals profit." He then turned to the class and added: "There are only two ways you can increase profit. Either you increase sales or decrease the cost of sales." Then he walked out. I thought: "That sounds good enough for me. I'm going to hang in with accountancy."

To go out on the road for Hardy's was to be a great way to learn a lot more about life as well as the business. I was keen to sell and equally keen to impress, but there were plenty of hurdles. Once every month I was to go across to the Yorke Peninsula, visiting all the hotels along the way to sell our wine. The very first pub I called into on my first trip was the Royal Hotel in Port Wakefield, right at the top of the Gulf of St Vincent. When I went in and asked for the publican I was told to go outside to the back of the pub where this surly-looking character was in the garden, digging up carrots with a pitch fork.

"Hello. Jim Hardy's my name from Hardy's Tintara Wines."

This fellow didn't even take time to stop and look up at me. He just kept pushing his fork into the vegetable garden. "Where's Harry Garrett?" he asked gruffly, still digging.

"Harry's just working in the city nowadays. He's been with us a lot of years I know, but he won't be doing this run any more. This is now my territory."

"Well, bugger off then," said the carrot digger. "I don't want any of your stuff any more."

"God, this is going to be a tough calling," I thought as I walked out. Total rejection on my first stop.

The great respect Harry Garrett had generated was fine for our company, but it wasn't going to make my job easier. Of course it wasn't like that everywhere. I met up with plenty of good publicans, some of whom had very pretty daughters.

Anne remained the woman who mattered to me most. Our relationship was on the up and up, so in early 1956 I decided the time had arrived. Without telling Anne I called her father and arranged to meet him one lunch time in his office. Ronald Jackson, R. A. Jackson as he was known, was an architect-in-chief for the schools and hospitals section of the South Australian Government Architect's office. Pumped up with all the courage I could muster I marched into his office at the appointed time. There was "R.A." sitting behind his drawing board, his sandwiches and a cup of tea in front of him. He seemed a little uncomfortable, while I was just plain nervous.

"Yes, Jim, what is it you'd like to say?"

I thought there was no use in beating around the bush and passing pleasantries about the weather or his workload so I dived straight in and asked if he would be agreeable to me marrying Anne. Well, the poor bloke just about choked on his half-eaten sandwich. His eyes bulged to the size of golf balls. He regained his composure and agreed to me becoming his son-in-law. Armed with that seal of approval I then went to see Anne, and much to my delight she accepted my proposal. I was to learn later that the reason Anne's father was so shocked by my approach was that he didn't think such etiquette happened any more.

That year, 1956, was also the year of the Olympics in Melbourne and this was to become my next target in sailing. The International 12-Square Metre Sharpie, which was one of the five sailing classes for the Games, wasn't a lot different from the Sharpies we had been racing for years. The hull shape was essentially the same, they didn't carry a spinnaker, the mainsail only had short battens and they carried only a two-man crew. It was the obvious way for me to go so I built a new boat, *Tintara*, and grabbed the biggest and strongest bloke

I could find, an Adelaide fellow named Bob Baldock, to be my crew. I had my boat measured in Adelaide, then headed for Melbourne for the Australian selection trials. We had won one race and finished second in the next so were leading the series when out came Perth's Rolly Tasker with the protest book. He was favoured to win the trials and I don't think he liked this young bloke from Adelaide showing him the way. He protested that the pumps we had in our boat were fixed and not loose as required under the rules. For us they were loose in the boat and only became fixed when I clamped a bracket to them to use them during the race. He also protested about how the hull planking extended just half an inch behind the stern of the boat. He said that that helped the boat sail faster. Well, I knew I had pushed the rules to the edge but everything I'd done had been approved by the measurers in Adelaide. But while they found *Tintara* to be legal, the measurers in Melbourne didn't so we were scrubbed from the first two races. We still managed to finish third behind Tasker and Ron Wright, a famous Queensland sailor and boat builder. The irony of it all was that Rolly went on to represent Australia and it wasn't until then that we realised that the pumps he had in his boat, when being jammed into the centre case, were far more permanent fixtures than ours. Over the years we were to learn that Rolly was full of all sorts of tricks, like using balsa where there should have been oak. I guess he, like so many other sportsmen, pushed the rules to the limit then hoped he wouldn't be caught. Everything was legal until you were told otherwise. Oddly enough Rolly missed winning Australia's first ever Olympic yachting gold medal in Melbourne after he was disqualified as a result of a collision in the final heat. Unfortunately for me the pressure of work was such that I could only spare one day to go to Melbourne and watch the sailing. In three days I drove to Melbourne, watched one race, then drove back to Adelaide.

On 20 December 1956 Anne and I had our big day. The newspapers in Adelaide carried the headline the next day: "Yachtsman's Wedding All White." The Chaplain at St Peter's College explained that we could not be married in the school chapel during the summer school holidays, so we chose the All Saints church hall near our family home at Seacliff. I thought that would be fine because I had helped the clergymen there with communion during my last couple of years at school. The local clergyman, Reverend Lloyd, didn't seem too happy when we asked the school chaplain to perform the ceremony. But we were happy and that was what mattered most. Needless to say it was a big wedding and an equally large reception back at our home.

The company loaned me the company Holden utility, complete with 'Tintara Wines' emblazoned across the back, for us to go on our honeymoon to Port Lincoln. I was into owning my third A Model Ford, but that seemed a bit too low brow to take my new bride away in. We stayed at the Boston Hotel in Port Lincoln, a lovely old large, weatherboard hotel. The first morning, around 6 am, it was very apparent that the publican's young child had a vintage tricycle. The thing hadn't seen oil since the day it was bought and it made a terrific racket—squeak, squeak, squeak—as the kid rocketed around the verandah outside our room. The immediate priority for me when I got up that morning was to go out and buy a can of household oil, find the offending tricycle and oil it to the degree where it was silent and I could get more sleep!

Much to my delight, the yacht club at Port Lincoln had just been formed and the locals, everyone from photographers to fishermen, had bought about half a dozen dilapidated old Sharpies from hither and yon. Having watched these guys rig up the previous day, it all got the better of me. I had to see what was happening. What a mistake.

"Oh, could you show us how to rig the boat?" they'd ask. I said to Anne that I should help them. Wouldn't you know it—I went down every afternoon, sailed a different boat four days running and won in every one. The guys thought I was from outer space. After each race I'd just step ashore and they'd let me walk off like God while they unrigged the boat. I was like Jesus teaching Peter how to fish. But if you meet people who literally don't know which way to put the mast in, chances are they won't know which way to steer it. My ultimate moment came on the final day when I sailed this really rugged, heavy old unit for a beaut old codger. He was so thrilled when we won. This lovely old guy was just so happy. I went back to my bride really chuffed, but she was far from impressed. While I had agreed to go to Melbourne for just one day while the Olympic yachting was on, I'd sailed five of the seven days we were on our honeymoon.

Anne and I moved in to the family home at Seacliff for the

first six months of our marriage while Mum went away to visit relatives in New Zealand and friends in England. When she returned we bought a fairly new little fibro cottage at 1 Ocean Boulevard in nearby Seacliff Park. It was a typical sort of house for the area at the time with a big verandah going around the outside of it and no fence. We named it "Humpybong" after a little township up in Queensland where we had a lot of fun during one trip away with the Sharpies. Our house had two things very much in its favour: an attic that I could turn into a sail loft and a large garage where I could keep our Ford Pilot—we had taken a step up from A models—and set up a workshop. After some fairly major extensions, designed by my father-in-law, I could also keep the Sharpie under cover in the garage.

Years later I was to look back on this period in life and realise that my mother had rung an alarm bell that I didn't hear. Both Anne and Mum were keen golfers and used to play together from time to time. One day mum called me aside to say that when she went to pick Anne up at 10 o'clock one morning for golf she was having a glass of sherry. "I didn't like the look of that," Mum said. "It's not a good sign." I just shrugged it off, saying there was probably nothing in it. Mum went on to say that she believed Anne's father had faced a drinking problem and that I should keep an eye on her. But I didn't heed the advice. Now I think that maybe my mother was right and that what she had seen really was the start of something. What we are learning today is that alcoholism is a gene, a hereditary addictive problem. I guess we were lucky as children to be brought up with alcohol all around us and to have a healthy respect for it. Mum always stressed that the one thing she didn't want any of her children to do was start drinking spirits before the age of 30. We laughed at her a bit as we grew older, but she really was trying to get the message across that some table wine with food was not a problem but the other things could spell trouble. It was the natural product versus the man-made product in spirits. If you have a bunch of grapes in a jug they'll turn themselves into wine, whereas to make brandy or to fortify wine you must boil the wine, condense the vapour—which is alcohol—then feed the alcohol back as a fortified spirit. I believe it's the human interference that manifests the problem and accelerates any tendency one may have towards seeking solace from alcohol.

Maybe, just maybe, if our lives hadn't been so busy, I may have been aware of the fact that Anne had a problem bubbling away below the surface. Actually I was so busy with work and study that even sailing tended to take a back seat during my first year or two of marriage. Much to Anne's credit, she didn't complain about the amount of time I was spending away from home, working on the road for Hardy's. The trips were becoming longer and more demanding, the biggest being from Adelaide all the way through to Darwin. Until I started making those trips we just had agents working for us. Then we saw opportunities to expand the business so grabbed them. My Ford Pilot would never have made the distance so I would be given brother Tom's company car, an FE model Holden, to drive to Port Augusta where I would put in on the train, the old Ghan, then set off on the seemingly endless train ride to Alice Springs. It was the slowest train you could imagine. The guard told me on one trip about a guy who came up to him and asked if he could get off to pick some wild flowers. The guard said: "There are no wild flowers around here," to which the guy replied: "It's all right. I brought the seeds." Slow as it was, the scenery and some of the sights I'll never forget, especially the time I woke up one morning to see a dingo standing boldly on a rugged, rocky outcrop, perfectly silhouetted against a vivid orange sunrise just watching the train trundle past.

Orlando had the bulk of the business in Alice Springs. The pub I stayed in, the Riverside, was only on a riverside when it flooded once every blue moon. The big hotel in town was the Alice Springs hotel, a huge concrete structure built and run by an old St Peter's boy, Lysurgus John Rickard Underdown. He was buying Orlando port by the ton, 40 cases at a time, until I managed to pull the rug out and get the business for Tintara VO Invalid Port, or "Nullabor Champagne" as some of the locals called it.

It was always a fascinating drive for me from Alice Springs up to Darwin, on a highway that had developed more pot holes than bitumen since the Americans built it during World War II. On my first trip, old Harold Drakeford, our Alice Springs agent, came with me. We stopped at Barrow Creek, a place where the only thing to be found was a pub and hundreds upon hundreds of goats, which all seemed to live on old semi-trailer tyres because, apart from that, there was nothing else to eat, not even a stick. The evening came and we sat down for dinner. I saw turkey on the menu so ordered it. It arrived on the table and I had started munching into it when

102

Harold asked: "Do you know what it is?"

"Turkey."

"That's bush turkey. You're not supposed to be eating it. It's protected."

Next morning came breakfast and I ordered some cereal, or soggies as I called them, with milk. "It's very creamy, very rich milk," I said to Harold with an element of concern. "It's goat's milk," he announced. I thought chops and eggs would be a safe bet to finish off breakfast. But no. The chops, about twelve inches long, arrived in front of me. Goat chops!

That part of Australia was a world unto itself where nothing was considered out of the ordinary. Stories that would shock city people were simply taken as a fact of life out there. One night I stopped off at the Daly Waters Hotel, right on the edge of Rum Jungle, which was being prepared as a uranium mine. They were tough hombres working out there. Jackie Hargraves, who ran the hotel, had the best story of all. Two of the guys who were driving the massive bulldozers out at Rum Jungle would come into the pub for a drink most nights—one being a huge, tough and aggressive guy and the other a slightly smaller, more passive sort of bloke. The big aggressive guy never let up on the small bloke. He was always giving him a hard time. One night while playing pool the little guy made a miss hit. The big bloke saw the opportunity to stir once more so got up, walked across, bent over and farted in the passive bloke's face. The other guy, playing pool, couldn't believe what he had seen.

"How do you put up with that?" he asked.

"I'm getting sick of it," the passive bloke replied. "If I had a gun I'd shoot the bastard."

"I've got a gun in my truck."

He went out, got the gun, brought it back in and said: "Here you go."

Jackie saw the whole thing developing and alerted her boyfriend, who had been sampling too many of the hotel's products on the day. "Ah, they'll be OK," he said.

How wrong he was. The next thing the passive bloke took hold of the double-barrelled shotgun, pointed it at the big bloke and shouted: "Fart no more you big bugger," and with that blew him away with both barrels. One of the locals rushed across to try to help the guy, only to realise there were bits of heart and chest splattered all over the wall. Jackie rushed around to the local police station to report the incident only to find the little bloke there already, giving himself up. Apparently he got off with a manslaughter charge in the end because of the way he had been provoked.

When I was back in Adelaide the company gave me little respite. While I was very busy with my accountancy studies it was thought it would be valuable for my career to run a wine appreciation course at the School of Mines as well. So with the backing of the Wine and Brandy Association of Australia, Jim Hardy became the head tutor in wine appreciation, an obligation I had once a week for almost three years whenever I was in or around Adelaide. The course started at 5.30 pm and I can tell you there was more than one very heavy drive back from Yorke Peninsula and other places over that period just to be back in time. It was particularly tough after I'd been away selling grog for all the previous week.

For Anne and me our social activities revolved around sailing during summer and football for winter. While my football playing days were well and truly over I followed Sturt with keen interest. At Preparatory School I had supported Glenelg, spending every weekend following them around with David Walker, Jim Macpherson and Pat Malone. But always, deep down, I had a yearning to support Sturt; my cousin Owen Price had played for them, as had many Saint's old scholars. I switched my allegiance when a school mate, Tony Goodchild, one of the greats of St Peter's, started playing for Sturt. My friends still rubbish me about supporting Sturt, but I justify it all through the simple fact that the border between Sturt and Glenelg clubs goes right through Seacliff, and the yacht club is in the Sturt district. I was to eventually become Vice President of the Sturt club, a title that could have been defined as fund raiser. There were many very successful fund-raising picnic days staged at the Tintara vineyard to support the club. I am still the holder of ticket number one for Sturt.

After actively racing sailboats for more than fifteen years, 1959 was to be my big year—I finally cracked the big time and won my first Australian championship, the Sharpie title in a series in Perth. By that time I had learned some of the tricks. I had this great big extra keelson, a piece of timber fitted inside the boat that ran along the centreline, to bring the boat up to weight. When the measurers declared the boat was still underweight I hollowed out part of the underside of the keelson and poured in some lead. It was a beautifully varnished piece of timber and one day I took it out of the boat and leant it up against the garage wall at Mum's house. Her old gardener came along later and decided to move it. The poor bugger tried to pick up this piece of timber and just about broke his back. He overbalanced and the timber took control, crashing to the ground and taking him with it. Poor bastard thought it was alive. We raced for the title on the Swan River in Perth and Queensland's John Cuneo, the defending champion, was favourite for back-to-back wins. After we won the title he sent telegrams back to Queensland saying we had won because of team racing and that it was all beyond the pale. He probably wasn't completely wrong, but he wasn't very popular at the time. He didn't endear himself to other competitors, so if they got the chance to cut him off legally they would. I got to like the guy a lot in later life, but he has always kept to himself, a bit of a loner, a one and only, even through to when he won an Olympic gold medal. John is a very serious man until after the racing. Anyway, we won that one and that's all that mattered. My name is in the book.

I was appointed Sales Supervisor at Hardy's soon after and was pleased to be able to report things were getting better for the company all the time. Our one problem was that we were outgrowing our city office and consequently suffering from a considerable breakdown in communications between there and our major bottling plant and warehouse at Mile End, which was literally one mile away. All that was happening at the head office in Currie Street was administration and the bottling of our champagnes in the basement. A tough decision had to be made, one that would sever another tie with old Thomas Hardy, our founder. He had lived and worked at those Currie Street premises but the time had come when it was no longer viable for us to stay there and have the company split between two premises. I was one of the people who advocated the move to Mile End and eventually common sense prevailed over emotion.

There were lots of wonderful memories within the walls of that old building. It was a real hands-on family affair. Whenever it came time for the next stage of the champagne-making process the call went out for staff to go to the cellars. The most frustrating and time consuming operation came at the end of the second fermentation when we had to fire the corks from each bottle then re-cork them.

The corks were held in with metal clips and after they had been released the clips had to be put through a machine to be straightened so they could be used again. Talk about remedial therapy—sitting in front of a silly machine with the clips going thump, thump, thump through it then falling out the other end into a bucket. After doing this for an hour one day I thought: "This is stupid. It's driving me crazy. But hang on. If it's making me crazy, maybe, just maybe, crazy people might enjoy doing it." I went to our manager, Dick Clark, and suggested we look into having the clip-straightening process taken up by a home for the mentally handicapped even though sheltered workshops were unheard of in those days. Dick liked the idea and after some searching we came across the person we needed at the Minda Home at Glenelg, a home for youngsters affected by Down's syndrome. This young kid just loved the job so much we couldn't supply enough clips for him to straighten. One night they found him out in the shed at the home working in the dark in the middle of the night, still straightening the clips. Don Crawford, who was the head of Minda, told me some years later that my idea to get that young chap working had led to the establishment of several workshops for the home that had become very successful.

As 1960 and the next Olympics approached my thoughts started to turn towards that event, but not before a defence of the national Sharpie title. The series was to be sailed in Adelaide so it was only right that I fly the flag on home waters after winning the previous year in Perth. Queensland's John Cuneo was desperate to regain the crown he lost in the west, especially when he was convinced that he had been a victim of team racing. The waters off Adelaide saw a broad spectrum of conditions for the entire championship, including winds of around 25 knots in the final heat. I was racing *Tintara* while Cuneo was steering *Daring*. *Seacraft* magazine in April 1960 recorded: "It was blowing about 25 knots with severe gusts recorded in the city at 40 knots, liberally sprinkled at infrequent intervals.

"The same old early race pattern unfolded as *Tintara* led from *Daring* followed by *Winjin*, *Fiona*, and the remainder well spread out. *Winjin* swam soon after rounding the weather mark and *Daring* was slowly but surely whittling down *Tintara*'s half-minute lead until at the leeward mark *Tintara* was but a boat length ahead.

"Several yachts ditched on the run, and *Daring* showed from the commencement of lap two just how good she really is and why she has won the title thrice and been runner up thrice in the past seven years.

"She left everyone else astern, and sailed a sure certain race.

"Halfway down the second run a shout went up. *Tintara* was jibing mid-way down the run, seconds later a further shout, and *Tintara* just couldn't hold it and went in."

That capsize was the end of the regatta and the defence for us. We finished second to a very satisfied John Cuneo. His revenge was sweet.

JOHN CROOKE, of Brisbane – competitor in Adelaide: "I had the pleasure of meeting Jim when he came to Brisbane at Christmas in 1957 for the Australian Heavyweight Sharpie titles, then firmed our friendship at the titles in Adelaide. Practical jokes based on interstate rivalry were part and parcel of any Sharpie regatta. The challenge to outsmart a rival crew on shore was almost as strong as the challenge on the race course. On the night of the prize giving in Adelaide Jim and Anne foolishly left their home unlocked. When they returned to their abode late that night they were too tired to bother with turning on the bedroom light, unfortunately for them. As the sun came up they awoke to an incredible racket. Half a dozen chooks, black Orpingtons, which had been 'borrowed' from a neighbour's yard the previous evening were either laying eggs or endeavouring to alight from their roost on top of the wardrobe in the Hardy bedroom. That was the ultimate prank that year. Two years later, I had forgotten about the black Orpingtons incident, but Jim Hardy hadn't. We were both racing 505s in a championship in Melbourne. One night during a regatta I joined Jim Hardy and a group of South Australians for dinner. I escorted a beautiful young lady who was temporarily and excruciatingly in love with me. We enjoyed lobster thermidor and my lady friend was impressed to the stage where she agreed to return to my two star hotel room for a nightcap. As we left the dinner I noted a smirk on Jim's face and those of his fellow crow eaters but didn't give this a second thought. Unbeknown to me the revenge of the black Orpingtons was about to take place. Back in my room things were progressing nicely with my lady friend. We were just getting comfortable when she rolled over then let out a blood-curdling scream which could have been heard three blocks away. There was a roar of laughter

> *from outside my room. The crow eaters had struck. I turned on*
> *the light to discover the spikes and shells from six lobsters firmly*
> *implanted in her beautiful, bare derriere."*

The lure of the Olympics was sufficiently strong for me to decide to leave the Sharpie class, which was now entering the lightweight Sharpie era, and get the state's first one-man Olympic Finn dinghy. I found a boat that had been brought to Melbourne for the '56 games by a Dutch guy. He brought his own boat out for training purposes even though the Finn dinghies were supplied. Then the Queen of the Netherlands pulled the team out of the Olympics in support of the Hungarian uprising over communism, so this guy was left high and dry. His chance of a lifetime to sail in the Olympics had been taken away and he was sufficiently browned off to decide to stay in Australia. He moved to Adelaide to start up a small engineering business and I bobbed up as a buyer. I was the only Finn owner in Adelaide but that caused me no concern. I saw the chance to race another international class in the 1960 Olympics as my only goal. I trained my butt off with a massive fitness program for the Olympics, running across the football field with a bar of weights across my shoulders. Dawn Fraser's coach, Harry Gallagher, was my trainer. When I stop to think back about what I put myself through it's no wonder things are starting to break up in my body now.

I headed off to Melbourne for the Olympic trials feeling reasonably confident about my chances but returned to Adelaide disappointed. My patriotism got the best of me in the trials. I was the only guy on the course with Australian-made sails. I was competitive sailing upwind but I just couldn't get the power or speed on the downwind legs that the others were generating from their imported sails. I finished about sixth. I guess it was a bit like trying to fart at a windmill.

My training for this regatta was sufficiently serious for me to go off the booze for the two months before racing began. The Queenslanders, however, did everything they could to encourage me to imbibe at the conclusion of each race. As competitors reached the shore they would welcome them with a large jug full of what they called a "creature", a very potent mixture of Bundaberg Rum and coke with ice. It became known as the "monster" when they ran out of coke. I rejected their hospitality until the end of the third race, when it became very apparent I wasn't going to the

Olympics. After a couple more drinks I was in a sufficiently relaxed mood to decide I would then accept an invitation from the same group to attend a party they we having at St Kilda. After more "creatures" at the yacht club I decided I would give one of the Queenslanders, Victor Day, a lift to the party in my old Ford Pilot. We had driven for some considerable time and not seen any signs to St Kilda so I began to wonder where we were. In looking for signs I managed to take one corner a bit fast and next thing the old Ford Pilot was whistling off the side of the road and into the sand.

"Stop the car. Stop the car. I'm not going any further with you," Victor shouted. "You're going to kill us."

I did as he suggested and stopped trying to drive the car out of the sand. We went across to a nearby telephone booth and called the Queenslanders at the party to get some directions.

"Where are you?" they asked.

"Mentone," I said, reading the name off the card in the booth.

"Mentone. You're 180 degrees off course. You've gone out of the yacht club and turned right instead of left."

Taxi!

We eventually arrived at the party and it was a great night. I drowned my "no Olympics" sorrows and made a good start on undoing all the fitness I had gained during my months of training.

When it came time to leave I decided I should collect my car as I would need it in the morning. It was about 1 am and my mate Dick Howard took it upon himself to drive me all the way to Mentone in his MG.

We arrived at the fateful corner in Mentone to find a police car stopped alongside my car and police climbing in and out of it. I went to get out of the car but was stopped by an solid punch in the stomach by Dick.

"What did you do that for?"

"You're stupid. Don't get out of the car. Wait until the police leave."

"But it's my car and I should tell them."

I walked across to the police and told them who I was and that it was my vehicle.

"We know you're the owner because we checked with the Adelaide police," the Sergeant said. "We found alcohol in the boot and wet clothes in the car."

"Yes, my clothes are wet from sailing."

"Sailing. We've been searching for bodies in the sandhills for the past two hours. We thought someone had been murdered."

The only thing murdered was my chance of going for an Olympic medal. But I was to score the biggest prize of all that year with the birth of our son David at the Community Hospital in Glenelg. There was a feeling between Anne and myself that if it was a boy I would name him, and if it was a girl then it was Anne's decision. While I was driving down to the hospital just after the birth I had David Nathaniel firmly implanted in my mind, Nathaniel having some tradition with the Hardy name—my grandfather was Thomas Nathaniel Hardy. Then I started thinking to myself that my mother's maiden name, Ponder, had ended in South Australia as her only brother Gilbert had a married daughter, Cynthia. I had decided by the time I reached the hospital it was to be David Ponder Hardy. I guess it was a nice thought on my part but the poor lad copped a pretty hard time through school, even up to today.

Anne was happy with the name but I don't think she has ever forgiven me for my very definite ideas on the rearing of a child in the early stages of life. I insisted on breastfeeding. I just had this theory that if you could breastfeed a child then you should do so for as long as possible. I had been breastfed and in thinking about it long and hard I believed that a child would have a stronger immune system through natural feeding.

My trips for the company, sometimes by road and other times by plane, remained far from boring, especially the ones I made into the Northern Territory with my great sailing companion and friend John Bagshaw. He had come across from Melbourne to Adelaide to be the Sales Manager for General Motors. The same man would go on later in life to head General Motors in Australia, the UK and Germany. On one joint trip "Bags" and I arrived in Tennant Creek. He was there to see Len Kittle of Kittle's Motors, the local Holden distributor, while I was trying to sell Hardy's wines to all the local outlets. We were staying at the Tennant Creek Hotel and after our first day of trying neither of us had achieved any sales. John was more than frustrated because he was pushing General Motor's first automatic model, the Hydramatic. I guess because it was so flat around Tennant Creek no one could see the value in an automatic. We both agreed things couldn't be much worse, so at breakfast the next morning I hit on an idea. "John," I said, "today we will swap jobs. You have a go at selling our wine and I'll have a go at selling your motor cars." It was agreed. The previous day the publican's wife at the Goldfields Hotel, while telling me she didn't want any of our wine, did mention that she and her husband were going to return to Sydney to live. So I cornered her in the bar: "Look, if you are going back to Sydney, with all those hills, you are going to need an automatic car," I told her. "And besides, if you arrive there with one of the new Holden Hydramatics all your friends will know you really made the big time in Tennant Creek." I played along on the theory of not keeping up but being ahead of the Joneses and she really bit at that. She decided it was the way to go and subsequently went out with her husband to order a car. When I caught up with "Bags" later in the day he'd sold the woman's husband, the publican, one ton, or more specifically 40 cases, of our wine!

JOHN BAGSHAW – retired Chairman and Managing Director of General Motors operations in Australia: "We flew into Alice Springs and I was met by the local Holden dealer, Len Kittle, who told Jim and me we were invited to the Rotary Club Ladies' Night dinner that night. It turned out we were the guests of honour. I was asked to get up and say a few words and did, then I introduced my good friend, the wine maker and famous sailor Jim Hardy. It was Jim at his best. He was on his feet for 45 minutes telling all sorts of yarns and jokes, some quite risque. He had the crowd just roaring with laughter. The Alice Springs Rotary Club voted it the best dinner they had ever staged."

My entire circle of friends in Adelaide always had a wonderful attitude towards life. There was always plenty to laugh about and practical jokes were often the call of the day. When David Phillips became engaged John Harrington saw the perfect opportunity to score points. He placed an advertisement in Adelaide's morning newspaper reading: "Going overseas. Must sell 150 laying hens and LP record collection." At the end of the ad he put the telephone number for David Phillips' fiance's father. The ad scored a direct hit on the family with the phone starting to ring at 5 am. Immediate retaliation was called for and over a game of squash that morning Dave and

I decided we would target Harrington with our own advertisement. It was school holiday time so we wrote an ad reading: "Casual work of all descriptions available for men and boys. Apply to John Harrington, Jnr., 66 West Terrace, Adelaide." The address was that of John's father's accountancy office, which John was managing at the time. The next morning I drove down West Terrace at 9 am on my way to my office expecting to see a line of people out into the street. There wasn't a single person outside Harrington's office and I thought: "Gosh, you would have thought somebody would have read that ad." Then I turned into Currie Street and there was Mr Clark, our little company manager, out on the footpath with around 50 people of all sizes standing around glaring at him—all brandishing a piece of green paper. He was obviously distressed and I couldn't work out what was going on. I parked my car at the rear of the building, went through the back door of the office and up to my desk. The next thing an irate Mr Clark came thundering up the stairs to my desk:

"What's going on here? Your friend Harrington is playing some sort of practical joke. I've got 40 or 50 people downstairs, some even in the champagne cellar, all with a piece of paper saying they should see you about a job. I've been trying to pacify them all the time you haven't been here, trying to tell them it's a joke."

I couldn't work out what could have gone wrong because I had read the advertisement and it was in the paper just as Dave and I had written it. Next thing the phone rang and it was David Walker up at Elder Smith's asking what the hell was going on. He had been mistakenly identified as a co-author of the advertisement and had 40 people at his office with a piece of green paper seeking work. It turned out that John Harrington deserved to be crowned the prince of practical jokers. When he arrived at work and saw all the people stretching from his office along West Terrace and around the corner he smelled a rat. After reading the advertisement he didn't bat an eyelid. He just called all the people into his office, thanked them for the wonderful response to the advertisement, advised them that the casual work was available at Thomas Hardy and Sons and David Walker's office at Elder Smiths, then gave them a piece of green John Harrington letterhead paper to take to those two offices. Not surprisingly the real victims of the practical joke, those applying for the job, went around to the office of the *Advertiser* newspaper to complain. Next thing the police were knocking on Harrington's door. They produced the original copy of the advertisement that I had handwritten and asked him if he recognised the writing. Harrington, who had been sitting next to me for six years while we did the accountancy course together at the School of Mines, said to the police: "I've never seen that handwriting in my life."

Practical jokes were just as intense on the sailing circuit. It seemed that if you weren't the target of some prank you weren't part of the scene. During the 1960–61 sailing season we went to Melbourne to sail for a national title. Our South Australian team was staying in a small private hotel in Brighton that was run by a couple of nature's bachelors. We were having some drinks in the lounge one night and Dave Binks, who was part of our group, was putting in some very heavy work on the hotel's attractive young waitress. I could see a very nice situation developing for the couple—Dave was being quite amorous and his advances certainly weren't being rejected. My tip was that Dave would soon be trying to get back to this girl's room with her, and I knew which room it was. Angus Neill had been sitting on the windowsill with his feet out on the hotel roof just admiring the evening so I quietly moved across to him and suggested he went across the roof to the girl's room, slipped in through the window and took her door lock off the latch. A matter of minutes later he casually reappeared in the room and gave me the thumbs-up signal. John Crooke was in on the act so at the appropriate moment the two of us feigned fatigue, said we couldn't be tired for the race the next day, and bid everyone goodnight. We rocketed straight down the hallway and into the waitress's room. I disappeared under one bed and John under the other. Next thing Angus came through the window and hid in the wardrobe.

It wasn't long before we heard the key in the door and the girl entered the room. Dave Binks was right behind her.

"You can't come in here, David. I'll get the sack if you do."

"Oh, don't worry. It will be OK."

"But David, I work here. You don't understand."

Persistence brought a dividend and soon David was sitting on the side of the bed with his young lady.

"Somebody's been in this room," she said suddenly. "The curtains have been closed."

"How could anyone have been in here? Relax."

113

Nature started to have its way and eventually the bed started rocking. I was struggling to contain my laughter. I then knew what people meant when they said they wet themselves laughing. John and I erupted in laughter and with that the wardrobe door burst open and out came Angus. "Binks, you're a dirty bastard," he shouted. The girl fainted.

At the end of 1961 I graduated from the School of Mines, which had become the SA Institute of Technology, with my accountancy diploma. It was my second attempt at the final exam. For weeks prior to my first attempt I had been getting up at 2 am to study every day. I worked on a theory that I would do my studying when I was awake and sleep while I was at Hardy's. My day schedule was to study until 8 am, start work at 9 then fade as the day progressed. I'd go home, have dinner with Anne then go to bed. I realised that I could well face fatigue during the exam so decided the solution would be to take a miniature bottle of Hardy's Black Bottle brandy with me. I remember the question that hit me hardest, one encompassing our entire syllabus. It read something like: "You own a service station. It also distributes Dunlop Tyres and Dunlop batteries. You sell Shell fuel and oil and you have a car repair section. You also provide additional services, including banking and the retailing of products. A fire destroys the business and all that remains are charred records." The question was for me to reconstruct a profit and loss account and calculate the tax I would be required to pay. That was enough for me. I knew it was time for the Black Bottle. I looked around the room, made sure no one was watching and gave myself a great whack of the brandy. The combination of fatigue and alcohol was all too much and the exam paper became one almighty blur—I couldn't focus. I couldn't read a thing or write. I was gone. The results came out and my name wasn't among those who had passed the course. I passed every other subject, including company law. When I went back in 1961 for my second try at my diploma my tutor told me I had gone within an ace of achieving the required marks the previous year. It was a very expensive brandy for Jim Hardy.

Chapter Six

Good Times, Bad Times

"JIM, THE BOARD has decided to appoint you a Director of the company." Those words from Uncle Ken Hardy, the Chairman, came out of the blue, as did the suggestion a few months later that I move to Sydney to head our east coast operations. In a matter of weeks in early 1962, not long after I had graduated with a diploma in accountancy, my career path was charted.

Ironically, while I had been doing my studies, I put a paper to the Annual General Meeting of the company stressing the importance of continuing our branch operations in Sydney. New South Wales was the most populous state and I'd always felt that if we did not succeed on the eastern seaboard there would be no opportunity to expand the company. Adelaide alone could not produce sufficient sales to make the business viable in the future. We had been operating in Sydney since Federation, primarily selling Tintara port, sherry and brandy—the table wine market had yet to develop in Australia— and my thoughts on the future there had been prompted by an earlier board decision to hand over our marketing to John Cawsey and Co., wine and spirit merchants, to give us more marketing clout. I was not impressed with that decision, firmly believing we were putting our future in a very important market in the hands of others.

Much to my delight Anne was very supportive of the move. Fortunately she had only her parents to consider when it came to immediate family, so that made things easier. Also, we knew we would be heading back to Adelaide on visits quite regularly. I think the

115

emotional side of moving was tougher on me, leaving so many lifelong friends and a close-knit family behind. While the move was a step up the Hardy's ladder I knew that with New South Wales offering the greatest potential for company expansion, success would mean the move was permanent.

The decision was for me to be a one-person advance party to Sydney. That would allow me to settle into the office and look for a home while Anne organised the move from Adelaide. So in May 1962 I flew to Sydney to break new ground in life and my career.

I couldn't have asked for a better welcome to a new city. My membership of the Royal South Australian Yacht Squadron gave me reciprocal rights with the Royal Sydney Yacht Squadron, so I moved into one of their delightful yet spartan guest rooms at the club at Kirribilli, right on the shores of the harbour with panoramic views to the east. It was a fantastic experience with sunshine every day and the Squadron people making you feel as though you were in your own home. Each morning I would walk through the boat yard at the Squadron, looking at all the beautiful yachts, appreciating their sweeping lines and admiring the way they were being maintained. It was all part of the wonderful journey I made to the office most mornings—through the boat yard, down to the ferry wharf at Kirribilli, on to the ferry for the ride to Circular Quay then the walk through the maze of tall buildings all the way up to our premises at 223 Liverpool Street. I was amazed how little time it took for me to feel comfortable in my new city. As far as I was concerned Sydney was sensational. It all reminded me of a school friend who came from Sydney. He said: "If you're not living in Sydney you're sleeping out."

My welcome became even warmer through the efforts of guys I'd met while racing the Finn dinghy at the Olympic trials in Melbourne—guys like Colin Ryrie, Ross Grieve and Ross McDonald. They made sure I was thoroughly entertained by all the activities at the Squadron. Ironically, the day I arrived in Sydney I saw our first America's Cup challenger, Sir Frank Packer's *Gretel*, being loaded aboard a ship for the voyage to Newport, Rhode Island and the big event. My arrival at the Squadron therefore coincided perfectly with countless farewell and sponsor functions for the challenge. Being a house guest meant I was entitled to attend all these functions— if there was a party at the club you were automatically invited. What a great rule. I crawled upstairs and into bed half full of syrup five nights out of every seven. I realised very quickly the pace of life in Sydney and the demands placed on one's ability to cope with social pressures were a lot different to what I was used to in Adelaide. This was big time partying.

I survived that initiation and managed to slot into my role as the head of Hardy's New South Wales operations very nicely. Having the opportunity to develop and expand our market share was very exciting, although some of my business plans didn't make our chairman, Uncle Ken—as I always called him—too happy. He came to Sydney from Adelaide with me to show me the ropes and introduce me to the hierarchy at John Cawsey's. After a couple of days in our office the two of us went out to Cawsey's headquarters at Silverwater where I was introduced to Mr Perkins, the chairman, the bloke who owned the majority of shares. Just before I left Adelaide the board of Hardy's had decided to take their involvement with Cawsey's one step further, to not only have them distribute our products, but to bottle them as well. Prior to that decision we were transporting our sherry, port and table wines to Sydney in bulk from Adelaide then bottling them on the premises in Liverpool Street. Once bottled they would be shipped out to Cawsey's for distribution.

We sat down at this first meeting with Mr Perkins and other bosses from Cawsey's and Uncle Ken started explaining the board's desire to transfer the bottling to Silverwater. I couldn't restrain myself—I had been against this move all along and I had the family interest at heart: "Can't we wait a little while, until I've been here long enough to get the feel for New South Wales, before we hand over this last bit of local involvement we have going for us?" I chipped in. Silence all round. "Oops," I thought. "That didn't score any points." Mr Perkins, his hands clenched in front of him on his desk top, looked over his glasses straight at me and said: "I don't know who you think you are young man, but I'm Perkins of Perkins Steel of England." I sat there struggling to contain myself. "Well that's good for you, Mr Perkins," I thought. "I'm just Jim Hardy from Hardy's Wines in Adelaide."

The atmosphere in the car during the drive back to Liverpool Street was cool, to say the least. Uncle Ken let me know in no uncertain fashion that I had caused him considerable embarrassment.

To be in Sydney was to discover a whole new world. Things

were going on in this city that I had only read about. My biggest
eye opener came during my first few weeks in my new home town
when I was given the opportunity to spend a night patrolling the
streets of Kings Cross with the Vice Squad. Brothels were part and
parcel of life in Kings Cross and it was the Vice Squad's job to patrol
the establishments. As far as the madams supplying the services were
concerned I was Detective Hardy from Adelaide. However, the look
on my face as we walked through the brothels all but gave me away.

"Who are you?" one madam asked.

"Detective Hardy from Adelaide."

"Oh, how much do the girls get fined there when they are
arrested?"

"One hundred pounds," was my immediate reply. It was the
first figure that came into my head, the fine for taking vine cuttings
from another state into South Australia.

"One hundred pounds! We'd all be broke here if they fined
us that much every time we were arrested."

Her next question was: "Are you really a policeman?"

"Yes, I am a policeman."

"You don't look like a policeman to me."

"Well, I'm from Adelaide."

When we left that establishment the two detectives I was
accompanying had only one request: "Can you please try to wipe
the smile off your face when we go into these places?"

When it was time for Anne and David to join me in Sydney
I flew back to Adelaide to collect them. We were to drive to Sydney
in our Volkswagen, and with David not yet two years old I decided
it was wise to turn the back seat of the car into a bed so he could
sleep for much of the long journey. By the time we reached Renmark,
just four hours from Adelaide, it was already too much for David
and he began bawling his eyes out. He was still crying as we approached
Mildura on the New South Wales border, so I decided instead of
having a hell trip for the rest of the way Anne and David would
fly from Mildura to Sydney. As soon as I mentioned my thoughts
to Anne, David stopped crying and we didn't get another whimper
from him.

Our new home in Sydney was an apartment in a large building
at Balmoral, on the shores of Middle Harbour. It wasn't a large place,
but it had magnificent views to the east, towards the entrance to

Sydney Harbour. We were both made to feel very welcome, especially through the Yacht Squadron. The club celebrated its centenary soon after Anne arrived and we had the pleasure of being there for the big party on the sprawling green lawns that ran from the clubhouse down to the edge of the harbour. There were big marquees set up and tables groaning under the weight of specially prepared food. The one thing this Adelaide boy couldn't get over were the rows and rows of tables laden with famous Sydney rock oysters. Waiters were standing there opening them and handing them to you. It was a very special night.

It quickly became apparent I should join the club, so with the support of Bill Fesq, a super sailor who was also in the wine and spirits industry, along with my mentor and winemaker friend Colin Haselgrove, his brother Ron and another South Australian wine grower, Henry Martin, my membership went through.

I decided I would race a Flying Dutchman, an Olympic two-man high performance dinghy, the coming season so ordered a new hull from a mould craft company in Melbourne. My decision to finish it off—paint it and put on the fittings—to my specifications presented a problem. Living in a home unit meant I couldn't do the job there. The only alternative was to do the work in our Liverpool Street cellars. So there I was one winter Sunday morning working away in the sunshine, the boat half out on the street and the doors to our cellars wide open, when who should come around the corner but Uncle Ken Hardy—unannounced. He had stopped over in Sydney on his way back to Adelaide and decided to walk around to see how the office looked.

"What's going on here?" he asked, showing obvious concern about the security of all the company stock. My quick fire response about lack of facilities elsewhere and an outline of my plans for the boat worked wonders because next minute he was pouring all over the boat, asking me questions and showing as much enthusiasm for the campaign as I was. The fact that I had named the boat *Fino*, after Uncle Ken's favourite sherry, also helped.

My suggestion that we should retain the bottling activities at Liverpool Street until I had assessed the situation in New South Wales had not generated one ounce of interest from either Uncle Ken or Mr Perkins. So with that part of the business now based at Cawsey's Silverwater factory all I could do was go around with their salesmen and help promote our product. It was very frustrating, like trying to fight with one hand tied behind your back. But I knew the arrangement was the wish of the majority of the board so I had to go along with it. If nothing else my thoughts on who should be bottling our product did cement a very strong bond with our sales manager, Gus Pfafflin, a huge athletic man, a rower who, it turned out, had pushed hard with brother Tom for me to be transferred to Sydney. He agreed with my thoughts on Hardy's and not Cawsey's being more in control of their own destiny. He became very supportive of me over the ensuing years.

One promotion I actively pursued on our behalf was the development of the Beefsteak and Burgundy Club. I saw it as a great opportunity to develop the wine market and help with the conversion of the major market share from ports and sherries to red and white table wines. The original club was literally formed out of our head office in Adelaide by our general manager, Dick Clark, and a friend, David Crosby, who had worked for us for a brief period. They decided the Bacchus Club in Adelaide, which was originally established as an elite wine and food appreciation group, had grown to be too impersonal with a membership in excess of 300. The pair decided on a smaller club, limited to 30 people, and each time 30 new people lined up they could form their own club. The idea received great support—brother Tom was the Foundation's President, our winemaker Roger Warren the Foundation Wine Master, and our Assistant Secretary, Ray Drew, the original Secretary. I had become the President of the second club, the Brighton Beefsteak and Burgundy Club. When I transferred to Sydney there were only two clubs in operation, Sydney and Mosman, so I joined the Sydney club. I'm a member to this day and at one stage was the club's Winemaster. It's a nice wine appreciation group which enjoys masked wine tastings and good food at different restaurants around town each month.

My frustration with Cawsey's handling our marketing, and my enthusiasm to develop our business, saw me doing everything I could think of to get better results. The line from that one accountancy teacher back in Adelaide that said there were only two ways to increase profits, one being to increase sales, kept gnawing away at my mind. One promotional idea I had was to print a little brochure about our Black Bottle Brandy saying it was made from Doradillo and Grenach grapes, and that it was pot distilled and matured for four years in oak vats. It was a true and effective little story about the product. To give the whole thing more credibility I adopted an idea a marketing consultant, Dick Graves, came up with and had a grey-haired cartoon character drawn up for the brochure. It was a bit like Colonel Sanders, but well before his time. This little old guy was known as Colonel Hardy and he had a line on the product that said: "Makes life worth living"—my personal touch. The brochures were out in the hotels only a matter of days when all hell broke loose. The Wine and Brandy Association of New South Wales erupted. They had very strict rules on marketing and I had broken one of the big ones—I had personalised brochures for each hotel, like: "The Manly Hotel recommends Hardy's Black Bottle Brandy". That was a big no-no. So Jim Hardy, a young upstart from Adelaide, was summoned to appear before a full committee meeting of the Wine and Brandy Association to face the music. The accused, full of humility, was marched into the committee meeting to face some of the biggest names in the industry, the bosses of McWilliams, Penfolds, Lindemans and Orlando wines plus the president, John Addison, who had earlier invited me into the Beefsteak and Burgundy Club. He read out the crime that I had committed: "Nominating licensed outlets to sell Hardy's products." They produced the association's by-laws and read out the appropriate rule—it was illegal to do anything for an individual hotel. You either did it for all or none at all. While I stood there in front of the committee they were all nodding up and down and grunting in unison to support each statement made by the president: "Mr Hardy, can't you read the rules?" I was asked. I nodded to confirm my ability to read, thinking all the time that all I had done was skate around the edge of those rules. I just kept saying: "Yes, Sir, No, Sir, three bags full, Sir." I felt very much like I did when the policeman nabbed me for hunting the rabbits out the back of home with a .22 calibre rifle.

After deciding I had received a sufficiently severe dressing down they all adjourned to the bar and asked me to join them. They then did a complete about face. I couldn't believe it. They were all so friendly to me. "This is quite nice," I thought. "They're really quite human, this mob." Then one of them said he had read my CV and noted I was a qualified accountant. I said that was right. Next thing the boss of Seppelts came into the conversation, probably because he got the nod from the guy talking to me and said: "Qualified accountant eh. Well, we need a treasurer for the association. How about you stand for the position?" Well, bugger me, a few weeks after being the worst kid on the block I'm the treasurer of the Wine and Brandy Association. It might have all been a plot to get me into the inner sanctum and, it may have been coincidental, but it worked. My misdemeanour had catapulted me into office. As it turned out it was a really good move for me because I got to know all the people on that side of the industry. Later I was to become Treasurer of the Liquor Trade Supervisory Council, which covered the entire industry—the breweries, wine and spirit merchants and the wine and brandy producers—and that was an even greater bonus.

The summer of 1962-63 was when I became convinced I did have a real future in the highest levels of competitive sailing. I sailed the new Flying Dutchman in the NSW State Championship and at the end of the series came ashore more than pleased to have taken out second place. We were sailing against some great names, like Richard Coxon, Max Whitnall, Craig Whitworth and Bob Miller—who later changed his name to Ben Lexcen. It was terrific to have come from Adelaide, where I'd been pretty successful in recent years, to join the big league and let them know I was about. That night I got a phone call at home from Ted Albert, who had finished fourth or fifth in the series.

"Jim, we think you have won the series. My father has read the rules and you have won on a countback of the results."

He was right. We had displaced Richard Coxon and Max Whitnall sailing *Vamoose* and won the series on a countback. A first-up win in the New South Wales title was really something.

Back at work I continued to proceed with the Cawsey arrangement under sufferance. I didn't stop working towards proving to the board we had made the wrong move. I certainly didn't try to sabotage the arrangement. I just kept storing enough ammunition so that one day I could show my fellow directors the company should be promoting, marketing and distributing its own products out of the Sydney office. One of my early steps towards this goal was to conduct a little experiment. I felt the word "Tintara" had become a great trade name for our port and sherry but didn't suit our table wines. A guy I had got to know owned a restaurant in Double Bay, in Sydney's eastern suburbs, so I asked him to do a survey for me— to put Hardy's Old Castle Riesling and Tintara Old Castle Riesling on his wine list. They were the same wines and I wanted him to keep a tab on which one was more successful. It came out very clearly that people asked for Hardy's over Tintara, something that confirmed my feelings about family names over brand names. At my next meeting in Adelaide I revealed the results of my survey and suggested we drop the word Tintara from the labels of all our table wines in New South Wales. Boy, did that meet with some opposition. Tintara had been with the company since Adam was a little boy. Uncle Ken came out and reminded me Chateau Tanunda Brandy, made by Seppelts, was the biggest selling brandy. I agreed but then made the point that all the table wines with family connotations—Penfolds, Lindemans and Seppelts—did very well in the marketplace. They sat back, took it all in, "uhmed" and "ahed" then next thing all agreed it was a great idea, and that we should take Tintara off everything, even our port and sherry. We had gone from one extreme to the other. Suddenly I found myself battling with them again because I firmly believed our sherry and port should remain as Tintara. But the majority won the day and now only occasionally does the name Tintara surface on a special release of table wine.

The success of the subsequent change to the Hardy's label over Tintara on our table wines was my second victory in product marketing for the company. Before moving to Sydney I had been responsible for the change of name for our brandy from Tintara Liqueur Brandy to Black Bottle Brandy. Back then I put forward the case that in calling it liqueur brandy we were confusing people— they assumed the reference to liqueur meant it was sweet. In fact it was a mixing brandy like all other Australian brandies. The brandy had always been sold in a black bottle and in bars it was more often than not referred to as "the one in the black bottle". It is amazing what a name change can do. Black Bottle Brandy brought about a dramatic increase in sales and it is still one of the top selling brandies in Australia.

Life in Sydney must have agreed with Anne and me from a very early moment because less than eighteen months after we arrived our second son, Richard, was born. When we were told he was on the way our immediate problem was to find a new home. There was no way our small unit at Balmoral could accommodate four of us. We decided we liked the north side of the harbour and after what seemed like endless searching, especially on Anne's part, we found our new home on Dobroyd Road at Balgowlah Heights. Of course, as with all new homes, it was priced above what we wanted to pay, so we had to console ourselves with the knowledge that it had everything we wanted—in particular a huge garage so I could accommodate our Volkswagen, my company Ford Falcon wagon, the Flying Dutchman and still have room to set up a workshop. It turned out to be the ideal workshop with plenty of bench space, a small circular saw, a band saw and buzzer all in place.

If I didn't know better I would have said it was Anne's way of getting even with me for all the effort she put into finding the house—because she went into labour with Richard the night before we were scheduled to move. So there I was the next day moving house, anxiously waiting on a call from nearby Manly hospital to tell me I was a father once more. The call came through—another boy! Richard James Hardy.

After that good news things got a little scary. I asked how Anne was and the Sister at the hospital said: "She's fine." Then I asked about Richard and the reply was: "Oh, he's fine, but he does have a slight graze." To this day I don't know what she was trying to tell me—she wouldn't elaborate. But when Richard had his accident a year later my thoughts went immediately back to that statement by the Sister. I'm no medico and I'm not one to judge, but I think his accident came as a direct result of something that happened to him at birth. When the Sister didn't explain what a "slight graze" was I assumed there was no need to be concerned.

Sydney was starting to fit more and more like a comfortable and warm coat for us as each month passed. We had established a delightful circle of friends through sailing and the wine industry. Not long after Richard was born my interests expanded to include Freemasonry. It was something that had always intrigued me. My father had been involved and I thought if he was in it then it was good enough for me. I had met a guy in Adelaide, Reg Lennie, who was from Sydney. I found him to be a very friendly guy and after a while he suggested that when I landed in Sydney I contact him at the Masonic Club, where he was General Manager. I told him about my father being a Mason and that I had recently been talking with Roy Mellish, an old family friend, about Freemasonry. I said I would look forward to seeing him to learn more. During the month of May, when I was staying at the Squadron, I spent quite a bit of time at the Masonic Club—it just happened to be on my path to the ferries at Circular Quay on the way home. Reg introduced me to many very pleasant people—all Freemasons. I told them I would like to know more about Freemasonry. These people said: "Right, we'll see what we can do." They were in the throes of forming a new lodge to be named Lodge City of Sydney, number 952 on the register of the United Grand Lodge of New South Wales and they obviously thought that was for me. They started getting a whole lot of particulars from me, then I went through the investigation process—it took months and months—and finally I was admitted.

To join that lodge was to explode a lot of preconceived ideas I, and a lot of others, had held about Freemasonry. It is not, as some people would have you believe, a secret society. Yes, it does have some secrets, but those secrets are no big deal. All Freemasonry is about is your ability to keep a secret—someone tells you something and says they don't want you to talk about it. If you tell someone you have perjured yourself. That's all the test is. I guess the big clash for Freemasonry came with the Roman Catholic religion, which works on the premise that each weekend you could tell the priest everything you had done wrong the previous week and start off with a clean slate. You couldn't in effect be a secret-keeping Freemason and a Roman Catholic at the same time. The priest would be there saying "You're not telling me everything," and you'd be saying "You're right. I've got a secret."

You are admitted into Freemasonry for being a good person, which in turn means you will help other people in that fraternity who might get into strife through no fault of their own. Being admitted has nothing to do with your worldly possessions—it doesn't matter if you're on the lowest rung or highest rung of fortune's ladder—it is assumed you have nothing. It started off as a guild of builders and its whole law is based on the building of King Solomon's temple, way back in the dim, dark ages. It was in effect a union of builders. In the structure of Freemasons each office lasts one year. You start as a Steward. It's just like a church. If you are a Steward you are inside the church and if you move to the next level you become a Tyler, who is in effect the doorman, the person welcoming visitors from other Lodges to the monthly meeting. Next you go inside the Lodge for a year to be an Inner Guard and then a Junior Deacon, a Senior Deacon, a Junior Warden, Senior Warden, then the Master. After you have become the Master for a year you then step down and become the Immediate Past Master. Then the Grand Lodge, the overall body which runs the activities in the state, may select you for further office. I went through our Lodge to become Master then five years later the incoming Grand Master, Noel Warren, selected me as his Deputy Grand Master for NSW for a couple of years. Apparently I was one of the youngest to ever hold that office.

The only religious thing about Freemasonry is that you have to believe in a supreme being—it doesn't have to be Jesus Christ, Allah or Budda—it's an all encompassing thing. It's just that you agree to accept there is a supreme being. You don't know who or what it, he or she is. The big thing is that you are not driven down a narrow, fundamental avenue with your beliefs.

Masonry is very strong in the United States but I think a lot of people feel it's not visible enough. Masons aren't seen out painting fences for someone worse off than themselves. Masons do support some education schemes and hospitals and other benevolent ideals, but it is mainly for the benefit of the fraternity, so in that regard it could be seen as being a bit closed. I think that's one of the reasons it could be frowned upon by some people.

I'm still actively involved in Freemasonry. It has been wonderful to me over the years, giving me a great opportunity to meet and be with people completely outside the sailing and wine side of life. One of the great things has been to visit other lodges, especially in America while I was there for the America's Cup. After my third visit I was made an honorary member of Lodge St Paul in Newport, Rhode Island which is Lodge Number 14 in the United States—that's a very old Lodge. I get their little scandal sheet each month. It's good to be able to stay in touch with their activities.

Back to 1964 and my target, the Australian Olympic yachting team for Tokyo. I had tried in 1956 and 1960 and missed out so I was hoping it was a case of third time lucky. Rolly Tasker, from Perth, had won a world title in the Flying Dutchman class so I was more than happy when his crew, Andy White, offered his services to me for the Olympic campaign. I had been winning races with my old boat, Fino, but Andy had all of Rolly's hull and rig dimensions and quickly convinced me I had to have a new boat built. I went to Dave Binks in Adelaide and had him build the boat, which I named Eileen after my mother. Warwick Hood, the well-known yacht designer, was then the official measurer for the Flying Dutchman class. He still classifies running the tape over my boat at our home at Balgowlah Heights as one of his most memorable measuring experiences. My mother was up from Adelaide and there was poor Warwick trying to measure the boat while dear old Mum kept plying him with champagne. Soon the tape measure was slipping and sliding everywhere, though laugh as we did, the news at the end of the day wasn't good. Fittings were found to be out of place and the boat was between 30 and 40 pounds overweight. It turned out Dave Binks didn't have a scale big enough to weigh the boat so simply used a smaller scale, weighed the boat at the bow then the stern and doubled the numbers. The theory might have been right but the calculations weren't, so *Eileen*, the boat, was shipped back to Adelaide for a rebuild.

It was a chequered start for the boat so we were relieved no end when we went to Adelaide and found we finally had the right formula. The Australian championship was the curtain-raiser for the Olympic trials and we won that.

Then we made our biggest mistake. We broke the golden rule and won the invitation race, the warm-up race, of the trials. The old saying in sailing circles is: "If you win the invitation race you never win the championship." Truer words were never said because the trials and the trip to Tokyo was ours for the taking and I blew it. And as if that wasn't enough, the boat that won the trials, sailed by John Dawe and Ian Winter, was near identical to the boat I replaced with *Eileen*.

It wasn't the boat's fault that we lost, it was mine. I disqualified myself from one race when I was fighting neck and neck with Noel Brooke, from Victoria, for the lead. We came around the windward mark side by side, sailing in a perfect breeze, a beautiful south-wester blowing at around twelve knots. Having sailed on that course off Largs Bay since I was a lad I knew the automatic thing was to gybe—go from starboard tack to port tack—and head parallel to the shore for the most favourable conditions. I did just that and, while Andy frantically hoisted the spinnaker, I noticed that Brooke's boat, which was right alongside, wasn't changing course. We were heading for a bump. I called on him to change course to avoid the collision but he didn't respond. So I did what one would normally do, I bumped into him to claim my right of way under the rules. I looked across at him and said: "Noel, you're out. You'd better go home." His

response: "Jim, you'd better go home. I'm still on starboard tack."
Gulp! I looked up at his sails and sure enough he was on starboard
tack. He held right of way. "You're right," I said, changing course
towards home. In my rush to beat him, and by force of practice,
I had gybed on to port tack and not noticed that he had held starboard
tack. I just assumed that he had also gybed. When I looked at him
before the collision I only looked at his hull, not his sails. Poor old
Andy missed it all. He thought we were still racing and was busy
with the spinnaker. When he looked up and saw we were heading
towards home he was lost for words: "Wha, wha, what's going on?"
"We're out Andy. We hit him. We're on our way home." A first
or second in that race would have got us into the team for Tokyo.
Poor Andy was stunned. He didn't get over it. I could accept it,
probably because of the experience of losing the Stonehaven Cup
when I was a youngster—when another guy's mast went overboard
and cost me the Cup.

A few weeks later there was a sweet side to our loss. I was
named as a reserve for the Olympic yachting team when it was
announced. What a thrill. I turned my attentions to Tokyo and did
whatever I could to help the team. Some of it had to do with sailing
and some of it with being in charge of support activities. The most
remarkable member of the team was Bill Northam—later to become
Sir William Northam—a man in his late fifties who was the boss
of Johnson and Johnson in Australia. He had qualified for the team
with his 5.5 metre class yacht *Barranjoey*. Now Bill loved a drink,
scotch whisky in particular, and knowing my relationship with the
industry that provided him with one of life's pleasures, he called
me aside one day to tell me he had some advance information from
Tokyo on how much alcohol we could take: "According to my
calculations we can take 72 cases of alcoholic beverages—you're in
charge," he said in a raspy voice that proved considerable quantities
of whisky did nothing to smooth the vocal cords. Message received
and understood. I went to John Cawsey's with the shopping list—
Black and White Whisky, our own brandy and wine. Then my friend
Tom Watkins, the head of Tooth and Co., came up with the beer.
The next problem was to arrange shipment. It was decided to send
some as a separate consignment and put a small amount aboard
Barranjoey just for safekeeping. Safekeeping was an understatement.
You've never seen anything like what Bill Northam did to protect

the beautiful mahogany hull of *Barranjoey* and to stop the refreshments rattling around inside. The entire yacht was wrapped, inside and out, using rolls and rolls of the material Johnson and Johnson used to make women's sanitary napkins!

Two team members were required to travel on the ship, the *Kweilin*, of the China Navigation Company, to look after all the team yachts. Being the reserve I got the gong along with the famous foredeck man off *Gretel* in the 1962 America's Cup challenge and mainsheet hand crewman on *Barranjoey*, Peter "Pod" O'Donnell. The ship wasn't designed for passengers so we were given the owner's cabin, and the associated full treatment. What a fantastic trip. Each day a little Chinese guy would come around and collect our shoes for polishing and go off and rub them until he just about went through the leather. Each night we would dress for dinner and join the captain and officers in a very small cabin. Cards would follow dinner. It turned out the captain was a full-on cheat. All the officers knew he cheated but nobody rubbished him. He was the captain and they wanted to keep their jobs, so they just played along while the captain remained oblivious to the fact that everyone knew what he was doing. We played poker and whenever he was dealing everybody would throw their cards in because he would just help himself to the cards that were left to fill his hand up.

Our main concern for the yachts was to keep them damp while we sailed through the tropics. If their timber hulls dried out too much in the heat they would crack and open up—so we spent time each day standing on the deck hosing them down. There were two other activities that filled the rest of my day: boat building and deck quoits. The engineer on the ship was building a small catamaran so each day Pod and I would work on it with him. In the two weeks it took to reach Tokyo we had the thing half finished. The deck quoits were a bit like volleyball, except that you used a rope ring and threw it over the net to the other team where someone had to grab it. Every now and then the ship would roll as you threw the quoit and it would go on an impressive arc, straight over the side. We'd run to the rail and look down to see this beautiful hand-made quoit, which had canvas sewn over the join, hit the water and disappear astern. The guy they called the sailmaker, a little Chinese bloke, made the quoits and it seemed that every time he would finish one, hand sewing the piece of canvas over the join with incredible skill, we'd be there wanting it because we had lost another one over the side. I don't know what it was he used to say in Chinese each time, but it certainly didn't sound as though he was too happy. In the end he realised that sewing the canvas was a waste of time so he just gave us rope loops.

Our first stop was in Nagoya and it was there I realised how different things are when it comes to work practices in Japan and Australia. It was almost unbelievable, seeing how the Japanese unloaded the ship. We anchored away from shore and in just two days they unloaded two thirds of the cargo onto barges. Then when we got to Yokohama it took just one more day to complete the job. It had taken 30 days to load the ship in Australia. However, I must say their handling techniques were a little bit different to what you would see in Australia. A number of hooks on the cable from the crane would be lowered into the ship's hold and attached to bails of hides, or something similar. Then as the workers in the hold called on the crane driver to start the lift they would all run under the decks because every now and then one of the bails would come unhooked and drop back into the hold. If you happened to be under it you were dead.

Our first problem on arrival was to find the yachts. They had been unloaded onto barges successfully, then we watched as they disappeared into a thick smog. There were ships and barges everywhere so we didn't have a clue where they went. After two days of searching we found them in a customs agent's yard and got them cleared. When it came to the alcohol I couldn't get my fingers on it at all. It had been put into some sort of bond store and no one was telling us where it was. Through interpreters I was told it would not be released, and it wasn't until I had worked on getting it for the best part of two weeks that finally the message came through. In fact, there were messages for me everywhere, at the gate of the Olympic yachting village, at our hotel, at the yacht club. "Hardy-san your liquor arrive tomorrow, Yellow Express, message, message." Well, the moment had arrived and the whole yachting village just stopped. No one could believe that the Australians would bring 72 cases of grog to the Olympics. It's still being talked about, even today.

I shared a room in the Olympic Yacht Village in Enoshima with Bill Northam, who was then 59 years old—and boy was that an experience. As well as being team reserve I was also made Assistant

Team Manager under John Crosbie, from Melbourne. For Bill Northam all this added up to just one thing—I was there to help him. He was forever on my back to do something, including finding a motor boat big enough to carry 30 people to follow the 5.5 metre and Dragon races. So off I went into Yokohama on an expedition—an expedition into a sea of Japanese faces where both English and powerboats were unknown commodities. I found my way to the waterfront and decided the best plan would be to find some sort of boat harbour then work from there. I searched everywhere until finally in the distance I spotted a couple of masts among buildings and barges. Sailing was just not known in Japan at that stage so finding these yachts was like finding gold. I went into the yard and, to my amazement, I found this American attorney. He'd been there since the end of the war and married a Japanese lady, and most importantly, he owned a motor boat that was just perfect for what Bill Northam wanted. All this American could say was: "I'm your man. I'm your man." I offered to have a beer with him while we struck a deal but he wouldn't be in it— he was a non-drinker. I was more than proud of my achievement, particularly in Yokohama in 1964 when half the people still wore traditional clothing. We all got together for a team meeting that night and there I was with all the information on the motor boat in my pocket. Bill Northam said to me in the middle of the meeting, in his very gruff voice: "Well, have you got a boat?" Out came my pad, and looking back I think I was probably a bit cocky about my achievement. I said: "Here it is—and I've got this, this, this and this and the owner will drive it." When I got down to how much petrol it would burn Bill asked what sort of engines it had. "Oops," I thought, "I haven't got the answer to that." "Petrol engines," I said hoping that would keep him happy. Well, he absolutely flew at me, shouting: "There you go. Just like every other young bugger in this world. You give them a job to do and they half do it, half do it." So there I was copping all this flak in front of the team, my only thought being: "I'm glad I don't work for Johnson & Johnson. I reckon he'd be too tough for me." We decided to go ahead with the deal, even though we didn't know the brand of engines. That lack of information was small bickies compared to the problem we had when the boat arrived. It turned out the owner, who had refused to have a beer with me on the grounds that he didn't drink, was an alcoholic. He was half shot from daylight until dark, so another

131

of the team reserves, the top Perth yachtsman Tony Manford, became the boat driver. For me, as much as I didn't like being berated by Bill Northam in front of the team, there was a lesson learned. I really did grow to admire the man immensely and learn a lot from his management skills.

I was to become Bill's training partner as he prepared for the Olympics—in the bar, not on the boat. Every morning, religiously, we would be in the bar overlooking the yacht harbour, Bill having a scotch, me having a brandy. We'd look out the window to see his crew, Pod O'Donnell and Dick Sargeant, carrying the sails down the dock to *Barranjoey* and Bill would lean out from the bar and give them a chiacking: "Come on you fellows. Get yourselves into gear." Pod and Dick would mutter something about "the old so-and-so" under their breaths and off they'd go and rig the boat completely. When they were finished Bill would go down and step aboard being, as far as he was concerned, ready to race.

One windy day I had to go out on *Barranjoey* to see how it all operated and how the crew worked. Being the team reserve I could be called on to sail on the boat should anyone be injured or fall ill during the Olympics. We were running downwind and I was sitting somewhat precariously on the aft deck of this very narrow yacht, right behind where Bill was steering in the cockpit. All the time Pod was saying, "You're by the lee captain, you're by the lee," meaning that if he didn't change course the yacht could go out of control and into an involuntary gybe—in short, a disaster. All hell would break loose. The whole time Pod was saying this to Bill he kept looking ahead, he never looked back at him. Then he'd be telling Bill to push the rudder the other way, that he was correcting it the wrong way. I thought: "Holy Moses, this is our Olympic 5.5 class helmsman—he keeps steering the wrong way." But then Bill would catch on to what Pod was saying, straighten the boat up and get it back on to course. All I could think was: "This is unbelievable. This guy will probably go out and win a medal for our country." And bugger me, he did. He won Australia's first ever sailing gold medal—and on top of that became the oldest Olympian ever to do so. It was incredible. This man virtually sailed the yacht by remote control. He just sat there and took the orders from Pod O'Donnell. But he had a real touch, a positive mental attitude and an enormous psychological strength. It was these things and his management skills that got him to the top. He covered his own weaknesses very effectively. Jock Sturrock, who steered *Gretel* in our first America's Cup challenge in 1962, was without doubt one of Australia's greatest ever helmsmen. But he didn't have the ability to lift himself past Bill's organisational skills and other strengths to win the Olympic selection trials for Tokyo.

A perfect example of Bill's strengths came in the race in Tokyo when he was disqualified at the windward mark for tacking too close to another yacht. Back at the bar after the race McNamara, the big American, one of the favourites, came up to Bill and me with a big broad grin and said as only big Americans cay say: "Ah Captain Northam, bad luck today to see you fouled out at the top mark." With that Bill Northam leant over and tapped McNamara on the forehead, right above his nose, and said: "Don't worry, Mac. I'll win tomorrow. It's all in the mind." And what happened? Bill Northam went out the next day and won. That put the Gold one step closer and McNamara one step behind.

For me the Tokyo Olympics provided the most memorable day in my life—the day I marched into the stadium with the Australian team as part of the opening ceremony. They were playing "Waltzing Matilda" as we approached the entrance to the stadium. To march inside knowing you were representing your country provided the most unbelievable feeling. I was covered in goosebumps. We were wearing white hats and I wasn't sure whether mine was on or off. The emotion was such that I couldn't feel my hat. When we marched around to where the Emperor was standing to take the salute we had to take our hats off and put them over our hearts. My hat was there and I made the move, thinking all the time how some returned soldiers wouldn't have been too happy to do an "eyes right" to the Emperor of Japan.

We had another Opening Ceremony down at the Olympic Yachting Village at Enoshima, where the Japanese had built a special yacht harbour for the regatta. In the weeks leading up to the racing I had renewed my friendship with Don St Clair-Brown. I first met him during the Interdominion Flying Dutchman championship in Auckland and he had come to the Olympics as the New Zealand team manager. It turned out the Kiwis had a spare Flying Dutchman with them, one they had used for training, so when the Invitation Race for the Olympics came up we decided to jump into it for fun and go out and race all the Olympic hopefuls. Don steered upwind while I went out on the trapeze, then downwind I'd steer and he would work the spinnaker. Off we went and had a super race. We finished second to the Russians and became the big talk of the bar.

Don and I had got to be pretty matey during the weeks of training before the Olympics, so when the Games started we agreed to establish an incentive scheme for our respective team members—any time either a New Zealander or an Australian won a race we would pay for team members to go to a Japanese bath house in Yokohama for rest and relaxation—if they so wished. Well, Bill Northam would win a race and off we'd all go to the bath house. Then Peter Mander, the Finn class sailor from New Zealand, would win a race—off to the bath house we'd go. Bill Northam would win again—off to the bath house. Helmer Peterson, the New Zealander, would win—off to the bath house again. Now, people have probably heard stories about those bath houses, so all I can say is that they are "A" grade for relaxation. You would arrive there and pick one girl to bath you. Then, after that mission was completed successfully—and very pleasant it was—you'd have a massage of sorts. You would lie on your stomach and this girl would get on your back, working her elbows into your neck and back. Then, for some obviously therapeutic reason, she would slide her body all the way down to your feet, than back up again. Yes, it was very therapeutic. And it was obviously the right incentive for the teams because they kept winning races.

All the excitement and fun that came from being part of the Olympic team evaporated in a flash when I received a letter from Anne, who was back in Adelaide. The opening line was to tell me Richard, our son, had suffered a terrible accident. I couldn't read the words quickly enough, all the time wondering why she hadn't telephoned me instead of writing a letter. I can only guess that things were happening so fast she wanted to have all the facts before causing me concern at the Olympics. The letter told me Anne and a girlfriend, Anne Macpherson, were at my brother David's house at McLaren Vale and Richard, who was ten months old, was crawling around. He crawled into the kitchen and the next thing there was a noise, a sickening crash. Everyone rushed out to the kitchen and there was Richard lying on his back on the floor, frothing at the mouth. He had apparently pulled a big, heavy stool over on top of himself. It appears that he tried to stand up, put his trust into the stool as a support, then fell over and pulled it down with him. The letter went on to say they had rushed him around to the local doctor in McLaren Vale, who diagnosed a cerebral haemorrhage. The rush was on to get him to the Children's Hospital in Adelaide so Anne undertook that drive with a police escort. Unfortunately there were only two neurosurgeons in Adelaide and one was away in Sydney and the other was busy operating. It was five hours before Richard was operated on and I think it was in that period that the real damage was done. The operation involved the removal of a large piece of his skull to ease the pressure from the clotting, but sadly the blood by that stage had got into the back of his eyes and wiped out his eyesight. He was in a terrible condition and it was 50-50 on survival for him.

"A cerebral haemorrhage," I kept thinking to myself while reading. When I finished the letter I sat down and continued to think—the words cerebral haemorrhage going over and over in my mind. I wondered then, and still wonder today, if it was the fall that really caused the problem. I look back further to the Sister at Manly Hospital who said he had a thing called a "slight graze" when he was born—I think that meant there was pressure on his head when he was born. I remembered that when we stopped at Cootamundra, driving to Adelaide before I left for Tokyo, he cried all night long. It wasn't that he wanted changing or needed food. I think it was pain. It was pressure in his head.

While thinking about this my real thoughts were for Richard and for what Anne was going through, so I immediately sent back a telegram asking for more information and what I should do about returning home. Here I was away on a bloody yachting spree again, like I had for half my life, and there was Anne having to cope with this enormous problem all alone. I began to make plans to go home, waiting as Anne suggested for the next message, an update on his condition, before any final decision was made. The next day John Crosbie came around with the telegram from Anne, offering to read it first if I wanted. I said OK, and there was poor old "Cros" shaking as he opened the envelope. The look of relief on his face said everything. The message simply said something like: "Richard much improved. No need to rush home . . . Love Anne." Sadly, at that stage, no one knew the extent of the damage to his brain.

Knowing the strength Anne was showing in being comfortable

with me staying in Tokyo brought me to write her a lengthy letter of support. I quoted from the father of the modern Olympics, Pierre de Courbertin, and the not-often-heard section of the Olympic Creed was created for the Olympics when they resumed in Athens in 1896. The words were, in effect: "The important thing is not the prize, but the struggle. The essential thing is not to have conquered, but to have fought well. To build up these precepts is to build a stronger, more valiant and above all a more generous humanity." It was a very traumatic period in my life. Anne was fighting her own Olympic battle.

Anne had arrived back in Sydney with Richard when I returned from Tokyo. She met me at the airport and brought me up to date with developments. I still wasn't mentally prepared for the impact of seeing him when I got home. There was my little bloke, this baby lying there on a bouncinette type of thing, helpless, with a fibreglass helmet on his head for protection. It was awful. This little kid who should have been active and all around the house was just lying there. The doctors, who were monitoring his progress, said they would have to wait some time before putting the large piece of bone they had removed back into his skull. The best part of six months passed before that operation came and during that time we had physiotherapists working with him at the Spastic Centre in Mosman. They, together with Anne, did a wonderful job, eventually getting him onto his feet and walking. Even in the early stages of his therapy the signs were that his left arm had virtually stopped growing and the growth of his left leg had slowed.

I met with a Macquarie Street specialist in Sydney, a Dr Sofer Schreiber, a remarkable human being who took over the task of putting Richard back together. The piece of his skull that had been removed was still in Adelaide. The arrangements were made for it to be air freighted to Sydney then for me to collect it and take it to the Royal Alexandra Hospital at Camperdown pending the operation. It wasn't a pleasant experience—going out to the Ansett terminal at Sydney airport to collect this package. My expectations were that I would be collecting a very hygienic, sterile looking package from the hospital in Adelaide. Wrong. I collected something that looked like a second-hand five gallon paint tin. It was packed with dry ice and inside that there was another canister containing the piece of Richard's skull. I guess that was the hygienic bit. It's a strange feeling signing paperwork to collect part of your son's head.

Dr Schreiber did a magnificent job and there was not a speck of infection. He did tell me one of Richard's problems, among others, would be epilepsy because there was no membrane between the bone and the brain. Sadly, that has been the case. Fortunately, as he has grown older, the number of fits seem to have decreased, but at times he has terrible displays of aggression and tries to break up things at the Lorna Hodgkinson Sunshine Home in Sydney, where he lives.

The next part of our program was to try to find out about his eyesight, so we took him to a Dr Hertzberg, an eye specialist in Double Bay. He went on to operate on Richard and it was when he came out of the operating theatre that the full weight of the crisis really hit me. "I'm afraid your little boy will never see," he said in a very stern manner. "Oh crikey," I thought, feeling very empty and lost. "Where do I go from here?" Because he was a physically bigger build than David I always thought he might be a footballer. Suddenly my little footballer, a guy who was also going to be a sailing mate like his brother, had no independence. He would always need support. He was a bird without wings. Dr Hertzberg suggested the Royal Blind Society as a starting point for Richard, so introduced us to the people there. It turned out the Chairman of the Society was Alexis Albert, the Vice Commodore of the Royal Sydney Yacht Squadron—that was comforting to know. We decided it was best to get Richard into the most suitable environment straight away so he became a weekly border at the Victor Maxwell Nursery at Edgecliff, one of the Royal Blind Society's hostels.

To describe an experience like this as shattering is possibly an understatement. You have to be part of it to know what it is like. Today Richard can see just a little out of one eye—he can get some definition—but he must use a white cane to be mobile. Actually, it's amazing to me how much he does see, but if there is no silhouette he's in trouble. It's hard to know how he is mentally. In some areas he's very astute while in others he struggles. He has been at school for a lot of years yet if you ask him what is two plus two he can't quite handle it. But if you want to know who is in the State of Origin team he'll tell you who they are and how much they weigh. He is fanatically interested in football—a mad keen follower of Manly and also his local team, North Sydney, in the Sydney rugby league competition. He is also a supporter of the Sydney Swans when I take him to their matches. He loves going to the football. I take him down to Brookvale Oval for the Manly matches on the odd occasion and he gets right into the atmosphere of the game. He really latches on to the crowd and even though he can't see he'll turn to me and say things like: "Des Hasler is having a great game. And isn't Toovey tackling well?" And you have to laugh when he goes up with the crowd to cheer when Manly scores and he's facing away from the field. I take him by the shoulders and turn him around 180 degrees to face the action while he's still cheering. It's impressive how he copes with his physical disabilities—his lack of sight and the problems with his left arm and leg. He's incapacitated on his left side, like someone who has had a stroke, in that his left arm is useless and his left leg is disabled.

Richard's problems brought a change to our lives but I don't think anyone will ever know what anguish it must have brought Anne. She could see all her friends, all loving families, enjoy a normal, happy existence while she was carrying this enormous emotional burden. It could well have been the catalyst for her own problems, which were to surface in the years ahead. To be absolutely fair about it, you can certainly understand people who had any sort of weakness towards a dependency on drugs, alcohol or cigarettes finding solace somewhere when confronted with a problem like Richard's. The sad thing is that Anne, from the comments my mother made all those years earlier when she found her drinking sherry early in the morning, was probably exhibiting all the signs of that addictive gene doctors now know about. For her Richard's accident was probably enough to really start things rolling, though somehow she managed to keep it a secret from me and others for quite some years.

Life has to go on and back on the work scene I decided it was time for some changes. After two years of our bottling and distribution arrangement with Cawsey's I was more convinced than ever that we weren't making the progress in the marketplace I had hoped for. We were selling more wines in South Australia than we were in New South Wales and had slipped to sixth place in the market alongside Yalumba. Lindemans was leading in sales from Penfolds, McWilliams, Orlando and Seppelts. To be fair to Cawsey's, they were very good at selling spirits—their heart was in spirits. So in 1965, after I had placed all the facts on the table before the board of Hardy's, the decision was to re-establish our own marketing in Sydney and have all our product bottled in Adelaide. For me it was a great victory and a big step towards our successful penetration of the market in New South Wales. Fortunately, there was no blood on the ground. Cawsey's were willing to admit they weren't doing a good job with our wines and frankly I think they were happy to get rid of us. Selling wine really didn't interest Cawsey's, particularly the cork sniffing at the Wine and Food societies and Beefsteak and Burgundy clubs, and the vocabulary that goes along with appreciating the product.

I thought it would be beneficial to our cause to white ant—poach—some of their top representatives, but we only succeeded in having one of them join us. One thing that stuck in my memory was the approach I made to Uncle Ken at the time to get motor vehicles for the representatives. I asked him if there was any company policy on not buying Japanese motor cars because the Toyota was certainly beginning to show itself as being a very good vehicle. His response was: "There's no company ruling, Jim, about that, but do you really need Japanese motor cars?" I got the message and bought Fords.

Our new push into the market with our table wines certainly met with some stiff opposition. Some of the locals didn't like the South Australians trying to put a wedge into their market. Some people went out of their way to make life as difficult as they could for us, but I didn't let that worry me. This brings me to the point of nastiness in life, to people who go out of their way to be horrible. Sure, I've met some nasty people over the years, but what I do is to not let them get under my skin. I tend to size people up and if I don't like what I see, or sense they are out to try to make my life unpleasant, then I ignore them. I don't give them the opportunity to upset me because while they're trying to do that I've moved off into another area. They can fan the wind and talk behind my back as much as they like. I continue on, comfortable with the thought that if someone wants to be a real bastard in this world they will get their come-uppance one day, so why should I let them annoy me.

While I have been very aggressive while racing a sailboat or playing football I think I have only lost my cool once in every day life. That came one night when I was staging a wine tasting at our Liverpool Street cellars in Sydney to raise funds for the sailors in the Flying Dutchman Association. I contacted the local police and

139

got the all clear to set up a few gambling tables for what was to be a great night. Everything was going along just fine until I noticed one of the guests break open a carton of wine we had in stock, remove a bottle from it and stick it inside his jacket. It wasn't as though there was any shortage of wine on the evening. No one wanted for a drink. To put it mildly, I wasn't very happy with what I had seen. I was at the front door farewelling the guests when the guy with the bottle came up to me to leave. "I would appreciate it if you would leave behind the bottle I saw you put inside your jacket."

"What bottle?"

"The bottle in here," I said, putting my hand inside his jacket. Before I could grab it he burst through the crowd and ran off up the street. I was after him in a flash and while I am no fast runner I caught him and held him. I could not remember being as angry as I was at that moment. I had him by the throat and was all but holding him off the ground with two hands. It looked as though his feet were paddling in mid air. I thrust my hand inside his jacket, ripped out the bottle and told him never to cross my path again. I just couldn't cope with someone abusing my hospitality.

My involvement with the Wine and Brandy Association was certainly beneficial to business in that it was giving me a first-hand insight into how the industry operated. After starting with the New South Wales Association I moved on to be a member of the Federal Wine and Brandy Association, as it was called then. I was a New South Wales delegate, then went on to be Vice President and finally President. In the early days of my involvement it was a very tightly run industry. Tom Watson, who was the head of Tooth & Company, the big brewers, was a very autocratic sort of guy who insisted on controlling discounts within New South Wales. If hotels didn't pay for their beer on time then he would simply cut off their supply—and you can guess how successful a pub is without beer. So their accounts were paid immediately. The industry also offered 2.5 per cent cash discount for accounts paid on time—an offer that would lead to all sorts of excuses as to why the account had been paid late and why the discount should remain. Well, each month the association would meet, compare notes on who was paying their bills and who wasn't, and decide who got the discount and who didn't. The whole operation led to very few bad debts throughout the industry, something that isn't the case today.

One of our best marketing tools were the wine tastings at our cellars in Liverpool Street. You couldn't have a wine tasting on licensed premises but you could invite people to your cellars. We set up a very nice dining room-cum-tasting room, employed a chef who really knew his food, then invited various groups and hotel owners in for a lunch. It almost became an occupational hazard. There were some very memorable parties.

There was an interesting and somewhat awkward surprise for Anne and me some six months after I returned from the Olympics. I received a letter from Miss Setsuko Taguchi saying she was arriving in Sydney and looking forward to seeing me. Fortunately I had told Anne I had befriended this young lady in Tokyo, but that did little to ease the tension when news of her pending arrival in Sydney came through. I had met Setsuko with Pod O'Donnell while attending the numerous small cocktail parties and functions hosted by the Japanese before the Australian team arrived for the Olympics. For some unknown reason Setsuko, who was an exceptionally tall and very nice young hostess—complete with kimono—took a real shine to me. She started bringing me gifts and sending me messages all the time I was there. Naturally the rest of the team, when they arrived, picked up on what was going on and rubbished me something awful, all thinking there was more to this than a simple, platonic friendship. And of course, the more I fought it and tried to convince them otherwise the less they believed me. From the outset Setsuko knew I was married and knew about my life back home, but that didn't stop the friendship developing. I farewelled her a few days before the rest of the yachting team left the Olympic Village to head for home because I wanted to go to the main Olympic Village and try to sell the remaining wine I had to the Japanese. When I met up with the team at Tokyo airport for the flight home there was Setsuko, unexpected and unannounced. She had found her way up to the airport just to deliver some final farewell presents to me. The next scene was an anxious Syd Grange, the deputy team manager, standing on the tarmac alongside the fully laden Qantas 707—which was minus just one passenger—me. I was still in the departure lounge trying to get myself away from a sobbing Setsuko. The first I heard of her after that was the communication saying she was coming to Sydney on board a ship that was a floating university. Anne was as cynical about this whole episode as my yachting mates but we agreed we

141

should take Setsuko to dinner to return some of her hospitality. So Setsuko duly arrived and we took her to Johnny Walker's Bistro for a night out. I didn't realise—but Anne certainly did—that during the dinner Setsuko, in typical Japanese fashion, was doing all sorts of little things for me, like putting my napkin in place, making sure my wine was always topped up, passing me everything I needed. Well at the end of the dinner I picked up my cup of coffee and "phfffft, phooooey!!!"—I just about sprayed it everywhere. It was so sweet. "Ah, what's happened to my coffee?" I asked, totally mystified. It turned out Anne had noticed Setsuko putting sugar in my coffee and stirring it. "Enough," she thought. "Sugar—I'll give him bloody sugar." She tipped the entire contents of the sugar bowl in my coffee. Surprise, surprise—I wasn't allowed to see Setsuko after that.

The overall pace of life wasn't getting any slower in any direction. I had also been elected to the committee of the Royal Sydney Yacht Squadron, where I served for six years. Alexis Albert, the Chairman of the Royal Blind Society, had been knighted since I first contacted him about Richard's sight problems and he was also a flag officer of the Squadron. Not long after I had been elected I said to him that if there was some way I could help the Royal Blind Society then would he let me know. Next thing I knew was that I had been named on the Royal Blind Society's committee, something that required attendance to monthly meetings and sub-committees. It was an involvement that would last 25 years and see me as Vice President for some years. It was a very satisfying and worthwhile commitment.

When news came through that the 1966 World Championship for the 505 class would be sailed out of my old club, the Brighton Seacliff Yacht Club in Adelaide, my next sailing target was obvious. John Bagshaw, who had been transferred by General Motors to Adelaide from Melbourne, and I were among the group that introduced the 505s to Adelaide on the advice of the man they called the Great Dane, Paul Elvstrom. If ever there was a god in sailing it would be Elvstrom—the winner of gold medals at four Olympics. After the Melbourne Games in 1956 he assured us the 505, a two-man sailing dinghy that originated in France, would be in the next Olympics. He was wrong on that count, but the 505 went on to be a strong and satisfying international class of sailboat, probably because it didn't get Olympic status. Getting the gong for the Olympics has seemed to be the death knell of many a good class of sailboat. The 505s had certainly given us a lot of fun in Adelaide and also allowed Dave Binks, the man who built them for us, to experiment with so many radical construction techniques. He had a smart idea on how to build a timber veneer hull using a vacuum process. He decided to put the entire boat on its mould inside this big plastic bag then suck all the air out, that way supposedly forcing the timber veneers together. It was all very Heath Robinson, so the night of the big suck he asked us to give him a hand. We needed fifteen psi to make it work. Well, by the time we got this thing down to ten pounds half the glue had set. The problem was that the staples he had used to temporarily hold the veneers in place were puncturing the plastic. There we were, going all around this five metre long hull with our ears stuck down to the plastic, listening for leaks then sticking putty on them. It was 2 am when we finished and there was a need for a drink. "Got any grog in your car, Jim?" was the call.

"No," I said. "What a pity—oh, hang on—I've got the Communion wine I'm dropping off to St Judes Church in the morning. Two flagons of our Gold Label Port." So, we knocked off the port while I quietly dealt direct to our Master, praying for some understanding and asking for guidance on how I would replace the Communion wine. The congregation were the winners at church the next morning. I pinched two of Mum's best bottles of port from her cellar. I don't know if the church-goers appreciated what they were drinking but John McCoy, who was part of the boat building night, had such a taste for the Gold Label port he didn't surface for three days.

Pioneer he might have been, but Dave Binks built me a beaut boat for the 505 world championship, which took the name of our famous brandy—*Black Bottle*. I fitted out the bare hull with all the fittings, applying some of the ideas I had gleaned from racing Flying Dutchmen in Sydney. Having not raced 505s for a few years I was able to approach this project with a completely open mind— I was starting with a clean slate and wasn't influenced by existing trends in the class. The two biggest departures from what was considered the norm in the 505s were that I fitted the jib furling drum—a fishing reel-like device that rolls up the jib when it's not needed—under the foredeck. To do that I had to move the anchorage point for the forestay—which goes from the bow to three-quarters of the way up the mast—back along the deck towards the mast.

I believed that would help the boat's performance because I remembered as a youngster reading the sailing theories of Dr Manfred Curry. He said the more vertical you could get the forestay the more efficient the sail plan. The other theory from Curry and others was that the jib should set down a line angled ten degrees off the bow. When I got out the protractor and started drawing the ten degree line across the foredeck the light really came on. That line went inside the stays supporting the mast. Until then all 505s had been setting their jibs at a much wider angle outside the stays. I ignored convention and set the jib where I thought it should be—on the ten degree line. I think that was where we got our breakthrough. We were faster upwind than just about anyone else in all conditions. I had another theory, a firm belief that Bob Miller was the best sailmaker around. While later in life he was to be recognised as Ben Lexcen, the designer of *Australia II*, I still believed he was an even better sailmaker than he was a yacht designer. In both sailmaking and yacht design he just kept reaching out, looking for boundaries he could go beyond.

With the boat and sails ready I hitched the trailer on to the back of the Ford Fairmont and Anne and I headed for Adelaide. We left in darkness to beat the traffic. As we drove away from the outskirts of Sydney and started heading up towards the Blue Mountains things started going wrong. The lights on the trailer started fading and blinking intermittently then went out. The problem then progressed to the electrics in the car. By the time I reached Katoomba the car had lost all power. We were going nowhere so sat outside an auto electrician's from 5 am until he opened at 8 am. It was then I realised I'm no electrician. I had rewired a light on the trailer mudguard the wrong way round and gradually fused the whole car. It was some relief to be back on the road in a matter of minutes instead of, as I expected, spending a day or two in Katoomba while the entire electrics in the car were replaced.

Max Whitnall, my crew, and I decided that if we were to be fully focused on the world championship we wouldn't stay with family and friends in Adelaide. Instead we stayed with our wives at the old Seacliff Hotel, and this turned out to be just ideal because a lot of other competitors, including former world champion Marcel Buffett, were there. The atmosphere was right.

With this being the first world championship of an international

144

class staged in Australia, anyone who was anyone in sailing was competing, including my old Sharpie rival from Queensland, John Cuneo. I was more than pleased when we were runners-up to him in the curtain raiser, the Australian championship, because I was still a firm believer that if you won the lead-up series or the invitation race of a major championship you didn't win the big one. It seemed to me that if you were prominent in those races your opponents were always looking for you in the major championship, and that meant added pressure to perform. Cuneo did try to take some of the heat off himself by always telling the media I was the dark horse, but fortunately none of the competitors took much notice. The fact that Paul Elvstrom was also competing helped. He was doing something very different in his sailing technique, steering from the trapeze while his for'ard hand sat inboard—the opposite to conventional sailing techniques. Elvstrom's attitude towards the world championship was quite casual, while Cuneo's was intense. We were all in the showers one day after a race when Elvstrom couldn't resist taking a psychological swipe at Cuneo, one of the men he knew he had to beat for the world title. "Hey Cuneo, why do you not speak to me when I say "Hello, Cuneo?" Elvstrom asked loud enough for all to hear. And, blow me down, Cuneo still didn't talk to him.

All of us get a little bound up before a big regatta—except Paul Elvstrom. It was interesting to watch his preparations. He obviously had a scale of preference and made sure that everything on his boat was prepared according to that. Hull smoothness was vital but the quality of the paint job didn't matter. He didn't care if he sanded through the paint on the hull and the undercoat or fibreglass showed through—he just wanted it as smooth as possible. Paint and presentation didn't matter on any part of the boat; as long as it added up to speed he was happy. At the other end of the spectrum was John Cuneo, the Brisbane optometrist who prepared every single point of his boat in a most fastidious fashion. Everything was perfectly painted, perfectly presented. The difference between the two was saltwater to fresh, but while you cannot take anything away from Cuneo and his wonderful record in sailing, his near fanatical attitude toward preparation has certainly cost him a lot of crews and strained a few friendships.

The world championship was a great test because we had 70 boats racing, including 27 from overseas, and we experienced every conceivable weather condition, from flat calms to 30-plus knot gales. We made a far from spectacular start to the series, sailing like a log in the first heat, which was raced in a near calm. But from then on we found speed and eventually hit overdrive. We were always with the front runners and when we won the fourth heat and went to equal first on the points table with Cuneo, the heat was on. Local knowledge played a part in that win. On the final upwind leg we stayed closer to the shore longer than the others and as a result spent less time sailing into a head sea and adverse current.

During the evening before the sixth and final heat Max and I decided to try to work out why we felt there was something wrong with the boat. We checked everything, from the top of the mast down to the bottom of the hull. Eventually we found it—the centreboard case that accommodates the fin that slides through the bottom of the hull was loose. We worked until the early hours of the morning to fix it then on the big day headed out to the start line knowing the world championship was between four of us, the others being Cuneo, Elvstrom and Britain's Larry Marks. At the first mark it looked like the championship would be a two-way race between Elvstrom and Marks because we were right out of the hunt, sitting back in eighteenth place. "Bugger this for a joke," I thought. "We shouldn't be back here." We really upset Cuneo as we approached that first mark. We were on port tack—which does not have right of way—and were desperately looking for a gap between the right-of-way starboard tack boats we could tack into and round the mark. I spotted Freddie Neill, my old mate from Adelaide, the one I built a boat for all those years ago, and I knew he wouldn't make life too difficult for me. Cuneo saw me tack right in front of Fred and started jumping up and down in his boat, claiming I had tacked too close to Fred's boat and should be disqualified. He shouted and screamed then put up his protest flag. I had only two thoughts: get stuffed Cuneo, and get on with the race. The spinnaker went up, then Max and I got *Black Bottle* into top gear. We started mowing them down. By the last mark, the start of the upwind leg to the finish, we were sixth—not good enough but certainly close to the money. The wind was fairly fresh and coming offshore, which meant that it was varying in direction quite a bit. I told myself I would tack every time we hit a header—an adverse change in wind direction—and we did just that. The others were tending to sail

146

through the headers, apparently believing they were of too short a duration to worry about. Back on shore, up at our old family home, Mum and all her friends were going crazy. It was like a grandstand on grand final day with all of them shouting and screaming as we continued to carve our way through the fleet. Soon after we rounded the last mark we slipped into fourth place. A quick mental calculation told me that was all we needed to win the title. Elvstrom was leading the race but couldn't get sufficient points to beat us if we finished in fourth place. "We've got it. It's ours," I shouted to Max, who was straining every muscle out on the trapeze wire, keeping the boat flat and at maximum speed. "Bullshit," he shouted back. "Your sums are wrong. We've got to finish second." Holy hellfire, he was right. We tacked on every header and continued to gain—from fourth to third then, you beauty, into second place. Elvstrom was just ahead of us and after a couple more quick tacks we crossed ahead of him. Sensational. All we had to do was stay upright and finish either first or second to win the World Title. Elvstrom picked a good wind shift, tacked, crossed ahead of us and "bang" got the gun. A few seconds later *Black Bottle* crossed the line. The 505 World Championship was ours ahead of Elvstrom and Cuneo. The shouting, the cheering, the sirens, the horns—what a reception. Max and I just looked at each other and grinned our heads off. We cruised back to the beach while the salute continued around us. Then, when we reached the sand and stepped out of the boat this huge crowd lifted us shoulder high and carried us up the beach. It was fantastic.

The celebrations at the Brighton and Seacliff Yacht Club leading up to the presentation that evening were, to say the least, significant. I finished up a stretcher case, literally, a victim of yet another practical joke at the hands of John Harrington. He had found an old Red Cross stretcher and, with the assistance of some other mates, grabbed me and strapped me to it. When everyone was assembled for the presentation I was carried in—the story being I had suffered a severe groin injury and would have to spend the evening celebrating while on the stretcher. When they eventually released me Max and I were presented with the magnificent world championship trophy. The rush of adrenalin was almost overwhelming. "Championate du Monde" was there, engraved on the perpetual French trophy in large letters. We were the "Champions of the World".

Telegrams and letters of congratulation came from all over

Australia and around the world, and of all of them one stopped me in my tracks. It read: "Congratulations Jim, we would love to have you with us. Signed Ingate—12-metre crew." What a beauty, a chance to sail in the America's Cup. Gordon "Wingnut" Ingate was heading one of the crews Sir Frank Packer—the publisher of the Sydney *Daily Telegraph* and *Womens' Weekly*, among other things—was assembling for *Gretel*'s second crack at the Cup. She was being rebuilt to race *Dame Pattie* for the right to represent Australia in the 1967 Cup series. The America's Cup had always excited me—as a youngster one of my favourite books in my late father's library was *The Lawson History of the America's Cup*. I would get it out of the big, glass encased bookshelf ever so carefully and just drool over it—paintings of all the magnificent America's Cup challengers and defenders back to the first race in 1851—each plate being protected by a leaf of greaseproof paper.

Sir James' father, Lieutenant T. M. Hardy in Egypt, 14th Reinforcement, 9th Light Horse, AIF

Jim Hardy at 22 months gives his sister Pam an earful

Jim (on chair) with Tom (left), Pam and David, 1934

Jim Hardy, 12 years old, with family dog Johnny at the family home, Seacliff

Brighton Public School Fife Band, 1940. Jim Hardy , 3rd row down,
3rd from right

David Walker (left) and Jim Hardy (14 years old) at the launching
of *Nocroo*, 1947

Winners of Company and Battalion Drill Competitions, 16 National Service
Training Battalion, 'A' Company, 5 Platoon, 1951. Jim front row, 3rd from left

Launching *Noctoo* with Mrs Neill, built by Jim for Fred Neill, 1952–53

Jim (left) with (left to right) cousin Bob Hardy and brothers David and Tom at Waikerie Winery, 1955

Jim with his mother, Eileen, the year he joined Thomas Hardy and Sons, 1953

Jim (left), Tom Philipson and Dick Bartholomaeus with 12 Square Metre Sharpie *Swan*, State Champion Runner Up Australian Championships 1954, 1955, 1956, 1957

Commodore Keith McCoy launches *Tintara* for Jim, Brighton and Seacliff Yacht Club, 1956

Jim and crew, Doug Giles and Ian Gray, sail *Tintara* to his first Australian Championship victory, 12 Square Metre Sharpie class, Swan River, Perth, 1959

Jim and American defence skipper, Bill Ficker, resurface after being thrown in following Australia's America's Cup loss, Newport, Rhode Island, 1970

Jim Hardy (skipper) and Andy White in Flying Dutchman, *Eileen*, Australian Champion and Runner Up Olympic Trials, 1964

Left to right: Tom Hardy, Eileen Hardy, Jim Hardy, David Hardy with father
Tom Hardy in the photograph in the background, 1966

John Cuneo congratulates Jim Hardy, World 505 Class Champion, 1966 at
Brighton and Seacliff Yacht Club

Jim Hardy is 'crowned' along with crewman Max Whitnall after winning the World 505 Class Championship, Adelaide, 1966

Jim Hardy (4th from left) at the formation of the Sportsmans' Association of Australia, Canberra, with Prime Minister Harold Holt

Jim, skipper of the *Southern Cross* with owner Alan Bond after winning over France at Newport, 1974

Jim's son David and his first sail boat with the family dog Sandy, 1971

Jim with his mother, Eileen, and sister, Pam, at Buckingham Palace, London for his mother to receive her O.B.E., 1977

Family day on Sydney Harbour with *Nerida* in the background. From left: Anne Hardy, Jim Hardy, Eileen Hardy, brother Tom and sister Pam, 1975.

Left to right: Tom Hardy, David Hardy, mother Eileen and Jim in front of the painting of Eileen which was later reproduced for the label of the 'Eileen Hardy' collection of wines

Jim at Government House, Sydney, after receiving his O.B.E., with the Governor of NSW, Sir Roden Cutler, V.C., and his mother Eileen Hardy

Jim Hardy and a life time of sailing friends, 'This is Your Life' television show, 1980

Left to right: Jim with his son, Richard, Anne Hardy, son David and host Roger Climpson, 'This is Your Life', 1980

'Arise, Sir James'. Governor General, Sir Zelman Cowen, Investiture
Ceremony, Government House, Canberra, 1981.

Start of Sydney–Hobart yacht race with the *Police Car* crew decked out by the
Sydney Water Police, 1980

Sir James explaining a point of the sailing instructions to John Bertrand prior to the start of the elimination trials for the 1983 America's Cup, Newport, Rhode Island

'Boys will be boys'. John 'Chink' Longley, Sir James, Warren Jones and Ben Lexcen at a salute to Australia II's America's Cup Victory, Paris, 1984

Sir James Hardy with Joan McInnes on their wedding day at the Royal Sydney Yacht Squadron, 18 December 1991

Sir James Hardy's personal coat of arms which took seven years to research and produce

Jim Hardy as seen through the lens of Lord Snowdon

CHAPTER SEVEN

Cups, Bottles and Boats

I COULDN'T RESPOND to Gordon Ingate's invitation soon enough. Not long after Anne and I returned to Sydney I found myself out on Sydney Harbour aboard *Vim*, the classic twelve metre, one of the world's most famous yachts and one I had read so much about. From the outset it was memorable, mainly because I was to realise just how powerful those large yachts could be. I was sailing as mainsheet hand—controlling the mainsail—when the call came to set a spinnaker. I had the mainsail trimmed properly so decided I would add some extra weight to the team of guys hauling the spinnaker up the mast. Bruce Stannard was right at the mast working the winch, and behind him were three other guys hauling away. Someone shouted the spinnaker was all the way up so everyone except Stannard and me, let go and resumed normal positions. Before I knew it the spinnaker had filled with wind and the halyard holding it up had not been secured. There was only one turn of the halyard around the winch when there should have been four or five. The next scene was Stannard, still hanging on to the halyard, disappearing up the mast, and me hanging on to the tail of the rope, trying to slow down his rate of ascent. There was no way I could hold it—and no way Bruce could hold on. He crashed to the deck somewhat bruised and I let go as the rope smoked through my hands. Agony. I had burnt the skin off every finger and learnt a lesson that would be with me for the rest of my sailing days. It took two months for my fingers to get back to normal.

Eric Strain and Colin Ryrie headed the other crews that Sir Frank had assembled and each weekend until the rebuilt *Gretel* was launched we alternated on *Vim*. The day *Gretel* hit the water she was taken outside Sydney Harbour to line up alongside *Vim*, which we were sailing. For me, right from the start, as we started pacing *Gretel*, I was saying to myself: "Oops, I think they've made a mistake here." *Gretel*, which had been redesigned by Trygve Halvorsen, was going no faster. The two yachts sailed away from Sydney Heads on the same tack with *Vim* obviously sailing closer to the wind than *Gretel*. We went on for hour after hour until we were over the horizon and feeling as though we were halfway to New Zealand. Finally, *Gretel* tacked and just crossed ahead of us. The *Gretel* team could go home and tell Sir Frank they had beaten us. But it was unconvincing and *Gretel* was to undergo three more major surgeries before and during the trials against *Dame Pattie*.

Sir Frank then stirred the pot by adding to his line-up of potential helmsmen Archie Robertson, the man who I believe to this day had the best feel for a yacht's helm of anyone I know. When it came to naming the final crew to meet *Dame Pattie* in the trials I was fortunate enough to be included as mainsheet hand. Sir Frank then included me in what he called his "Professionals' Meeting", a gathering every Tuesday night in the heavy atmosphere of his office at Consolidated Press in the heart of Sydney. Among the professionals were Trygve Halvorsen, *Gretel*'s original designer, Alan Payne, Eric Strain, Archie Robertson, Gordon Ingate, crewman Colin Betts and publisher Colin Ryrie. The night came when Sir Frank had to decide who should steer *Gretel* in the first race against *Dame Pattie*, and he had no hesitation in picking Archie—a decision I agreed with. Well, Eric Strain erupted. He got up and stormed off towards the door. Sir Frank, completely unimpressed, said somewhat casually: "Well, Mr Strain, I think you will find it easier to go out the door than to come in." And that was it. Gone. It was water off a duck's back for Sir Frank. What an impressive man. He just made his decision and got on with it. For me that particular moment was his test for Ingate, Strain and Robertson.

Sir Frank did have a sense of humour, although it didn't surface all too often. One night after a professionals' meeting we all got into the lift with him to go to the ground floor. He would always get off at the first floor to go in and check the editorial for the next day's *Daily Telegraph* newspaper. This particular night the lift stopped halfway down to the ground floor and an artist type got in—long hair, paint splattered on his clothes—and Sir Frank, who was operating the lift with his key, said jokingly: "I wouldn't ride on this lift with this mob. I'd take the stairs. They're bad." The guy ignored him and just stared blankly at the lift door while we chuckled politely. When Sir Frank stepped out of the lift the guy half turned to us and said, while Sir Frank was still within earshot: "He's very cheeky for a lift driver." I saw a grin come on Sir Frank's face as he moved off down the passage.

As interesting as that incident was, it was to teach me a lot about Sir Frank. A week or so later I was at a wine tasting up in the Hunter Valley and I told the story about him being the lift driver. Unbelievably, the next Tuesday night when I saw him he said: "What's this about you telling stories about me in Newcastle?" His network of contacts was second to none.

Our races against *Dame Pattie* were pretty "unmemorable" because my theory that *Gretel* was slow was right. We only beat *Dame Pattie* twice the whole summer, once when her mast fell down. We beat her in another race when she continually blew headsails apart. Even on that day when she destroyed almost every headsail, she still almost beat us under mainsail alone. Just as we neared the line in that one Ken Beashel fell overboard. If he hadn't finished up getting his arm caught in a fitting as he washed down the side of the yacht, we would have had to go back and get him—and lose that race as well.

The writing was on the wall for *Gretel* so an end-of-season party was organised at Sydney's old Chevron Hotel. Sir Frank and Lady Packer came, as did all the wives and girlfriends of the team members. Sir Frank had not announced his plans for *Gretel*—whether or not she would go to America, whether he would try to modify her once more—so there was an air of tension hanging over the night. Halfway through the evening Sir Frank produced a letter that he asked me to read to the gathering. I couldn't argue, but I thought it strange that he would ask me, a rope jerker in the crew, to announce to everyone his decision not to send *Gretel* to America for the Cup. While I agreed with his decision it was no fun making the news official. The wives and girlfriends burst into tears and it wasn't hard to guess what everyone was saying under their breaths.

The following day I was in my Sydney office when I took a phone call from an angry Sir Frank: "What's this about the crew rebelling, Jim, that you're sending the boat to America yourselves?"

"What's that, Sir Frank? I don't know what you're talking about."

"Haven't you seen the *Daily Mirror* posters all over town? Haven't you heard the news?"

"No, I've been in the office all day."

"It's out there, Jim, in six inch print—posters saying 'CREW REBELS—WE'RE SENDING *GRETEL* OURSELVES'."

"That's news to me, Sir Frank."

Unbeknown to me Gordon Ingate and some of the crew who were at the Chevron party were so peeved by Sir Frank's decision they went straight around to Rupert Murdoch's *Daily Mirror* newspaper at midnight and tried to stir up a story seeking public support to send the yacht. It was a lost cause and I'm pleased to say it didn't get off the ground.

With my first America's Cup episode behind me I got together with Max Whitnall once again and decided to campaign a Tempest, the new Olympic class two-man keelboat. It was a bit like a Flying Dutchman with a small keel, so we felt quite comfortable with it. We won the right to go to the Tempest World Championship at Weymouth in England, which was timed nicely for me—just before the America's Cup in Newport. I could stop in Newport and watch the Cup races on the way home.

It was during this trip to England in 1967 that alarm bells began to ring loudly about Anne and alcohol. Unfortunately I still didn't hear them clearly. I still didn't realise what was happening, but later in life, when I looked back on our life together, this was when the problem was really beginning to appear. This was Anne's first overseas trip and she suddenly became terribly apprehensive about it. Her concerns about her condition and how she would cope with being away from the security of our home came to a head as we walked across the tarmac at Sydney airport to board the Qantas 707 for our first stopover, Hong Kong. The captain of the plane, Stuart Archibold, was a friend and that created opportunities for experiences on the flight that excited me. I was certainly looking forward to seeing how they flew the aircraft. As we left the terminal gate and began to walk towards the plane Anne really started to slow up. I think if she could have run for home at that moment she would have. "What's wrong? What's wrong?" I kept asking her. She wouldn't answer me and I finished up having to almost carry her onto the plane, all the time reassuring her everything was OK.

We were to spend two nights in Hong Kong to relax before heading for England. Around lunchtime on the first day we were there we were standing in the foyer of our hotel when Anne just collapsed in a heap on the floor. I called for the hotel doctor, who rushed out, gave her oxygen and brought her around. He couldn't decide what was wrong with Anne so immediately made an appointment for a visit to a local Chinese doctor. That doctor started asking Anne a few questions then asked to see her tongue. It was black, as black as a moonless night. I couldn't believe what I was seeing.

"That's malnutrition," the doctor said.

"Malnutrition. It can't be. That's something the people in the poorest parts of Africa suffer."

"The food is going straight through this person. She is not getting any nourishment from her food."

I was stunned—and of course I still didn't realise that the root of the problem was alcohol. Anne was always as thin as a church mouse and she didn't really eat much. My theory then was that lack of desire for food was the reason for her condition.

Our stopover in Hong Kong coincided with Stuart Archibold's lay-over on his Qantas trip through to London, so he was our pilot once more. He invited me into the cockpit of the Boeing 707 for the take off and that was a scene almost too close to the action. It was an appalling night, with the rain absolutely bucketing down as he moved the jet to the end of the runway. It was carrying maximum fuel and maximum load and Stuart told me we'd be using plenty of runway. That was an understatement. We started thundering down the runway, which extended out into the harbour, and when we had covered about half its length he called for the windscreen wipers to be turned on. I couldn't believe what I was seeing, the wipers being just like the ones on my old Volkswagen. The jet kept going on and on and I started getting the feeling we were going to run out of distance. The co-pilot made the pre lift-off call of "V-One" then finally "V-Two", which meant the aircraft had sufficient speed to rotate and become airborne. To me we had already run out of runway. Stuart started talking to the plane: "Come on, come on, get up, get up." I thought we were so low when we went off the end of the runway we would rip the bottom out of the plane on the runway marker lights that were on piles in the water. Next thing the control tower came on the radio: "My word, Captain, you certainly used all the runway. We had our hand on the panic button here."

"I got 14 additional feet of altitude once we cleared the end of the runway," Stuart called back. Pilots I have since talked with about this experience say that the fact that Stuart, a fine pilot during Hitler's war, did not try to lift the aircraft off the runway before the absolute end probably saved the day.

We eventually arrived in England safe and sound and went straight to the Royal Dorset Yacht Club in Weymouth to collect our chartered Tempest. We were more than impressed when we realised the American competitor had air freighted his yacht to the regatta all the way from San Francisco. That was unheard of in those days and was even more remarkable because the lead keel was part of the shipment. When it came to weighing his yacht it went nose down immediately it was lifted from its cradle. The big American, who was forever puffing on a huge cigar, said: "Oh man, that's certainly unusual." Max Whitnall said: "I think you might have water in the bow of your boat." Sure enough the American had air freighted gallons of San Francisco Bay all the way to England. Talk about expensive excess baggage.

Max and I went within an ace of winning that world championship. In one race we had led all the way and were only a matter of metres from the finishing line when a windless hole descended on to our boat. We stopped dead after a tack then started to be carried away from the finishing line by the current. While we drifted aimlessly in the wrong direction the boats behind us picked up a new breeze and sailed by. I knew it was curtains when Max sniffed the air and announced: "The American's in that bunch over there. He's going to beat us." Sure enough I too got the whiff of the American's big fat cigar he puffed on all the way around the course. He and just about everyone else beat us in that race. We finally took third on points and consoled ourselves with the knowledge that our win in the final race had left two English sailors, who didn't really like each other, locked in an unbreakable tie for first place. If you can't beat 'em, confuse 'em.

There was an incredible coincidence for us during the regatta.

Max, his wife Thea, Anne and I were sitting in a bar in Weymouth having a drink and talking to some Englishmen about my lifelong mate Dave Binks and the great boats that he'd built over the years. At that moment who should walk through the door but Dave. He had arrived in Weymouth unannounced, having decided to come and look for us while on the way to commencing studies in a Churchill Fellowship in England.

With the world championship completed Anne and I went to London to visit the Emu Wine Company, which was distributing our products in England. We then took the opportunity to visit Yates Brothers, a long established company that ran numerous wine lodges in the region and which sold a lot of our port. I had always wondered why they insisted the port we supplied was 40 per cent proof, a lot stronger than normal port, which was 30 per cent proof. Their explanation was simple: "When people visit our lodges to have a drink we want them to know they have had a drink." While there I met dear old Mr Yates, the grand old man of the family, and to my amazement he told me that he could actually remember meeting our founder, my great grandfather Thomas Hardy. He recalled it was around the turn of the century when he was a young man in the business. When a stranger came through the door Mr Yates inquired as to his name: "I am Thomas Hardy from Adelaide, South Australia. I make the best wines in the Empire." Yates Brothers have been buying our wine ever since.

Anne and I flew out of London to Newport, Rhode Island and stayed in a little cottage with some *Dame Pattie* supporters. Sir Frank was there and had chartered a 70 foot motor yacht, *Pearl Necklace*, to follow the racing, and he kindly invited Anne and me out on it every day to watch. *Dame Pattie* was soon to become known as "Damn Pity" partly because the American skipper, Bus Mosbacher, had got his way after *Gretel* gave him a fright in 1962. He had a rule introduced that banned foreign challengers from using American sail cloth. The basis for this was that when *Gretel* surfed past his yacht *Weatherly* and won a race in spectacular fashion the Australian yacht was sporting a magnificent white spinnaker that had originally been made for his yacht. Sails, or the lack of good ones, brought *Dame Pattie*'s downfall. Disaster as it was for Australia, it really whetted my appetite for the America's Cup.

Being in Newport, with all its mansions and associated wealth,

155

was a real eye opener for me. I'd never seen anything like it and was fortunate enough to see some of the lifestyle first hand. Archie Robertson was with us on *Pearl Necklace* and on one of the lay days Sir Frank arranged for Archie and me to get him out to the small airfield in Newport so he could fly to New York on business. We were unsure about how to get to the airport then, fortunately for us an obviously wealthy, aristocratic woman who had been with us on the boat each day offered to show us the way. So the four of us went to the airport. After farewelling Sir Frank we accepted an offer from the woman to return to her mansion for a drink. Talk about a mansion—it was like a castle with sweeping driveway covered in chipped marble leading up to the front door. As we stopped at the front door I went to water. There, snarling at me, its eyes focused on mine and its nose and front teeth pressed against the car window, was an almighty Alsatian that had appeared from nowhere. The dog was called off and Archie and I followed the woman inside, all the time looking over our shoulders for the bloody dog. Drinks were poured and the guided tour of this mansion began. Archie and I were in awe. The walls were covered by large, original modern paintings. We entered a huge room that had an indoor-outdoor swimming pool and there, sitting on the far side of the pool, was a very dapper looking central European bloke, perfectly groomed with just a hint of grey in his slick hair. He was lying on a deck chair sunning himself and did nothing to acknowledge our presence. "Oh, he's my guest," the woman said, gesturing towards him with the back of her hand.

"You've just seen your first gigolo," Archie whispered to me as an aside. And sure enough, it turned out this guy was the matron's "escort" for the summer. What a job!

Home was always a pleasant relief from my travels, which were always for business and sailing. With Richard still being a border at the Victor Maxwell Nursery at Edgecliff it was becoming more and more apparent there was very little that could be done for his sight, his mind or his physical condition. Anne, true mother that she was, lived in the hope that something could be done. Even now physiotherapists renew our hopes for Richard, but none are successful. But you never know—one day they might find a way to short-circuit the brain, and get messages to his withered left arm and his leg and get things functioning. This all made the time I spent with my other son David even more valuable. When I wasn't away my commitments to business, committees, Lodge and charities resulted in me getting home quite late a few nights each week, so having the time to drive him to school each morning, up to Balgowlah Primary School, was very important. It gave us a chance for a man-to-man chat. One particular drive to school was to also remind me of the responsibilities associated with fatherhood and how careful one must be not to damage the delicate bond between father and child. On this morning I was running late and rushed David into the car for the ride to school. He was already feeling uncomfortable, knowing he was going to be in trouble for being late to school. Sure enough, we came whistling around the corner to the school at two minutes after nine and the playground was empty—the kids were all in class. The look of disappointment on my eight-year-old son's face has been with me from that day to this. It was my fault for not allowing enough time to get this poor lad to school. It was terrible to put him out of the car, say goodbye then see this poor little forlorn bloke, tears rolling down his face, making his lonely pilgrimage across the deserted yard to the school. I don't think I have ever felt worse. It was a simple but solid reminder of the responsibilities associated with being a parent.

Anne's condition had reached a stage where apparently everyone but Jim Hardy knew about it. Finally my family and friends began pulling me aside to tell me what they knew and express their concerns. Disbelief turned to belief. Malnutrition was in fact alcoholism. Yes, she had been drinking throughout the entire trip to England and America. Yes, she was more often than not "off the air" when our friends visited our Balgowlah home while I was away. Yes, she had collected my brother Tom from Sydney airport then scared the daylights out of him by driving up on the median strip dividing the road. All the time she was saying to our friends: "Oh, please don't tell Jim." She was fighting alcohol addiction and fighting herself.

My immediate reaction was to first decide why this was happening. I was regularly interstate; I was away sailing; I was at the Olympics when our baby Richard had his terrible accident. None of that could have helped her situation. I was now confronted with a wife with an addiction, an illness. It was something like diabetes, whereas if you give sugar to a diabetic it kills them and if you give alcohol to someone who is dependent on it, that kills them. Most people don't have a problem with alcohol because they enjoy it, but for

Anne, she needed it. There is a huge difference between people who like it and people who need it.

My only theory on how to handle the problem was to confront it—something that was met with the strongest denial. But then, realising that I suspected what was happening, her condition started becoming more apparent. She would no longer concoct elaborate excuses for not being somewhere or attending a function. Bottles started disappearing from our liquor cabinet—something I hadn't really noticed before. I tried to reason with her and talk her out of it, but it was like trying to talk her out of smoking. I was yet to realise this was an illness much bigger than both of us and one that needed very specialised help. Sadly, if we knew back then what we know today about alcoholism things would probably have been a lot different. It wasn't looked on as an illness in those days; it was considered a weakness, and treated as such. Anne's condition would deteriorate as the years rolled by and finally lead to hospitalisation on many occasions. But still she continued to support and encourage my sailing activities, all the time logging my progress through thick scrapbooks she kept.

The year 1968 meant another Olympics program, this time for Mexico, in the Flying Dutchman class with my mate Max Whitnall. We ordered a new boat from Dave Binks and called it *Shiraz*. Max and I then developed a unique system that controlled the mast rake— the amount of angle the mast would lean back in the boat. The aim was to have the mast automatically lean aft in proportion to the increase in wind strength, and alternatively become closer to being vertical as the wind decreased. To our amazement and delight it worked, but unfortunately the revolutionary new thin stainless steel mast we used failed. We bent the mast during our first race on Botany Bay so spent that evening in our garage at home with Anne and me hanging off the bent section trying to straighten it, which we could do easily.

Our failure to impress in other races leading up to the Olympic trials led us to believe we had a slow hull. So just before the Olympic trials I rushed out and bought a second-hand timber hull from Adelaide, Norm Butcher's beautiful spruce boat *Skidoo*, and renamed it *Shiraz II*. It then became apparent the problem was actually the mast, so we replaced it with one from England. It was all too much too late and we finished second in the Olympic trials to Carl Ryves and Dick

Sargeant, who scored a popular and well deserved win. I was honoured and excited to be once again named a team reserve—until the Australian Olympic Federation bowed to external pressures and decided *Barranjoey*, which had again won the right to represent Australia in the 5.5 metre class, be dropped from the team to help keep the overall Olympic team numbers at the nominated level. The announcement stunned the yachting fraternity. *Barranjoey* was the reigning Olympic gold medal yacht and skipper Bill Solomon and his crew, Scotty Kaufman and Mick York, had done a great job winning the trials for Mexico. I went to the Australian Yachting Federation and offered to meet with all the Australian Olympic Federation delegates in all the capital cities during my business trips around Australia and campaign face to face for *Barranjoey* to be included in the team. I wrote a letter and hand delivered it to every delegate I could get to, telling them I thought it was unfair, unsportsmanlike, and un-Australian not to send the yacht to defend its 1964 gold medal. I was not making any headway, just fanning the air, so came up with the idea that if I withdrew from the team along with the boatman who had been nominated, then that would provide two positions in the yachting team. That worked and the decision came through to send *Barranjoey*. It was sad that I wasn't going to another Olympics, but I was pleased to have contributed to *Barranjoey's* inclusion in the team.

A few days later I took a phone call from the Secretary General of the Australian Olympic Federation in Melbourne, Sir Edgar Tanner, and heard: "You are back in the team, Jim."

"That's great news, Sir Edgar. How's that come about?"

"Mick York, the for'ard hand on *Barranjoey*, has told me he will be in America when the team gets there, but his business commitments won't allow him to get to Acapulco until four or five days before the event. So I told Mr York that unless he was in Acapulco when the team arrived two weeks before the Games then he wasn't in the team. He told me his business came first so I suggested he went about his business and I would replace him—with you, Jim."

So I became mainsheet hand for Bill Solomon on *Barranjoey* and Scotty worked the bow. Things were going OK for us until at breakfast one morning one of the English 5.5 metre fellows came up to me and asked if I had heard the Mexican Navy had smashed a hole in the side of *Barranjoey* big enough for a man to climb through.

"You're joking!"

"I'm not. The boat is still afloat—the hole is just above the waterline. I suggest you get down to the dock in a hurry." Hurry! I would have won an Olympic gold for running if they'd timed me for the distance to the dock. Sure enough, there was *Barranjoey* with this gaping hole in the bow and surrounding her Mexican Navy men, all gibbering away and pointing. It turned out one of their number had started a huge landing barge that was tied to the dock, not realising it was in gear. The mooring lines snapped, the barge took off and careered like a waterborne bulldozer into the 5.5s, which were all moored neatly at right angles off the dock. The stern of the British yacht *Yeoman* had been pounded through the bow of *Barranjoey*.

We made hasty arrangements to have the yacht lifted from the water so we could make repairs and race that day. We seemed to be surrounded by total confusion as the Mexicans did their best to show otherwise. Finally, as the yacht was craned onto the dock the British sailor Sir Owen Aisher, who was watching proceedings, casually leant across to me and summed things up perfectly, saying: "Jim, it's easy to see why two horses and fifteen men conquered this country." His thoughts were echoed by one of the crew of the American yacht *Williwaw*, who shouted to us as we were towed out to the start line after completing our repairs.

"What do you think of the Mexicans now, Jim?"

"I suppose you could call them colourful."

"Colourful! This is the only nation in the world which could stuff up a one car funeral!"

We claimed a respectable sixth place with *Barranjoey* in those Olympics, which were notable for their memories from onshore activities as much as the sailing. Top points for the best performance on shore went, without question, to our team boatman, Bob Miller who, as I have mentioned previously, went on to change his name to Ben Lexcen of *Australia II* fame. We all went along to a bullfight and Bob became just as intrigued by the antics of the Mexicans in the crowd as he did with the Mexicans in the ring. Every time there was some supposedly heroic deed done by the bullfighter a band would strike up in the crowd. Bob thought they were fantastic, belting out this incredible sound on instruments suffering a severe dose of verdigris. The atmosphere was all too much for Bob and he disappeared off

160

into the crowd of cheering Mexicans in search of the band. No one gave it another thought until the final night of the regatta when we were all back at the hotel celebrating after the presentation. You could hear a Mexican band getting louder and louder until finally it burst through the gates of the courtyard of the hotel, and there, out in front, leading them as a beaming bandmaster towards the hotel foyer was Bob Miller. Bob had paid for the band for the occasion, and as they made their way into the hotel people started cheering and throwing bread rolls and coins into the tuba and other instruments, which were a sickly green colour. The front section of the band, still playing, followed Bob into the lift while the rest made their way up the stairs, without missing a beat, for the final point of assembly, the Australian team rooms. People were laughing so much they had tears streaming down their faces—until the phone rang. I answered it and it was the hotel manager, absolutely fuming. He'd called the Mexican riot squad—they were on their way. The concert promptly ended.

Another evening saw us head for the hills behind Acapulco, where we found a place that looked like a night club. It was the only place we had come across with the Olympic rings outside and all the signs seemed to be saying "Olympians, welcome, welcome." It was therefore compulsory that we sample their hospitality, so in we went and discovered it was one of those places where you could get just about anything your heart desired. There were lots of pretty young girls there and, having agreed that one of our team was still a virgin, we decided that if we pre-paid one of these attractive ladies she would make him very happy. The hat went around without him knowing and we came up with enough money to pre-pay the young girl for the desired service. Much to the guy's surprise and delight this young lady seemed to come out of nowhere, and of all the Australians present chose him for some attention. She sat on his lap and stroked his hair—it was wonderful fun watching our plan unfold. Next thing he was being led away from the table. He was finding it difficult to believe his luck. When they eventually rejoined us his grin was right across his face.

"She's a lovely girl," he said to us on the side. "A university student from near Mexico City. She's not a professional girl or anything like that—I mean she wouldn't take any money. She's just a really nice girl."

161

We had got our money's worth and so had he.

There was a wonderful letter waiting for me back in Sydney from Alan Payne, the America's Cup yacht designer, saying Sir Frank Packer was inviting me to try out for the role of skipper for his 1970 challenger. "What a beauty," I thought. "That gives me a chance to have a go at the big time." The other ten or so contenders included Bill Fesq, Martin Visser and Peter Cole. My mind ticked over: "Bill Fesq—I see a lot of him through the yacht squadron committee and the wine business—like every month at the Wine and Brandy Association meetings. We would make a good team, not rivals."

"How about we form a partnership?" I suggested to Bill next time I saw him. "You're a very good navigator, so what about the idea that I steer the boat and you tell me where to go?"

"That'll do me, Jim," he said, quick as a flash, then shook my hand to seal the deal. With the position of navigator decided I started to think about the nine remaining spots. I remembered Rolly Tasker had alerted me to this young chap from Melbourne, John Bertrand, who had been very impressive as a skipper in the Sharpie class. It turned out he was in Sydney working with Warwick Hood, the naval architect, while on his holidays from Monash University, where he was studying engineering. I telephoned him and arranged a meeting, where I outlined my plan for the Cup campaign and asked him to join me. He liked the idea, accepted the offer and became my most important crew member in my three challenges for the Cup.

With the campaign being based in Sydney it was inevitable that almost the entire crew came from that city. While I was from Adelaide I was well aware of the rivalry between Sydney and Melbourne, something that was reinforced the day I went down to look at *Gretel* soon after I received my invitation from Sir Frank to try for the job of skipper. There was one shipwright working on the yacht on a Berrys Bay slipway when I stepped aboard and asked if I could look around.

"Yeah, mate—go right ahead," he said.

After fifteen minutes he said: "Geez mate, you're really interested in this boat."

"Yes, I was crewing on it in the races against *Dame Pattie* a couple of years ago and now Sir Frank has asked me to try out as skipper for his new yacht. So, I'll be steering this boat from time to time."

162

"Oh. Well, you'll make the same mistake as all the other skippers."

"What's that?"

"You'll fill up the boat with GPS blokes—y'know, private school blokes. You should get your crew from Green Valley boys—out near Liverpool. Get some real blokes."

"I don't think that will be the case. For a start I'm South Australian and I've already gone as far afield as Melbourne to find the best crew. I've just signed up this brilliant young yachtsman named John Bertrand from Victoria."

With that the shipwright stopped mid-swing with his mallet, put it down along with his chisel, turned to me and said: "Victoria— the land of overcoats and thieves!"

JB has been reminded of that one ever since.

While I formed my crew and began making plans towards the 1970 America's Cup challenge I was also careering all over the countryside promoting our wines and generating more business. Uncle Ken Hardy, the Chairman, and the rest of the Hardy's board continued with their great support for my sailing activities and the associated increase in the profile of our product. I knew I had a moral obligation to work as hard as I could whenever I could for the company. Among our gains was the distribution of Cooper's Beer—that wonderful cloudy beer from Adelaide—for New South Wales. Bill Cooper, of the brewery family, and I were mates when we were going to school and I saw benefits for them and us in handling the distribution. We struck a deal and it still stands today. On the wine side I came up with the idea to produce Hardy's McLaren Vale Hermitage. The wine market was changing—the public's taste buds were maturing—and McWilliams were doing very nicely with their Hunter River Hermitage. In South Australia the Hermitage grape is called Shiraz, but it's the same grape, so I suggested we bring out Hardy's McLaren Vale Hermitage. We decided to educate the people of New South Wales on South Australian wines so had a little map drawn on the label showing where McLaren Vale was relative to Adelaide. The whole thing was a great success until old Harry Brown, H.G. Brown, who had been the Sales Manager for Rhinecastle Wines, decided to start his own business and first up target our Hermitage with his own McLaren Vale Hermitage. While copying might be a subtle form of flattery, he certainly put a dent in our market, especially in the restaurant trade where he had very strong contacts.

163

Since the 1930s our company had been quite heavily involved with Hunter Valley wineries, so trips to that region became a regular event for me once I was based in Sydney. The major trip came in May of each year after the vintage was complete. That was when our chief winemaker, Dick Heath, would come over to check the quality of the Hunter Valley wines with a view to purchasing product for our own wineries. These trips were always fun as well as being enlightening and educational. One of the many great things about the wine industry was the excellent rapport that existed between everyone involved. While we may have been competitive in the retail outlets, we were always great friends back in the vineyards. As with many things in life your first experiences are usually the best, and that was the case with my early trips to the Hunter Valley. On one of those trips, involving Dick Heath, Gus Pfafflin and Max Lake, we stopped in Cessnock and bought some steaks so we could enjoy a roadside barbecue at lunchtime. We stopped along a road in the Hunter Valley where, with me being the youngest, I was given the job of wandering off through the bush to find firewood. The others were given the arduous task of preparing the wine. As I walked back out of the bush, my arms loaded with firewood, I noticed a large powder blue Ford pick-up truck with a black cover over the back also stopped where we were. A couple of big guys were talking to my companions, who were looking very solemn. As soon as I approached the group one of the strangers turned to me and asked very sternly: "Who are you?" As I introduced myself as Jim Hardy from Adelaide who was now living in Sydney I realised I was talking to the police. I couldn't work out what it was we had done wrong. The attitude of the police changed very quickly when they realised we weren't who they were looking for. Over a glass of wine they explained that they had received a tip-off that some people were wandering through the bush in the area looking for marijuana plants. They thought our barbecue was a cover for me while I was out searching for the plants. Hell, they couldn't have been any further from finding the right person. This young man from Adelaide had never heard of marijuana. That's how naive I was.

Much of the credit for the expansion of Hardy's in Sydney had to go to Gus Pfafflin and Ivor Peatty, who had worked tirelessly with me since the time we resumed selling our own product. Their efforts had contributed to us being in a position in the late '60s where we were outgrowing our premises in Liverpool Street and needed to consider a move. Sadly, just as we began plans for that expansion, Gus Pfafflin died. He was not to see our new headquarters, which we established at Botany, near Sydney airport. I had a strong feeling a Labor government, if it got into power, would push for the expansion of public transport systems over private, particularly in the area of rail for interstate transport, so it was decided we should look for new premises with a rail siding facility. I have always been a great believer in rail as the most important form of transport for long distance haulage and still cannot understand why, even today, Australia can't use more rail in preference to road.

The property we found at Botany was an old wood yard and it had the desired railway siding. That meant our guys at Mile End in Adelaide could load the wine at the goods yard, which was just 100 yards away, and it would arrive at our front door. There were benefits all round, not the least of which was the fact that the rail wagons loaded with the wine would arrive at Botany at around 3 am and we had 24 hours to unload. With road transport it was a case of unload the truck immediately it arrived so the driver could get back on the road—something that usually disrupted business on the day.

Our first rail delivery arrived in perfect condition and everything was pointing to happiness for us at the new premises. Then the second load of wine arrived—forty tons of broken glass—every bottle in the entire consignment smashed. The problem apparently came with shunting at places like Broken Hill, where they decide "this truck" or "that one" won't be going to Sydney for another three days, so they put it up the back of the yard. The way they would do this was to give it an almighty thump with the shunting locomotive then let it rattle up to the other end of the siding, where it hit the buffers with an equally solid thump. What they didn't break when they first hit the rail truck they got when it hit the buffers. That was the end of our experience with rail—we haven't used it since. While I was really disappointed I think our team in Adelaide was quite happy about returning to road transport. They didn't like the idea of taking the wine across to the goods yard and loading the wagons. It was much easier for them to load the semi-trailer in the yard, pat it on the backside and say: "Have a good trip to Sydney."

As the 1960s progressed table wines became more of a force

in the land. The era of cocktails, vermouth, port, sherry and brandy was starting to fade. Sparkling moselle, which was bottle fermented like champagne and a bit cheaper, was one of our big sellers and two of our best customers were Chequers Night Club and Sammy Lee's Latin Quarter. Of course it was important that I provided "after sales service" to these establishments, so whenever the opportunity presented itself I would visit them. One day I received a telephone call from my old mate Rolly Tasker to say he was in town. He asked if I would like to get together with him after work for a drink. We did just that and were joined by Bruce Ritchie, who was buying some sails from Rolly, and two guys from the Tasker sail loft in Sydney, Kevin Shepherd, who was the boss, and his assistant. We went to dinner at a French restaurant at Circular Quay then, on my suggestion, headed for the Latin Quarter. The guys just couldn't believe their eyes. The place was full of young ladies. There were dancing girls on the stage, a guy singing, and Norman Erskine compering and singing. It looked like a smorgasbord to Kevin Shepherd's assistant, a blond-haired young Danish lad. While we sat back and enjoyed the scenery and the entertainment he kept going around to all the tables asking young ladies to dance. His rejection rate was 100 per cent. The poor guy didn't realise—and we certainly didn't tell him—that the girls weren't there for dancing, but for more professional reasons. About 1 am a wonderful opportunity for some fun presented itself. Sammy Lee had recently opened Les Girls, and some of the girls, or should I say guys, came into the Latin Quarter for a drink after their show. They were dressed as women, and if you didn't know you certainly thought they were female.

"I'll see if we can get a little match up for the young bloke," I said to Rolly and Kevin when he was out of earshot.

Well, what a classic situation. On my suggestion he went over and asked a tall redhead for a dance, and sure enough "he", or should I say "she", accepted. I can still see the kid's face when he turned back to us, smiling and making sure we saw that he had finally found someone who would accept his invitation for a dance. Off they went, whirling around the dance floor with him chatting away with his prize, a beautiful redhead. It was all smiles for him and all too much for me. We just laughed, and laughed and laughed. The young bloke went back to his/her table and was having a wow of a time. He thought his luck had changed. At 3 am he was still at it so we could wait for him no longer. We waved goodbye and headed home. The poor kid—the waterfront tom toms were working overtime the next morning telling the story of his exploits the night before. But we still didn't know what was the end result of his night—until I saw him a few days later at the Royal Prince Edward Yacht Club.

"I thought it was great until she got an erection in the middle of the dance floor," he said. "I've never got out of a place so fast in my life."

The last month of the decade, December 1969, was to be, as I realised a few years later, a turning point in my life. I had never heard of Alan Bond until Bob Miller approached me that month and asked if I would like to sail on a 58 foot yacht, *Apollo*, in the Southern Cross Cup races leading up to and including the Sydney–Hobart race that year. Bob had designed the yacht for Alan Bond along the lines of a Flying Dutchman—it was going to be a fast machine, created regardless of the International Offshore Rule handicap system of the day. I accepted the offer, thinking it was a terrific idea because we were getting a spell from the twelve metres over the Christmas period while they worked furiously to launch the as yet unnamed new Alan Payne twelve metre early in 1970. So out I went and sailed on this big yacht and met the owner, Alan Bond, and his wife, Eileen. I found the stories going around the crew about the owner, this young millionaire from Perth, were very impressive. He had made his money out of signwriting, then borrowed some cash from his wife's family and went on to become a property developer. He had met with amazing success and was one of the youngest self-made millionaires in Australia.

The Southern Cross championship started off Sydney Heads and in this particular race I was at the mast, trying to make an adjustment to the mainsail with Bob's assistance. He gave an almighty heave on the rope I was hanging on to and the fitting it was attached to snapped. I went cartwheeling across the deck and over the life lines—the safety rails around the side of the yacht—very spectacularly. I became entangled in the wires as I went, an act that stopped me from falling into the ocean—but also an act that again dislocated my poor old carnival knee as I called it, the right knee that I had dislocated playing football at Port Vincent. Into hospital and into a plaster cast I went, then finished up sidelined in my bunk at home at Dobroyd Road. The boys went off on *Apollo* and had the most exciting Hobart race against the big English yacht *Crusade*, sailed by Sir Max Aitken. All I could do was listen to every radio report and read every newspaper, all the time wishing I was there.

Martin Visser used to come to see me regularly on the pretext that he wanted to know how I was getting on. But I think he had a hidden agenda—while I was out of action he was working on the management of the America's Cup challenge syndicate to get more of his crew into the final squad for the new yacht. I based that feeling on the fact that when we started out the twenty man squad comprised fourteen of my team and six of Martin's team. By the time I was back on my feet and ready to sail again it was ten-all. Good guys like John Anderson, who had been a wonderful for'ard hand for me, didn't make the cut, and that really upset me because he was good enough to go on and win an Olympic gold medal in 1972 but wasn't seen to be good enough for our team.

Martin's move reflected the extreme rivalry existing between the two of us while we raced the old *Gretel* and *Vim* in the skipper and crew selection trials off Sydney. It was always a case of "never give the other guy an even break" and we both would grab every chance that came our way to impress. I played this game as hard as Martin and one time got right up his nose as a result of Commander Donald "Spike" Ross, the head of the Navy's diving establishment at Balmoral, who just happened to be the best man at my sister's wedding. He visited me in my office one day to ask how the trials were going and I explained that it was my turn to steer *Vim* the following week. I said quite innocently that I was a little concerned about *Vim*'s speed potential as she was moored between two piles in Neutral Bay and appeared to be accumulating quite a bit of weed on the bottom. *Gretel*, on the other hand, was on a swing mooring and because it was constantly moving had less weed below the waterline.

"I can fix that," Spike said in a flash. "*Vim*'s moored just opposite the submarine base. I can create an underwater exercise for the diving team where they have to locate the yacht, clean the bottom, then return to the base."

"That's one hell of a good idea," I said. "There's nothing in the rules to say we can't do it. Go for it."

So, much to my delight, Spike Ross organised his divers and they cleaned the boat.

My plan wasn't to tell anyone about this bonus. But wouldn't you know it, one of the diving team was a relative of Martin Visser. He went to Martin and wanted to know why they were cleaning only *Vim* and not *Gretel* as well. Martin apparently blew up, complaining to Sir Frank about me creating an unfair advantage in the racing.

The combination of sailing, business and charity work was starting to open a lot of doors, but I was still pleasantly surprised when I was invited to Canberra by the then Prime Minister, Harold Holt, to assist with the formation of the Sportsmans' Association. Dawn Fraser, Johnny Raper, Colin McDonald, Jack Brabham and other leading Australian sporting identities were part of this very interesting group. At around 11 o'clock the Prime Minister invited us up to his rooms in Parliament House for morning tea. I immediately became impressed by one thing—how much the guy was shaking. Being in the grog business I guess I am pretty sensitive to people with the shakes. When I looked at him I said to myself: "That's not alcohol. Something is really worrying this man." There was no way he should have been shaking the way he was in front of such a laid back group of sporting people like us. We were no threat to his position. When I got home I mentioned this to Anne: "Something is really worrying Harold Holt. I think the job is too big for him." Those were my exact words to her. Two weeks later, on a Sunday afternoon, I was working in the garage when a news flash came through on the radio saying a famous Australian was missing. No name was given and it wasn't until 6 o'clock that it was announced it was the Prime Minister. I immediately said to myself: "He's taken his own life."

I believe that to this day.

CHAPTER EIGHT

A Decade of Achievement

THE TELEPHONE RANG in my office and within a split second of picking it up the deep, husky voice on the other end told me it was Sir Frank Packer—and he wasn't happy.

"Who have you been talking to?" he bellowed down the line.

"What do you mean, Sir Frank?"

"Haven't you seen the posters for the *Daily Mirror* all over town?"

"No. What do they say?"

"It's in type six inches high—'New skipper says we have no hope'."

My heart hit the floor and I got a lump in my throat the size of a cricket ball. I'd been the victim of a sneak attack by a newspaper reporter.

"Sir Frank, a reporter from a newspaper in Adelaide called me at home at 10 o'clock on Saturday night to ask how *Gretel II* went on her first day under sail. He asked me outright: 'Are you going to win the America's Cup?' I said we were going to give it our best shot. I told him: 'I don't know how probable it is, but it is always possible. Nobody has won it before but we are in there.' That's all I said, Sir Frank—and he was a reporter from Adelaide, not the *Daily Mirror* in Sydney. I haven't spoken to anyone from the *Daily Mirror*."

My explanation was greeted with silence. My mind was telling me I was about to become the shortest serving nominated skipper of an America's Cup yacht in the Cup's 119 year history.

"That makes sense," Sir Frank suddenly blurted. "Rupert Murdoch owns both papers. That's how the story has got to Sydney."

"What should I do, Sir Frank? How do I apologise? How do I get a retraction printed?"

"You don't do anything, Jim. I'm in this business and the only things that sell newspapers are sieges."

I knew just what he meant. Ignore the story and it would go away.

The incident deflated what had been a wonderful weekend. Sir Frank had named me skipper of *Gretel II* at the yacht's magnificent naming ceremony at the Royal Sydney Yacht Squadron on the Saturday and, after that, we had then enjoyed two exciting days of sailing. *Gretel II*, with its amazingly small rudder, massive mainsail and very bendy mast—which had been built by aeronautical engineers—was a handful to steer. But right from the outset she left the impression there was potential just waiting to be extracted.

The preparation for the America's Cup campaign, and the challenge itself in Newport, Rhode Island, consumed almost all of 1970 for me. We sailed every available weekend in Sydney before shipping the yacht to America. We had to train the crew, prepare the best possible sails and make sure we had everything we needed in the form of the yacht and its equipment. With two crews—Martin Visser's and mine—having been blended into one it was inevitable there would be friction. The rivalry between the two teams while we raced to decide who would be skipper and who would make the final cut had been too strong for the odd war wound not to open up occasionally. In a bid to create harmony and generate team spirit I invited the entire team to our premises at Liverpool Street one night to sample our product and have some fun. Fun! At around 11 o'clock the place erupted. A bottle of vermouth went rocketing off the bar and onto the floor. Smash! Dave Forbes, who was from my original team, and Martin Visser were trading abuse and blows. Martin accused Dave of double-crossing him—because he had accepted my invitation to sail on *Gretel II* after rejecting Martin's. At the same time Dave was telling Martin to go back to Holland because he wasn't an Australian. It looked like a fight to the death until a few of us leapt in and dragged them apart. So much for team spirit.

Less than 24 hours later the phone rang in my office. It was Sir Frank.

"I believe you had the golden gloves down in your cellar last night, Jim."

"Sir Frank, you are unbelievable. Your pedal wireless network really does work well."

"It must have been fun," was the only other comment from the man who was once a champion amateur boxer. The incident did warn me of one thing—there was a mole in our team. Someone was keeping Sir Frank updated on the inner workings of the group.

The final weekend of our training convinced me we had an excellent yacht, especially in light winds, because *Gretel II* absolutely blew *Gretel* away in a race in a light south-easterly outside Sydney Harbour. I had convinced myself we could, and probably would, win the America's Cup, though the press didn't see it that way. They were already writing us off as another "Damn Pity", which I guess was fortunate in some ways because it took the pressure off us and let us get on with the job. I managed to keep everything in some sort of lightweight perspective, telling our designer Alan Payne I thought we could win but, in the eyes of the public, victory would mean it was a great design while a loss would simply be seen as the skipper's fault.

Gretel II was the first yacht of its type in the world to have two steering wheels, so we thought it a bit rude when we saw the Americans had copied us by putting two wheels on the defender, *Intrepid*. As it turned out the Americans had gone to two wheels, one on each side of the cockpit just like *Gretel II*, for a completely different reason. *Gretel II*'s dual controls came about after Alan Payne's good friend, Professor Peter Joubert, from Melbourne, spent a day sailing with me.

"Jim, I want you to speak only to me. Very quietly tell me everything that is going through your mind as you steer the yacht to windward. Just say it so I can hear you."

"I wish I could see more of the headsail," I said as he stood right alongside me at the steering wheel, which was then on the centreline of the yacht. "I'm really struggling to know if I'm hard on the wind—and I can't see the waves approaching the yacht. It would be good to be able to see them—to be able to work out in advance how steep they are and the quickest way over them."

After an hour of me blurting out my thoughts Peter Joubert went off, met with Alan Payne, and devised a two wheel steering system, one each side of the cockpit near the edge of the yacht. They gave me every answer I was looking for. It turned out the Americans went for two steering wheels so they could position the boom, running along the bottom of the mainsail, as close to the deck as possible. They believed this created an end plate effect and generated more power in the sails. By removing the central steering wheels they were able to get the boom even lower.

We took only *Gretel II* to America after deciding it was a waste of money and effort taking our trial horse, the original *Gretel*, because the new boat was outclassing her by big margins. Sir Frank had very kindly decided the team should have a stopover in Honolulu en route to Newport and he gave each team member 50 dollars to cover their costs. I guess we stuck out like sore thumbs as we walked down the main street in downtown Honolulu wearing our official America's Cup blazers, complete with the Australian Coat of Arms on the pocket. Three gangling black guys spotted us and couldn't resist a chat: "Hey, you guys. What you up to?"

"We're on our way to the America's Cup."

"America's what?"

"The America's Cup. A yachting regatta."

"Oh, a yachtin' regatta."

"What have you guys been up to?" I asked.

"Man, we've bin drinkin' wine and talkin' shit."

For years after, when I found myself standing in the middle of a crowded wine tasting, I thought of those black guys. There I was, drinkin' wine and talkin' shit.

Once in Newport our plan was to tune the yacht and prepare for races against the French syndicate, headed by that colourful character Baron Bich, of ballpoint pen fame. That all changed when Sir Frank came to me one day in Newport and said he had been having discussions with Ted Turner, the famous sailor and burgeoning media tycoon.

"Ted has offered me *American Eagle* as a trial horse for *Gretel II*," Sir Frank announced. "He will steer it. Half the crew will be his guys, the rest ours. Would you like that, Jim?"

"That would be terrific, Sir Frank."

"Well, Turner wants $30 000 for two weeks."

"THIRTY THOUSAND DOLLARS," I spluttered. "We couldn't match the cost with the benefit."

"I'm not asking you about the money, son. I'm asking would it be worthwhile?"

"Well, it certainly would, Sir Frank. We really don't know the performance of some of our sails and that would be the best way to assess them."

"Right. I'll talk Turner down to $15 000 now and $10 000 when we win the America's Cup."

I knew Ted Turner well, having crossed tacks with him at Flying Dutchman and 5.5. metre regattas. His nickname was "The Mouth from the South" and to say he was flamboyant was an understatement. But while I was looking forward to trialing *Gretel II* against his yacht, the New York Yacht Club had its nose right out of joint—an American was helping Australia towards winning the Cup. That feeling didn't phase Ted one bit, and just to rub the club hierarchy a little more he decked out the crew in Confederate rebel clothing. Deep down I think Ted was putting sport well ahead of club politics. He was a 100 per cent sportsman and tough both on and off the water, just like Sir Frank. They hit it off well together and I think that was why Ted wanted to be part of our effort.

Just as I was amused by Sir Frank's deal with Ted Turner I was equally amused by his reaction to my request for larger steering compasses for the yacht. We had a compass in front of each of the two steering wheels on *Gretel II* and they had small, three-inch diameter cards in them. *Intrepid* had large, easy to read, seven-inch cards and I was so impressed I asked Alan Payne if we could at least get five-inch cards so it would be easier for us to work out our new course after each tack. Alan got some prices together—something like $500 per compass—and put it to Sir Frank.

The next day Sir Frank came down the dock and bellowed in his raspy voice to me, "What's this about steering compasses that you want to spend $1000 on, Hardy. What's wrong with the ones you've got?"

I tried to explain our problem and the advantage the *Intrepid* helmsman had in being able to more easily read his compass.

I helped Sir Frank on board (I believe this was the only time he ever came aboard *Gretel II* even though he owned it) and he stood behind the wheel, looking at one of the compasses through his glasses, which had lenses as thick as Coke bottles. He then turned to me after about one minute of contemplation and said, "I think

174

it would be cheaper to buy you glasses."

What a classic response. But good old Sir Frank then went away and ordered the new compasses.

Our trials against Ted Turner went well, however, any thoughts we had about an easy elimination series against the French fell apart in the first race when they led us at every rounding mark. It was only that I managed to bluff them approaching the last mark that we were able to go on and win. We were right on their stern going into the mark but were not close enough to legally claim the inside running and take the lead. I called Paul Salmon back to the cockpit from the foredeck and told him that while there was no way we could get the overlap I wanted the guys on the foredeck to shout and scream as much as they could when we neared the buoy. I wanted the French to think we were claiming the much desired inside course for the rounding. Two hundred yards from the mark the big act began. Our guys were hollering at the French, who reacted perfectly. They all stopped what they were doing, began looking back at us then mustered every word they could in French to tell us where we could put our yacht. The plan was unfolding as I waited. The French sailed a tight course towards the mark, trying to keep us out then made a mess of their spinnaker drop. We trimmed our sails perfectly, whipped around the outside of them at full speed and went on to blow them away at the finish by four minutes.

Baron Bich sacked his skipper that night. He did the same thing to his replacement skippers after we won two more races. Then short on helmsmen and big on pride, the Baron decided he would steer the yacht for what would probably be *France*'s final encounter. What an impression he made stepping aboard *France* that morning wearing his perfectly tailored white silk jacket, suede gloves and a cap. It was to be a very memorable day, which started with the fact that he gave me the match race start I had always dreamed about. When the countdown for the start commenced the Baron just turned his yacht and bolted away from the starting line, obviously determined not to engage us in any pre-start manoeuvring. We pushed *Gretel II* up to full speed and chased him, simply hunting him away from the start with the greatest of ease. "This is a dream situation," I was thinking. "I've woken up at 2 o'clock in the morning dreaming about this—being able to push a guy so far from the starting line that the navigator could turn to you and say that if we tacked and

175

headed back to the start at full speed there was no way we could be at the start prematurely."

"If you tack now and head back to the start line, Jim, there's no way you'll be early," said our navigator, Bill Fesq. My dream had come true. We led the Baron by almost a minute at the start line—58 seconds to be exact—and we all knew that if we couldn't win the race from there we had a pretty dud torpedo. As we headed up the leg to the windward mark a fog started rolling in. After a while it was so thick we couldn't see the French behind us, or the windward mark ahead. We kept peering through the fog, looking for the orange buoy. Suddenly Barry Russell, the man we nicknamed The Oracle, shouted that the mark was behind us. We had sailed right past it. Bill Fesq took an absolutely positive fix on it then announced that no matter how thick the fog became we could sail wherever we liked and he could guide us to the remaining marks. The rest is history. The Baron found the windward mark then got lost in the fog, quit and went home while we sailed on to victory. He stepped ashore angry, claiming the race should have been called off—it was like he'd fallen over in a running race so wanted the race stopped. Au revoir—we were off to challenge for the America's Cup.

While we were excited about becoming challenger, Alan Payne tempered the moment with some very sobering words: "Jim, I think beating the French 4-0 has done your crew more harm than good." At the time I thought his words were a bit heavy, but on reflection some years later I realised what he was saying. Beating the French had been too easy and our racing skills had not been honed by the competition. On the other hand the American defenders were enjoying tough competition right up to the start of the Cup defence. The tougher the competition the easier the final assault.

On the racing side of the America's Cup I was to make several bad decisions. The first came because I was having trouble with my number one for'ard hand, Ron Prescott, who had come from my team into the final squad. He had lost his back-up in the form of John Anderson and Billy Burns, two guys who, to my mind, deserved to be in the team but didn't make the cut. Instead Ron was backed up by two of Martin's guys, Paul Salmon and Barry Russell, and he wasn't happy. I decided to move him from the bow back to the coffee grinder winches and put Martin's entire foredeck crew on the bow in the hope we would get the desired results. When I told Paul Salmon what my plan was I added the one thing I feared most was that he would fall off the boat during a race.

"You've fallen off once or twice while sailing with Martin and it's a track record that scares me," I told him.

So there we were overtaking *Intrepid* in the first race for the America's Cup, heading under spinnaker for the mark we had to gybe around. It was blowing and the seas were quite large as *Gretel II* roared into the turn. We gybed the yacht, and the mainsail crashed across to the opposite side, Paul turned his back on the game and came aft from the bow facing me instead of looking at what was going on around him. *Gretel II* stuck her bow into a wave, which then came surging down the deck towards Paul. Sure enough it hit him from behind, right under his backside, and the last I saw of him was when he disappeared over the side. The rules said we have to complete the course with the same number of crew as we started with so we had to go back to get him. I was furious and our first attempt to pick him up showed that, because I charged at him at around seven knots. If we'd grabbed hold of him we would have pulled his arm out of its socket. I asked myself under my breath how much of a body we needed to finish with for it to be considered a crew member? Would an arm do? We got him on the second sweep but at that stage we were more than six minutes behind *Intrepid*. What was really starting to get in my craw was the fact that I had a foredeck crew that had really outshone the others, but I was stuck with the "B" team. We did have one card to play in that race. Prior to the start, while we were manoeuvring, I could have nailed *Intrepid*. We were on starboard tack so had right of way and I'm sure that had we not tacked to avoid a collision we would have cut *Intrepid* in half. We flew our protest flag and after we finished the race I radioed Sir Frank, who was aboard a support boat.

"We are protesting to the New York Yacht Club over an incident at the start," I told Sir Frank. "We caught them on port tack and could have hit them dead centre."

"Protesting to the New York Yacht Club, Jim, is like complaining to your mother-in-law about your wife."

If nothing else, the protest was a lesson in how to deal with Americans, and it was a lesson I have since carried throughout my life. It was the first time I realised just how different they are—

they speak English but they are foreign. Unless you use exactly the right vocabulary, exactly the right word, the meaning they are receiving isn't the message you are transmitting. As far as this protest was concerned, they were trained under one set of interpretations and we were trained under another. Whereas our interpretations were a little more open, theirs were very clearly defined. The Protest Committee's decision was that as there had been no collision there had been no foul. Protest dismissed. And as if that wasn't hard enough to swallow, we copped all sorts of flak in the local media and from the Americans. As far as they were concerned they were racing this amateurish bunch from the backblocks of the world who didn't know the racing rules.

While it was obvious we had the yacht that could deliver the goods we were now one race down in a best-of-seven series. The pressure was coming from all sides so I called a meeting with Alan Payne, Bill Fesq, Martin Visser and our sailmaker, Peter Cole. I suggested that Martin, who was seen to be a more aggressive starter than me, take the helm for the start and I take over once we were racing. While outlining the plan I said to Martin: "If I give you this job the one thing that really worries me is that you'll get us disqualified on the starting line."

"What makes you say that?"

"Your behaviour at the starts in Sydney."

"I won a lot more starts than you," Martin replied.

"But I won a lot more races, Martin. Just promise me your aggression at the start won't take over and get us disqualified."

That was to be mistake number two. Just as I had put the "mocker" on Paul Salmon about falling overboard I had put the "mocker" on Martin.

Bill Fesq pulled me aside before we made the final decision to say he would support the move only if I retained captaincy of the yacht. When we all agreed on the change I called Sir Frank and set up an appointment to see him in his room at the Viking Hotel.

"I'm pleased about that decision, Jim, because I was only going to give you one more start," was his response to my announcement. I suddenly sensed he saw me questioning my ability. My confidence had received a severe battering, but I knew I was doing my best in a situation where, for the first time in my life, I was sailing someone else's yacht and having to answer to them.

178

Life went from black and white to full colour at the start of race two. Martin executed a great start, beating *Intrepid*. When I took over we were able to lee bow her—squeeze up around *Intrepid*'s bow until we were on her course and ahead. We began to sail away. It was a fantastic feeling. You could feel the euphoria among the crew. We continued to draw away from *Intrepid* up that first windward leg but as we did the fog started rolling in. The 119-year history of the America's Cup was starting to roll through my mind as we approached the first mark. When we arrived at the turn ahead of *Intrepid* I knew it was the first time in a Cup race since 1934, when *Endeavour* raced *Rainbow*, that a challenger had led at the first mark. The spinnaker went up and we were off on the two reaching legs. What a sensational feeling. We led at the second mark and the third— then the fog started getting thicker. *Intrepid* gained on us on the next upwind leg and eventually crossed ahead, then we quickly reclaimed the lead. The fog was thick but certainly no worse than what we had experienced while racing old Baron Bich. Both yachts knew their respective positions on the course and where they were headed. That didn't matter for the New York Yacht Club. With *Gretel II* neck and neck with *Intrepid* the NYYC Race Committee called the race off because of the fog.

The second time around for race two was to see one of the most controversial incidents in the history of the Cup. It is an incident which is still hotly debated when it is brought up. In the closing stages of the starting sequence Martin had *Gretel II* perfectly positioned to shut the gate on *Intrepid*—we were sailing at an angle towards the starting boat and quite legally closing the gap the American skipper, Bill Ficker, obviously wanted to sail his yacht through. We knew we were not obliged to give a boat to windward room at the starting mark, which was the official start boat, because those were the rules of yacht racing. *Intrepid* could not force a passage prior to the start, and even at the start, if there is insufficient room, you were not required to give way to the yacht trying to sail through the gap. When Martin called for the sails to be hauled in so the yacht could increase speed I trimmed the mainsail while the two guys on the grinders, Ron Prescott and John Freedman, wound in the jib very quickly. They were too fast in the light winds because instead of helping the yacht accelerate the sudden pressure on the sail forced the bow away from Martin's desired course. All the time I was looking at *Intrepid*, thinking: "She's going to try to get through the gap, and there isn't going to be a gap." Martin was frantically turning the wheel trying to hold the yacht up on course. I realised his problem and shouted for the jib to be eased out. At that stage *Intrepid* was travelling at double our speed, Ficker leaving no doubt he was going for the rapidly closing gap between *Gretel II*'s bow and the starting boat. I shouted at *Intrepid*, telling Ficker not to go through the gap. At the same time our crew was calling: "Up, up, up!" to the *Intrepid* crew—letting them know they couldn't force a passage. That call was the single biggest mistake we made because while we were calling "Up, up, up," the Committee from the New York Yacht Club was standing along the side of the start boat, named *Incredible*, looking askance upon what was unfolding before their eyes. I knew there was going to be one almighty collision, my immediate thought being that *Intrepid* would plough into the committee boat. But no. Ficker kept going for the gap and the next second our 30 tons of 12-metre class yacht ploughed straight into the side of *Intrepid*, leaving a calling card in the form of a piece of our bow on *Intrepid*'s deck. Amid the shouts, screams and boisterous accusations as to who was right or wrong red protest flags were raised on both yachts. When things settled down and I took over the helm from Martin, *Intrepid* had cleared out, so the chase was on. I kept reminding myself I had now put the "mocker" on Martin as well as Paul Salmon. After four legs of the course we had made big gains on *Intrepid*, then on the downwind leg under spinnaker I handed over the helm to Dave Forbes, who did a great job getting us even closer. We realised a smaller spinnaker would be better in the choppy water and light winds so changed sails and made even bigger gains. After a great team effort we hit the front then drew away for a comfortable win. The jubilation was just unbelievable. We knew then that *Gretel II* could be the first yacht to take the Cup away from America in 119 years.

The protest was our next concern. We felt confident that it would go in our favour, so much so that when we returned to the dock I told the first reporter who came up to me: "If they get away with that, forcing a passage like they did, then I'll give up sailing!" It was probably a bit irrational at the time, but I said it.

We had a meeting to first discuss then file the protest just as we had done with protests over the years. We all headed home for a good night's sleep before the protest hearing the next morning.

For some unknown reason words from my mother were playing on my mind: "He who acts as his own lawyer has a fool for a client." As it turned out the Americans stayed up all night planning their case and seeking every piece of evidence and advice they could. We should have done the same. Martin presented our protest at the hearing because he was skippering the yacht at the time. I was the main witness.

I went back to the dock to await the protest result and was polishing the bottom of the yacht when someone came up to me and announced: "*Gretel II* disqualified." My America's Cup dream was becoming a nightmare. I was shocked. I just stood there shaking my head in disbelief.

I still say today the facts found by the New York Yacht Club's protest committee were wrong. I believe the decision they reached was correct on the facts that they established, but the facts were wrong. I know Dave Forbes, Bill Fesq and others all disagreed with me, primarily because they can remember Martin turning the steering wheel, which they assumed meant he was turning the yacht above a proper course to make sure he shut the gate on *Intrepid*. But Martin never had the yacht above a proper course. He was turning the wheel to try to hold the yacht up to the desired, and perfectly legal, course because the jib had been hauled on too quickly and the bow had been blown below course. Martin could have walked away from the helm at that stage because the pressure in the sails, and not the piddly little rudder, were steering the yacht. The other thing that made it appear the yacht was above close hauled—a proper course— was that the jib went inside out. That happened because *Intrepid* went across our bow so fast the wind shadow from her sails created a vacuum and sucked our jib to windward so it looked like we were above close hauled. The other thing that went against us was the terminology used—the application of American English against Australian English. In the protest hearing one of the New York Yacht Club committee men, who had been standing on the side of *Incredible* at the start, said he watched the entire incident develop: "We heard you calling 'up, up, up'," he said.

I suddenly realised our big mistake. If we had been calling "no room at the mark, no room at the starting mark, no room at the starting boat", the Americans would have understood. But "up, up, up" is a luffing call to them, and they just wouldn't believe we were not talking about luffing, sailing the yacht so close to the direction of the wind that the sails flapped.

The result of the protest, especially after we had come from behind and got the gun, just demolished the crew morale and blew away their loved ones who were in Newport with them. They were like sails without wind. They were completely demoralised and deflated.

At the start of the next race Martin was so paranoid about blowing the start he just about handed proceedings to the Americans on a platter. We made an appalling mess of things, an abysmal start, because his confidence was shot. We were beaten convincingly by *Intrepid* so as soon as we hit the dock I headed straight for a meeting with Sir Frank.

"Sir Frank, I'd like to take over the starting again. Our mistake today came about because you instructed Martin before we left the dock to be passive and get a safe start. The only way we could have been any safer than we were today was for the yacht to still be at the dock at start time. I should have been the man starting the boat today."

"You are quite right, Jim. That was my mistake today."

"I would like to start the yacht in the fourth race, Sir Frank."

"That's fine, Jim. Would you like me to tell the crew?"

"No, Sir Frank. If you don't mind, I will."

I went off, called a crew meeting, told everyone of the decision and did what I could to restore confidence. It was tough because while we could have been leading the series 2-1, possibly even 3-0, we were down 3-0 and just one loss away from packing our bags and heading home empty handed.

What a difference a day makes! The day for race four dawned—and we went out and won. Once again we came from behind, this time passing *Intrepid* on the final leg to the finish. As we approached the line I could feel the tension coming from the crew. It was like electricity sparking in very direction. *Intrepid* crossed behind us and I had both Bill Fesq and Dave Forbes in my ear: "Cover, cover, cover"—meaning I should tack and go the same way as *Intrepid* was going to stay between her and the finish. But we were almost aiming at the finishing line and two more tacks would have cost us a lot of speed. I remembered how Max Whitnall and I had lost the tempest world championship in England after I elected to tack twice near the finish line in similar light winds. "I'm not going to do a Weymouth

Harbour here," I thought and decided not to cover. Thank God for the Weymouth experience, because we managed to keep enough speed in the light winds to glide across the line and get the gun. What jubilation. Sir Frank was cock-a-hoop and my gut feeling about us winning the America's Cup returned.

Our disqualification from race two was still weighing heavily on my mind. Controversy over the incident was raging along the waterfront in Newport, in yacht clubs all over the world, and in the media. I pushed pride to one side and sat down before race four with the Canadian yachtsman, Bruce Kirby, to study the yacht racing rule book and the result of the protest, especially in the area of the interpretation of the rule as written. The more we read the more I became convinced we were right and should not have been disqualified. To reinforce my beliefs I telephoned Mr Sambrooke-Sturgess in London, a world authority on yacht racing rules. He was well aware of the incident and after I explained my theories, and where I believed the New York Yacht Club was wrong, he said, much to my delight: "I believe you have a case. I will back you on that one. You have the grounds for an appeal."

I couldn't get to Sir Frank quickly enough to tell him we had the ammunition for an appeal and that I wanted the protest reopened. But he stopped me in my tracks: "You may not agree with the finding, Jim, but you must accept."

"OK, Sir Frank. It's your yacht and your call."

It was "case closed", but I know that had it been my boat I was racing the appeal would certainly have been lodged.

Of the many telegrams I received from supporters in Australia it was one from North Queensland that stuck in my mind: "Come home Jim Hardy. Don't let the same thing as happened to Les D'Arcy and Phar Lap happen to you."

While I admired Sir Frank's attitude I was reminded of his statement: "Protesting to the New York Yacht Club was like complaining to your mother-in-law about your wife." We were playing against a home town advantage which was biased to an incredible degree in their favour. Sure we knew the conditions before we arrived, but when they dump on you from a great height and there's a distinct smell of unfair play then it is very difficult to just stand there and cop it. As if the protest situations weren't bad enough, I and many others believed we were racing against an illegal yacht, a yacht that didn't meet the measurement requirements of the twelve metre yacht class rule. When American designer Britton Chance was commissioned to update *Intrepid*'s hull lines for the 1970 match he decided the rudder should be moved further aft. It was a significant change, one which created a better water flow around the hull—the gap between the old rudder post and the new position was filled with fairing strips so it became part of the hull. But when it came to measuring the waterline length of the yacht, the vital measurement, which took into consideration the position of the rudder post, it was taken from the original rudder post. That meant *Intrepid* could retain her large sail area. If the measurement had been done in accordance with the proper interpretation of the rule, it would have been taken from the new rudder post. It is a crucial measurement in the twelve metre rule. Had it been done properly it would have resulted in a huge reduction in sail area for *Intrepid* and made her considerably slower. When Alan Payne latched on to what the Americans were up to he protested to the only group available to him, the match organisers and the Cup holders, the New York Yacht Club. Our elation over winning that protest went flat very quickly. While agreeing the Australian interpretation of the rule was correct their solution was to put a quarter inch wide slot between the top of the old rudder post and the new "so the water could wash in and touch the old rudder post". Well, bugger me—on one hand they are telling you their yacht is not a twelve metre then on the other they're telling you a quarter inch slot, which made no difference to the performance of the yacht at all, made all the difference to the measurement. It was another interesting lesson in how to play the America's Cup game.

We went into the do-or-die fifth race still believing we could win the Cup. I got a slightly better than even start and our confidence was boosted on the first upwind leg when we twice crossed ahead of *Intrepid*. At the second cross I had the option of either tacking right on top of the Americans and covering or sailing on and letting the race develop through sheer speed, clever sailing and wind shifts.

"Are you going to tack on top of him or continue on?" Martin Visser, my tactician, asked as we closed on *Intrepid*.

"We'll tack on top of him," I said, remembering everyone, including Sir Frank, had said to me before the race "cover, cover, cover!"

"If we tack on top of him he'll tack away and get out to the right-hand side of the course. If the wind goes right it will favour him and be curtains for us."

"I'll have to wear that, Martin. We'll tack on him and cover."

Tack we did. *Intrepid* immediately tacked away, sailed out to the right-hand side of the course, picked up a windshift of around fifteen degrees, and rolled over us. Bah!

From there on it was a super yacht race with the two yachts rarely more than a boat length apart for the remaining distance. It was tack for tack, but we couldn't break through. My mind was rapidly changing channels from a dream of winning the America's Cup to the reality of defeat. When the Americans fired that final finishing gun and signalled *Intrepid*'s successful defence they might as well have shot me. The adrenalin which had kept me going for so long suddenly rushed out of my body. I literally felt as though I had deflated. I had never experienced exhaustion like it. I could hardly lift my arms and the crew sat around in the cockpit looking like a crumpled heap of bodies.

"This is no good," I thought to myself. "I've got to do something about this."

"Hey," I shouted to the guys. "We have just completed a very Christian act. We have conferred happiness on others, and that's very Christian. Look over there and see how happy all the Americans are—all because of us." It worked. It broke the tension and eased the disappointment. The guys started lifting their heads and smiling. Then Bill Fesq improved the situation no end by producing a bottle of Bermudian rum. It was his emergency supply, just for a moment like we were experiencing. The entire crew had a tot of rum like the old Royal Navy and our spirits were lifted. We were ready to face the crowd on the dock.

The sun might have risen in spectacular fashion in Newport the next day, but for me the dense fog descending on my life would not clear for almost a decade. We could have and should have won the America's Cup. Yachting's ultimate prize and the trophy which was the symbol of sport's longest on-going competition could have been Australia's. But it wasn't to be the case. My mind immediately began a serious analysis of myself and the campaign. I put on a brave front to cover the terrible things happening inside. I was the one who had put Paul Salmon on the bow knowing he was capable of being washed overboard—and he went over the side. I was the one who moved for Martin to steer the boat at the start while knowing his aggression could lead to us being disqualified—and that was what happened. If I had stuck to my hunches and not let outside influence affect me we would have been much better off. I had also been trying to read Sir Frank's mind and stay one step ahead of him. I should have just got on with the job.

I felt very alone within myself, very isolated, until someone finally realised what was happening and came looking for me for a chat. It was none other than Ray Martin, then a reporter for the ABC based in New York and now the host of the *Midday Show* for Channel Nine out of Sydney. He had followed the entire campaign for the ABC and the morning after the final race he came up to our residence, "Chastellux", just to see me. To my surprise and delight he was there only to commiserate and say he thought the team had done a great job. It was just the two of us, sitting there talking over a cup of coffee while I exposed my heart and my mind. I was to realise there are very few people in this world who are as compassionate as Ray Martin. We were both near tears when he left.

Before going to the America's Cup I had found my dream car, the new Jaguar XJ-6. I saw it in a car showroom in Sydney and it just struck me as a magnificent motor car. I considered all previous Jaguars as looking like pasties on wheels, but this model was very different. I promised myself I would buy one if I won the America's Cup. Well, I didn't win the America's Cup but I did buy the XJ-6. I decided it was my consolation prize. The registration plate I ordered was CVP 001, the CVP representing how the word "Cup" was spelt in the English language of the early days of the competition, and the 001 representing the race that we won and kept with *Gretel II*.

There were two additional consolation prizes associated with our 1970 effort, ones that would eventually contribute towards *Australia II* winning the America's Cup in 1983. Firstly, because of the controversy surrounding our disqualification after the collision in race two, the New York Yacht Club decided it would no longer be judge and jury for protests affecting its defence of the Cup and would agree to the appointment of an international protest committee. Secondly, the club agreed to an international measurement committee to measure the yachts, a consequence of the controversy over the hull measurement on *Intrepid*. Ironically, a year later at the Cruising

Yacht Club of Australia in Sydney, our belief that *Intrepid* was illegal was supported by the yacht's original designer, Olin Stephens. Olin, one of the doyens of America's Cup yacht designers, was giving an address at the club in his role as Chairman of the International Yacht Racing Union's Keelboat Committee. He was asked for his opinion on the measurement on *Intrepid* for the 1970 campaign and to my astonishment he said that while he did not agree with Britton Chance's interpretation of the rule, he went along with it. I had to put a black mark against Olin's name that day. I had held him in the highest regard for a lot of years, yet there he was as the head of a world body on yacht measurement saying he believed *Intrepid* was illegal but would do nothing about it.

Getting back to business was one way to get my mind off losing the Cup, but even that had its moments. Not long after I returned from Newport there was a sad and sudden blow to the company with the death of our Chairman, Uncle Ken Hardy. He had made an enormous contribution to the development of Thomas Hardy and Sons and set us on a course that would see the company develop in spectacular fashion over the next two decades. My brother Tom, who was Managing Director, replaced Uncle Ken and took on the additional title of Executive Chairman.

On the sailing front Max Whitnall and I decided to give the Tempests another shot. What a mess that became. The first four Tempests built by the Australian licensee were different to the next four. The original batch were better because their hulls were stiffer. Unfortunately Max and I finished up with a boat from the second batch and to make matters worse our efforts to rectify the problem by adding hull stiffeners were deemed to be illegal. We saw a way out of our dilemma when the opportunity to charter boat number four for the remainder of the season presented itself. The owner, Ian Spies, a Sydney undertaker, told us we would find the boat stored at a business associate's premises in Williamstown in Melbourne. Max and I drove down to Williamstown, found the address, and sure enough it was a funeral home. As we approached the front door we could hear chiming, morbid music coming from the building. We were welcomed by a very sombre gentleman, just oozing compassion, dressed in the full regalia—the perfectly pressed morning suit, crisp white shirt, black tie and highly polished, seamless black shoes. He bowed solemnly with his hands clasped in front of him, at the same time mustering every look of consolation he had in his repertoire for welcoming people bringing news of a bereavement.

"Good morning, gentlemen."

"Good morning. We've come looking for a boat—Ian Spies' yacht."

"I beg your pardon, gentlemen?"

"Ian Spies' boat is here somewhere. We've come to pick it up."

A complete change of tone followed.

"Oh, is that all. Yeah, it's out the back in the shed. 'elp y'selves."

Out the back we went, dragged open the rickety doors on the shed and were not welcomed with the sight of a gleaming sailboat, just coffins, wall to wall coffins. We peered in and spotted the bow of the Tempest so began excavating coffins to get at it. What an awful experience—big coffins, little coffins, coffins for babies, expensive ones, cheap ones—they were all in there. When we finally got to our target it was groaning under the weight of a pile of artificial grass, which was used around grave sites at cemeteries. There were even dried out old wreaths of dead flowers on the boat. We hooked the boat on to the car and moved it out, put everything back in the shed, then accelerated away rapidly. Somewhat appropriately, after another unsuccessful attempt at the Olympic selection trials this time with the funeral parlor boat, it was a case of: "There endeth our sailing career in Tempests. Amen."

There was one very delightful highlight to those Olympic trials on Melbourne's Port Phillip in 1972. It developed from a phone call earlier in the year to my brother Tom, a call that was to bring a wonderful new chapter into my life. It was a Mr Wilcox, from Melbourne, asking if we were interested in buying our father's magnificent old yacht, the 45 foot long Nerida. He was the owner and after unsuccessful efforts to sell the old girl in Melbourne he had sent it to a yacht broker in Sydney. Tom liked the idea, called me and suggested we track it down. I found Nerida at Max van Gelder's marina at Neutral Bay looking very forlorn with weed growing on the hull and a deck which obviously leaked. But her character was undamaged. Despite changes to her rig and cabin the graceful lines which my father commissioned were still very evident. He started the Nerida project in 1929, eventually commissioning famous Scottish naval architect Alfred Mylne to design the yacht after being disappointed with a submission from an Australian designer. His first letter to Mylne, dated 10 July 1929, said: "It seemed impracticable at the time to consult a Yacht Architect in another hemisphere owing to the delays which would inevitably occur in the interchange of correspondence." How right he was about those delays. It took something like eight months for a letter to get from Adelaide to Glasgow then a response.

There was another interesting aspect to Father's letter: "I have obtained a price from a reputable builder amounting to six hundred pounds for base, hull and spars . . . " I often think about how my father would have laughed at suggestions back in those days that in less than 60 years his sons would be able to transmit a letter to Glasgow in a matter of seconds using a telephone line, and how a yacht of *Nerida*'s proportions would cost hundreds of thousands of dollars to build.

After four years of planning and construction *Nerida* was launched in 1933. Originally she carried the rig of the day, that of a gaff cutter, but later, after she was sold following my father's death, she was rigged as a modern-day two-masted Bermudian yawl. She went on to win the Sydney–Hobart classic in 1950 under the ownership of our great family friend, Colin Haselgrove.

It took very little to convince me *Nerida* should return to the family so I made a presentation to the Hardy's board suggesting we buy the yacht and restore her to her original glory. That way we would have a genuine vintage yacht that would complement our vintage wines. The restoration of *Nerida* became a project for the *Gretel II* design and construction team. Alan Payne inspected the hull then planned the restoration and Bill Barnett, who built *Gretel II*, did the work. A beautiful touch came to the project when I wrote away to Alfred Mylne's office in Glasgow and received a reply from the founder's nephew, also Alfred Mylne, saying all my father's original correspondence was still on file. He sent over a complete set of original drawings so we were able to complete the restoration very accurately. I did stray from the original plans a little, just to make *Nerida* easier to handle. The boom and gaff, which were originally heavy timber spars, were replaced by aluminium extrusions for the 1971 version. But to retain some authenticity I had the famous Sydney marine painter and decorator, Geoff Tyers, paint them to look as though they were varnished oregon. He did an incredible job, painting the grain in superb fashion, even putting a glue line along the length of each spar so it appeared they were made from two halves. His work was so good that one day Max Whitnall looked at the boom and said: "Jim, I know you are more into wood than I am, but how do you pop rivet into timber?" There was the give-away—we had to use pop rivets to attach the boom fittings.

Nerida was to sail to Melbourne in all her splendour after we had recommissioned her so she could be our company flagship for the Olympic trials. However, it was Mum's activities aboard the yacht during the regatta that were to be more impressive than the mere presence of the vintage vessel. Everyone knew Eileen—she was like the matriarch of the sailing scene—and on one particular day she was aboard *Nerida* watching the keelboats contest their trials. The wind faded to nothing and the start of the racing was postponed so *Nerida*, which was anchored nearby, became the focal point. Half the fleet tied up to *Nerida* while the wait for the wind went on. For Mum that meant just one thing—a party. Out came the Swinger, a potent brew we were marketing at the time which was a mixture of champagne and orange juice. Bottle after bottle was handed around to all of Mum's guests and it wasn't long before the Swinger was hitting the spot. Talk about "what do you do with a drunken sailor?" There were about 50 drunken sailors lying around *Nerida* that day.

While I once again missed selection for an Olympics—this time the 1972 Games—there were other significant developments in my life, like becoming Master of the City of Sydney Lodge. After coming up through the ranks over six years I was treated to a super installation ceremony at the Temple at Redfern. It was a big night with the New South Wales Grand Master attending along with many of my local and interstate friends.

Sadly the subsequent celebration involving wives of Lodge members proved to be too much for Anne and her efforts to find solace in our product at the party took a terrible toll. This situation was becoming more frequent and each time it happened I was blamed for everything that had happened in her life as an individual, and ours as a family. When she wasn't in that condition and our life did have a level of normality to it, she would love being involved.

On the sailing side of life the America's Cup was back in the spotlight. Alan Bond had decided he would go for the big one, with a challenge in 1974 sailing a Ben Lexcen design. The wheels went into motion in 1972 with Bondy first commissioning Ben to design an aluminium version of the 45 foot yacht *Ginkgo*, a successful Admiral's Cup yacht he had created a year earlier. He named the new boat *Apollo II*, and after we were successful in the Admiral's Cup team selection trials he flew back to Perth from Sydney and left me in charge of the sailing activities. "I'll make sure I always have a good navigator and don't put the boat on the rocks," were my parting words to him. A week later we set off in our first race, a 180 nautical mile overnight jaunt out of Sydney, with Graham Newland, one of Australia's best navigators, on board. It started at 8 o'clock and after getting away from the line nicely we found ourselves fighting for the honour of being first yacht out of the Harbour. We tacked in towards South Head to protect our lead.

"Tell me when I've got to tack, Graham. I don't know the depths in here."

"You're right, Jim, keep going."

CRASH! Straight up on the bricks. We had hit an apron of rocks just off the edge of South Reef. "Oops, wait until Alan hears about this," was my immediate thought.

We started the engine and at the same time a police launch came over to tow us back into deep water. A quick check below showed we were still watertight so we elected to sail on through the night as an unofficial entry—we could no longer be an active participant because we had started our engine. When we got back to the yacht club the next morning the first thing I did was head straight for the telephone to call Bondy. I wanted to make sure he heard about the incident from me before it reached him via the very quick and always accurate waterfront grapevine. That conversation taught me more about Alan Bond.

"Alan, I've called to tell you we had a little problem in the race. We ran aground off South Reef . . . "

"Who did you have in the crew?" was his rapid fire response.

"Well, there was Graham Newland and 'this guy' and 'that guy' and Rob Mundle . . . "

"Rob Mundle! He's a reporter! He's a journalist! Why'd you invite him? That's ridiculous."

"Well, Alan, he's a good yachtie . . ."

"Bbbbbut he's a reporter! He's a journalist! The story will end up everywhere."

Alan was more concerned about his corporate image than

anything else. He only had visions of "Bond on the Rocks" headlines.

The story and the headline didn't hit the press and I retained my position as a crew member for *Apollo II* for the Admiral's Cup in Cowes that year. It was a regatta we didn't win, but boy did we have a great time. Some of international yachting's more colourful characters were there, and heading the list was none other than my old mate Ted Turner, from Atlanta, Georgia. It was a regatta where we saw, and heard, "typical Ted". His yacht, *Lightning*, was having trouble making the handicap so Ted saw the simple solution coming via the removal of the yacht's propeller, and thereby removing the propeller allowance in the rating.

"The rules say I have to have a motor, but they don't say I have to have a propeller," was his reasoning. The move saw *Lightning* meet the desired handicap requirements and provide a new source of entertainment at the conclusion of every race. Because he couldn't get back to his marina berth using a propeller-less engine, Ted would charge *Lightning* into the entrance of the river in Cowes under full sail, drop the lot then try to glide to his berth. It was mayhem. There was Ted bellowing at the top of his southern drawl as he dodged his way through the hundreds of other yachts around him. Inevitably *Lightning* would approach the marina berth with an overload of speed. The crew had no chance of stopping it so the yacht would make a crash landing into the end of the dock. As *Lightning* came to a shuddering halt Ted would step onto the dock, brush his hands and walk away as though that was the way it was always done.

If there was a prize for the best one-liner of the regatta it would have gone to Ted. It came when he was approached by a reporter at the end of the third race.

"Well, Mr Turner, your American team is still trailing the leaders, Germany. What do you think about that?"

"The Germans were leading in 1942 too!"

As it was the Germans did go on to win the Cup but I must say I came away from the regatta asking some questions. In the last race, The Fastnet, *Apollo II* and the leading German entry were becalmed, along with a group of other yachts, about 50 miles from the finish. The yachts behind us were to sail into the same calm— except for the two other German team yachts. It seemed quite incredible that these German yachts suddenly changed course and headed almost across to the coast of France to avoid the calm. I could only assume they got some information the rest of us didn't receive—communication from another yacht about weather conditions, which is illegal in a yacht race.

As always one of the highlights of the Admiral's Cup campaign was the pre-regatta Cowes–Dinard race, which sees the fleet dock in the beautiful French port of St Malo, one of the fun places in the world. Alan Bond put on a really good crew dinner for us one night where we also entertained some of the locals. When dinner finished we decided to head for the casino to try our luck. As we started walking across town I continued chatting to a young French lady who had been at our table. I had a few French francs in my wallet so suggested she hold them for me at the casino because I didn't really understand the French currency, and that way she could control my spending. As soon as I gave her the money she looked me straight in the eye, smiled and said with the most beautiful French accent: "Do you really want to go to the Casino? Why don't you take me back to your yacht?"

"What a nice idea."

With that tactical decision made we tacked away from the rest of the group and headed for *Apollo II* at the dock. Who cared if she thought it was my yacht and it wasn't? It was going to be far more fun sitting on the deck watching the world go by than frittering away francs at the casino.

When we went aboard *Apollo II*, which was docked adjacent to a very active and historic part of the city's waterfront, I gave my French companion a guided tour. We went down into the cabin where, straight away, it was very obvious she was interested in only one thing, and it was going to cost me money. She saw the francs I had given her as a deposit. I began back pedalling.

"I take credit cards," she said as she tried to negotiate a deal.

With that there was a muffled laugh from one of the bunks back aft. That triggered another muffled laugh from a bunk on the other side of the yacht. Sure enough, there in the bunks were two Australian mates, Bob Ross and Ian Treharne, who had decided to stay aboard *Apollo II* for the night.

"Who are these men?" asked my little French friend in a manner only the French can muster.

"Oh, uhm, they are my crew. They sleep on board."

"Hmmmmph. It is no good that they are here."

193

"You're right. Now, can I get my French francs from you?"

"Hmmmmph. Goodnight!"

Once back in Australia Bondy decided business and the America's Cup were to go hand in hand. He based his campaign headquarters at Yanchep, north of Perth, where he was involved in a large real estate development. He had bought *Gretel* and *Gretel II* from Sir Frank Packer as trial horses, then approached me and asked if I would move to Yanchep with Anne to act as training skipper against the man he expected to sail his challenger, my old arch rival, John Cuneo.

Anne and I moved to Yanchep during the Christmas period of 1973 and I began an intense training program with *Gretel II* against Cuneo, who was steering the new yacht, *Southern Cross*. Much to our delight *Gretel II* was going very well, despite having spinnakers which were like corn sacks. But while it was satisfying for us to be so competitive it wasn't a good sign for the potential of the new boat.

One of the guys I invited to sail with me on *Gretel II* was Bob Blackburn, Managing Director of Ron Brierley's company, Industrial Equity. He had been my reserve navigator for *Gretel II* in 1970. One day, out of the blue, Bob started asking me questions about the relationship between the Emu Wine Company in London and Thomas Hardy and Sons UK Ltd. I explained we had enjoyed a long association and that Emu were our agents and registered office in London. He then asked about the financial relationship—did we have any shares in Emu? I told him we didn't, then asked why he held so much interest in Emu and Hardy's. He told me that two of the more dynamic investors in Australian business, Robert Holmes à Court and his own boss, Ron Brierley, were busy buying shares in the Emu Wine Company.

The news rang alarm bells for our company. We knew the big asset Emu owned in Australia was the Houghton Wine Company in Western Australia, which included the Moondah Brook vineyard. I travelled to Adelaide from Yanchep for the next monthly board meeting of Thomas Hardy's armed with the information on the move for the Emu Wine Company. We decided we didn't like the idea and would much prefer to have the company in our stable instead of someone else's. We had our Finance Director, Ian Gray, start making some inquiries.

We thought the Chaplin family, which controlled Emu, would always be disposed towards us if they were ever going to sell. At that stage they had no intention of selling, but their ownership was down to about 40 per cent, with the other 60 per cent in public hands.

Holmes à Court and Brierley saw an opportunity for a profit-making hit on the company and we found ourselves locked into a long, drawn-out battle that lasted a couple of years. Eventually Brierley pulled out and we purchased the Chaplin family's 40 per cent. Holmes à Court had gained 40 per cent so there was 20 per cent still swinging. It was our task to woo these people into keeping Houghton as a wine company and not let Holmes à Court, as we expected, use the land in the Swan Valley east of Perth for a race horse stud. One day, with the negotiations still dragging on, Tom rang me in Sydney and said: "It's all too hard. He's pushed us up too far on the share prices. It's become a Dutch auction. We can't afford to borrow more money." On hearing that news Ian Gray, decided to make one final approach to Holmes à Court in a bid to strike a deal where we would take over the winery assets and the trade name and sell him the land for his horses, or whatever. At that time Holmes à Court, the poor guy, had the mumps and was in hospital. We must have caught him at a very tender moment because he just said: "OK, you can have the lot." However, the decision came after he had pushed us up several hundreds of thousands of dollars on the share price. He was set to make a tidy profit. We finished up with 100 per cent of the company and in 1976 it became a wholly owned subsidiary of Thomas Hardy and Sons. It would eventually become the jewel in our crown.

That deal was the one bonus that came out of being in Yanchep. The place was called Yanchep Sun City, but at times we were forced to call it Yanchep Fly City because of the millions of bush flies that decided it was a nice area to frequent. It seemed that we received a double dose of bush flies every day. In the morning they would be doing laps of honour around you as the strong offshore winds blew them from the inland out to sea. The sea breeze would arrive soon after lunch and they would stop for another visit as they were blown back to the inland. The great Australian salute, the one-handed swipe across the front of your face to remove persistent bush flies, became a symbolic gesture among the crew for the rest of the season.

It was a relief to get away from Yanchep and head for the

essentially fly-free zone of Newport, Rhode Island. It was obvious to me while we trialled *Gretel II* against *Southern Cross* in Yanchep that there was a problem with the new boat. It was called lack of speed. *Gretel II*, with her baggy old sails, was giving *Southern Cross* a run for her money. I thought a new plan should be put in place as a precaution for the challenge so went to the syndicate manager, Brian Leary: "If *Gretel II* continues to perform so well against *Southern Cross* there's nothing to stop us campaigning her as well as the new yacht. As I read the Deed of Gift two years has elapsed and it will be four years between the Cup matches, so she's legal. You can't challenge with a defeated challenger in under two years. I think we should campaign *Gretel II* in full racing trim then see how she matches up against the new boat. If she beats *Southern Cross* she can challenge."

"Oh no, Jim, that's not possible. It can't be done," was Leary's response.

I wasn't strong enough to push the point. I thought Sir Frank might have given some covenant over the sale of the yacht which said *Gretel II* couldn't challenge. Then, blow me down, when we were racing in America and still doing very well against *Southern Cross* with all her new inventory of sails, Alan Bond came up to us at our crew house one night and said: "I've just had lunch with the New York Yacht Club committee and they've told me I can campaign *Gretel II* if I want to." I thought: "Hell, I said that to Brian Leary six months ago and he said it couldn't be done."

The sad thing was it was too late. The tide had gone out. There was no way we could get *Gretel II* up to full speed in the time available. Had *Gretel II* been in full racing trim all along she would have been very competitive, particularly in the light winds that prevailed so often in Newport. It's a pity the same money wasn't spent on the sail wardrobes of both boats, particularly with spinnakers. So it was too late to do anything about *Gretel II* but Bondy's comments about campaigning her led me to believe he knew he was in trouble with *Southern Cross*.

If the good luck charms Bondy had on board *Southern Cross* were any indication then there was no doubt the yacht was in trouble. He had horse shoes, rabbit's feet, St Christopher medals and anything else he could lay his hands on. The ultimate scene was when he had a dockside ceremony so he could sprinkle sand from Yanchep on the yacht. It all prompted crew man Dick Sargeant to say: "Jim, if we could get all these good luck charms off the yacht we'd float three inches higher."

Initially the deal was that Cuneo would skipper the challenger and I'd back him up. But when we arrived in America Bondy announced otherwise. The position was vacant and it was a competition between the two of us for the job. The day he made his decision on the skipper he first invited John Cuneo into his office at Newport Offshore, then me. After a few minutes Cuneo came down the stairs and said to me, somewhat tersely: "You've got the job." My immediate perception was that underneath it all John was pleased. He knew the yacht could not deliver the goods and he didn't want his name going down in the history books as a loser. Up I went to Bondy's office and he told me I was his skipper: "I want you to remember one thing, Jim. I once read where Napoleon was losing a lot of battles so he took his most popular general out and shot him in front of his own troops. He wasn't very popular with his troops but he started winning a few more battles."

"I hear what you are saying, Alan."

We had to beat the French in an elimination series to become Cup challenger, and *Southern Cross* was good enough for that job. I was on my way to another America's Cup challenge—in a slow yacht.

In the first race for the Cup Hughie Treharne was the tactician and Ron Packer the navigator. Bondy, like all America's Cup yacht owners, was starting to get pretty jumpy in the final days before the challenge. After we lost the first race he decided he would be better at selecting the crew than me—an owner's prerogative. It was poor Hughie who Bondy dragged off and shot for that loss. He was sacked, so he headed for home. In came Cuneo as tactician. Initially I thought it was going to be a very tough situation to handle but I was soon to realise what a great guy he could be. I have never had anyone sail with me who has been more subordinate, more co-operative, more helpful. I couldn't believe that under all the competitiveness and rivalry we had experienced for so many years, there was a guy who was completely supportive of me. Even when we were going bad he had this incredible ability to encourage me. There was a time when I was really annoyed because the Americans were sailing higher and faster than us. They were blowing our doors off and I didn't know what I could do to match them. Cuneo turned

197

to me and said: "No one can sail this boat to windward better than you, Jim," meaning "Don't blame yourself. We've got a slow boat and can do nothing about it."

That America's Cup match really isn't worth delving in to. To be beaten by the American defender *Courageous* 4-0 with a slow boat was just one of those things. I must say that loss didn't hurt anywhere near as much as the 1970 defeat, which was still weighing on my mind. At least I could walk away from the '74 match with my head held high. I just wished that I had been able to convince Sir Frank Packer and Alan Payne after the 1970 campaign to have another challenge with *Gretel II* in '74. My belief that such a campaign would have been worthwhile was based on the fact that *Intrepid* had been reconfigured almost to the shape it had been in 1967 and went within an ace of beating *Courageous* for the defence. At the back of the pack in the defender trials was the new Britton Chance designed *Mariner*, a very radical and very slow yacht. It had a big bustle under the water near the stern which, instead of tapering out to a beautiful fine edge, was cut off square like the end of a house brick. On seeing it for the first time the skipper, none other than Ted Turner, said to Britt Chance: "Britt, don't you realise that even a turd is pointed at both ends!" That statement was one of the more memorable moments in the 1974 America's Cup.

I guess our effort with *Southern Cross* was on a par with that of the *Mariner*. Both crews needed a sense of humour to survive the summer of slow boats. I realised how much we had in common with the *Mariner* team when, after the Cup match was completed, I saw a note pencilled onto the corner of one of Mariner's headsails. It read: "Never have so few done so much with so little for so long. But we have done so much with so little for so long we could do anything with nothing forever."

The memories of that frustrating campaign were well astern when a very formal letter, with sufficient decoration for me to realise it was from the Governor-General, arrived at home. I thought it was an invitation to a function, but it was far greater than that. It started something along the lines of: "The Queen has instructed me to write to you to advise you have been nominated to become an Officer of the Most Excellent Order of the British Empire . . . Should you wish to decline the Order please contact the Secretary of the Governor-General . . . "

I thought: "Thank you very much. I won't decline that."

Apart from telling Anne, I was sworn to secrecy. When the announcement did become official—Jim Hardy had received an OBE for "services to the community and sport"—it was the Queen's Birthday long weekend and I was racing a Soling at Royal Prince Alfred Yacht Club on Pittwater, north of Sydney. I copped a ribbing from everyone, one competitor even setting up a mock protest after the race and saying that the OBE stood for "owing beers everywhere".

The investiture was by the Governor of New South Wales, that wonderful man Sir Roden Cutler, at Government House. All Honours recipients were lined up and told how the presentation would proceed. Then we had to stand by and wait until a fellow read out a citation along the lines of "Hear ye, hear ye" and announced you for the award. On hearing my name I moved up to Sir Roden, who pinned the Most Excellent Order of the British Empire, a gold cross attached to a ribbon, on my lapel. It all meant that I was no longer Mister James Gilbert Hardy, but James Gilbert Hardy Esquire, OBE.

Formal functions like the investiture were particularly tough on Anne. She was just full of torment. It was now all too obvious she had a very serious problem with alcohol addiction. Treatment came the only way known then—through the local doctor. My hope was that she would gather the strength to beat it, just as people gave up cigarettes. Each time there was a function to attend I would have to give Anne plenty of warning and stress how important it was that we went together and that she was comfortable and in control.

Life at home was becoming somewhat of a nightmare as I struggled to cope with the situation. I transferred my cellar to the office and did everything possible to encourage her to have the strength to beat the problem. But still each night when I arrived home and put the key in the door I didn't know how I was going to be greeted. It was only a matter of time before it all proved too much for Anne and she collapsed through a combination of malnutrition and alcohol. December 1975 saw her enter hospital to receive special treatment for her condition. This was to be one of the most distressing and emotionally draining periods of my life. My love for Anne had been completely drained, but at the same time I had great compassion for her—a word she hated me using. My anguish was not made any easier by the emergence of another woman in my life. I met her while I was guest of honour at a trophy presentation in Melbourne and before I realised what was happening we were heading on a course towards deep emotional involvement. The comfort and pleasure we experienced together could well have been generated by our respective marital problems and an absence of love at home. Anne's confinement to hospital proved to be the first real breaking point in our marriage— for me there was more to life than what I was experiencing. After much critical analysis of myself and our marriage I decided it was time to leave Anne. I don't know why I had to tell her this while she was in hospital, but I did. It was just one of those impulses in life. Her response was to literally leave hospital immediately and head for home without completing her rehabilitation period. Anne's parents rushed to Sydney from Adelaide on a mission to salvage our marriage. They had a long chat with me and went out of their way to try to convince me that Anne deserved another try. The one consolation was that they were very supportive of me and understood the problems I had faced over the years. Next on the scene was my mother, who arrived in Sydney to reiterate a statement she had made many years earlier: "Jim, you've made your bed and now you must lie in it." She then reminded me of the wedding vows—for better for worse, for richer and poorer, in sickness and health. Next came an incredibly long letter from my sister Pam, who came down really heavily on me and my decision. Boy, I felt as though I had cracked the trifecta. It all sounded like the fall of the Roman Empire.

My decision was to give our marriage another try. I was to do everything within my powers to encourage Anne to work towards health and involve her in as many activities as possible. The one big ask on my part was for her to go on the water wagon. There were encouraging signs from Anne for a while, but sadly her will deserted her. One night, while her parents were there, she suffered a severe attack of delirium tremors—a most frightening experience for everyone concerned. Her convulsions were so strong we had to hold her down while I forced a small piece of timber between her teeth to stop her from biting off her tongue. The strength coming from this tiny person was beyond belief. After that experience I could believe the stories I had heard about mothers somehow gathering the strength to do incredible things when the lives of their children were at stake, like lifting a car off a baby trapped underneath.

Problems were also developing for me with Richard's situation at the Lorna Hodgkinson Sunshine Home, where he was a full-time border. His was a difficult case because he was more mentally alert than most of the other residents around him but far more physically handicapped. Helping him cope with this situation is something that has confronted me to this day. The one consolation for me has been that he is very proud of his father and lets everyone know it.

While all this upheaval was going on in my life the America's Cup, or more specifically, the thought of another challenge for it, acted as a pleasant diversion. With the memories of the 1974 campaign well behind me I was beginning to think the time might be right for me to mount my own challenge. There was one major hurdle in what might have appeared to some to be a flight of fancy—I didn't have the money. However, my America's Cup experience coupled with my knowledge of business led to me believing there was a course to the Cup. I met with Alan Payne and sailmaker Peter Cole over dinner one night at our Balgowlah Heights home and laid out my plans for a challenger which would be backed by the people as well as corporate Australia. It was agreed between the three of us to establish a syndicate along the lines of the community-supported *Intrepid* defence campaign of 1974.

We decided to test the water and see if the support was there. In November 1975 we announced to the world the formation of the Matilda Syndicate. The news of the campaign was well received— except by Alan Bond. He rang straight away to say he thought he at least deserved a telephone call from me to explain my plans. Maybe he was right, but at that stage Alan had given no indication he was anything like serious about going again in 1977. In a very short period we had promises of almost half of the budgeted $1.5 million, then we hit a brick wall. The turmoil associated with Gough Whitlam as our Prime Minister was creating concern in the business world and that wasn't helping us. But I continued going from Managing Director to Managing Director and Chairman to Chairman of some of Australia's biggest companies in search of the dollars. With Sir Frank Packer having died in 1974 I held the hope that his son Kerry might want to continue with what was a tradition in the Cup. My personal approach to him did not get very far. His response to my request was: "The answer is no. My father wasted a fortune on sailing."

The fate of the syndicate was sealed about six months after we started when one of our strongest hopes, the National Bank of Australia, said no. I had a meeting with the bank's Managing Director at their head office in Melbourne. What an eye opener that was. When it came time for tea while we discussed the project a tea man, not a tea lady, came in to serve us. He was wearing a crisp, white apron and carried on with all the formality you'd expect to see at Buckingham Palace. The MD listened to my story then said he was faced with a quandary—support the America's Cup or a home for children afflicted with cancer. You didn't have to be a Rhodes scholar to work out which way the bank would turn. From that point on it was all downhill for the syndicate and soon after it was curtains for the Matilda campaign. As it turned out Alan Bond did challenge for the America's Cup in 1977 and, not surprisingly, I didn't get the gong for the role of helmsman.

There were some wonderful times to be had in the 1970s with the Wine and Brandy Association which, while being the industry watchdog, managed to retain an element of fun and entertainment for members. I was fortunate enough to be Vice President and then President in the twilight years of the organisation—a very memorable period. The highlight of each year was the Christmas party we staged for the press at our headquarters at Sydney Showground. Over the years the party just got bigger and bigger and bigger until eventually we had to draw the line. In those days the Wine and Brandy Association's Christmas party was treated with similar reverence by the media to the party staged by the New South Wales oyster farmers.

For almost 100 years the association had very effectively managed and directed the industry in Australia. Our control of the industry and the retail price ensured producers made their profits and the consumers received value for money—and there was hardly a bad debt in the industry. But the wind of change was beginning to blow—the Trade Practices Act was out to end manufacturers' control of retail prices. I was very much against this move and I still am. The industry is faced with huge bad debts and the Trade Practices Act's theory that it was there to protect the little guy owning the corner shop so he could buy wine at a competitive price and retail it, just like anyone else, fell apart. He has been forced to buy from huge wholesalers. Today the industry is in the hands of a few big merchants who have mushroomed between the manufacturer and the retail buyer. These major wholesalers buy wine in such great quantities they are able to claim enormous discounts. They come along and say: "This is the price. Take it or leave it." Nowadays these middlemen really control our industry.

The emergence of the Trade Practices Act and a decision by the Whitlam Government to remove a clause from the Income Taxation Act took a heavy toll on the wine industry, particularly in the family-owned companies. With the clause in place we were able to mature wine. We were treated much the same as other primary producers in that when a lamb was born, or a calf, a farmer would put it in his books at a standard value on the basis that he was never sure if the lamb would live or die. When it came to selling that lamb the farmer made a profit—the difference between the standard price and the selling price—and he paid tax on that profit. Just as it was an incentive for farmers to let their animals grow, the original Act was an encouragement for wine producers to mature wines. When the government threw out that clause it meant we could not afford to cellar our wine for maturing, so younger and younger wines started appearing on the market. Today's wines are generally too young when they arrive on the shelf, and while they represent value for money the percentage return to the producer is frustratingly small. When we had the Wine and Brandy Association in place everyone was happy.

Because of these trends in wines I have established a few golden rules that I believe people should stick to so they can maximise their pleasure from the product. There was a very old rule that said you should drink white wine with white meat and red wine with red meat. For me that is a very basic guide in as much as I don't believe red wine and white fish go together. But conversely I prefer red wine with all poultry. My rule of thumb is that if the food is delicate the wine should be delicate and, alternatively, if the food is rich the wine should be rich. On the quality of wine, we originally had a rule of thumb at Hardy's that saw red wine two years in the wood then two years in the bottle. Now, because of pressures placed on the industry, reds generally spend two years in the wood then come straight off the bottling rack to the consumer. So the obvious suggestion is that if you cellar your reds for two years you will enjoy them to the fullest.

Enjoying wine and sailing—or more specifically life in general—to the fullest has always been my goal. When I look back on my sailing career today there are two notable failures which could get me into the record books. I have lost more America's Cup races than anyone else and have finished second in the Olympic selection trials more times than anyone else. The year 1976 was no different. I was the bridesmaid once again in the Olympic trials, this time finishing second to Dave Forbes in the Soling Class, steering Bob Terrett's boat *Terror*.

Dave won the gold medal in the Star Class in 1972. After he beat me in the 1976 trials he left me in no doubt he wasn't comfortable about going back to an Olympics having already won a gold. He came up to me at the end of the regatta and said he wished we had beaten him and won the right to be Australia's Olympic Soling representatives.

With another failed Olympic campaign behind me I decided it was time to move into larger yachts full time. I had always wanted to own my own ocean racer and the circumstances around me told me the time was right. I had a long, in-depth chat with my brother Tom about building my own yacht, suggesting to him I could sell some of my shares in the company to pay for it. I said that Anne's condition was also influencing my move, as history indicated it may be a never-ending problem. Tom took it all in, digested it and came back with a plan: "Why don't you sell your house to get the money, rent a place and keep your shares because they are appreciating in value."

It didn't take me long to realise it was a good idea, partly because our big, two storey home was now proving to be too much for Anne. She agreed to the plan so the house was sold and we moved into a pleasant waterfront apartment in the ocean-side suburb of Fairy Bower, near Manly.

The project to build my own offshore racer quickly gained momentum and really started to fall into place when I began sailing with that famous ocean racing yachtsman Syd Fischer aboard his yacht *Ragamuffin*. It became apparent that I could have a crack at the Australian Admiral's Cup team selection trials. Things took an even stronger turn for the better when Tom Philipson, a boyhood mate and crewman, told me there was an opportunity for financial support from a Gold Coast developer. The arrangement was for me to become the presenter for a development at Runaway Bay on the Gold Coast and in turn tie the yacht to the project by naming it *Runaway*. The deal was done and I began a wonderful episode in my life. Owning my own yacht and campaigning it was to be extremely exciting and satisfying, especially when we won the right to be a member of the three-yacht Australian team challenging for the Admiral's Cup in 1977.

How can someone with so many sea miles respond to the "do you ever get sea sick" question that so often arises: "Jim Hardy has never been seasick, but he has been sick at sea, occasionally."

One memorable encounter with mal de mer came in the 1976 Hobart race while *Runaway* was being built. I did the race on *Ragamuffin* and it was a rough one with big, rolling seas, which had developed in the southern ocean, coming at us as we sailed across Bass Strait. No one on board was eating much but that evening a desire for food resulted in me deciding to eat a hard-boiled egg. I was sitting up on the side of the yacht with the rest of the crew, being lashed by spray as the yacht speared its bow into the oncoming waves.

"I think we'll be seeing that again," Syd Fischer said.

Sure enough, I joined a chorus of sea sick crew members a few hours later. Syd reckons he saw the egg returned to the world shell and all.

That race was also memorable for an incident that came when we were hammered on our side by a southerly squall as we rounded Tasman Island at midnight. *Ragamuffin* was lying on her side, shuddering and shaking and with the sails flogging. The panic call from the deck was: "Reef, reef, reef," meaning reduce sail right now, or sooner. Crewman John Munson was asleep below deck, as was I. It was his job to operate the winch used for raising and lowering the mainsail, which was attached to the mast below deck. He must have been half asleep when he leapt out of his bunk and headed for the winch while the yacht continued to lie with the mast almost parallel to the water. "Munno", forever eager to please and quick to respond, reacted to the call for reefing action with the question: "Which way? Up or down?"

I began campaigning *Runaway* as soon as she was launched in January 1977. The first big challenge was to raise the funds to get the yachts and crews to the Admiral's Cup at Cowes, in England. Things weren't looking good until the Royal Australian Navy came to our rescue by offering free transport aboard the aircraft carrier HMAS *Melbourne*. The loading of *Runaway* provided an enormous bonus for my sponsor from the Runaway Bay development. The cradle carrying the yacht collapsed as it was being lifted and the picture that resulted from the drama made the front page of the *Australian* newspaper. Neil McCowan, from Runaway Bay, was on the phone as soon as he saw it, telling me I was the Public Relations champion of Australia. One picture had returned him most of his investment in our campaign.

Before leaving for the Admiral's Cup there was great news for our family. Mum was awarded the OBE for her services to the wine industry. Someone who remains anonymous and other supporters in the wine industry nominated her for the award, which she accepted with great pride and dignity.

Mum had the option of being invested by either the Governor of South Australia or the Queen at Buckingham Palace. It wasn't hard to guess which she would choose: "The letter has come from the Queen, the Queen I will see."

The investiture was to happen during the time we were in England for the Admiral's Cup. Mum was allowed two guests, so she took my sister Pam and me along to the Palace. What an experience. The first impact was the Household Cavalry Guards standing on the steps inside Buckingham Palace wearing gleaming brass helmets. You had to really stare at the guys before deciding if they were alive or just statues. There was absolutely no movement from them, but for the very occasional flicker from their eyes. Mum's biggest concern on the day was that she may fall over as she took the regulation three steps back from the Queen before making a curtsy.

"I might fall head over turkey," were her words.

Well, falling over was the least of Mum's problems—she was only interested, as you would expect, in having a chat with the Queen.

"Mother's speaking to the Queen too long compared with everybody else," my very concerned sister said.

"Good luck to her," was my only comment.

It turned out the Queen and Mother had quite a chat about Australia and the wine industry.

It seemed this period of my life was becoming one of emotional highs and lows. Yet another blow came when I attended a board meeting in Adelaide soon after my return from England. I was staying with my brother Tom and his family in our old family home in Seacliff. At the end of the visit Tom, as he did more often than not, drove me to the airport. This particular night was one I would love to be able to forget.

"Jim, there's something I must tell you but I don't want you to tell anyone else. I've got cancer."

I didn't know what to say and the response I eventually uttered was as embarrassing as it was ridiculous.

"Geez, that's crook."

To me it was the same as hearing that my brother had received a death sentence. His request that I told no one was to be a real test of my Freemasonry. He told me the only other two people who knew were his wife, Barbara, and a sailing mate. He didn't want Mother or anyone else in the family to know. It was tough on me but I stood by his wishes. He wanted it kept a secret because he didn't want anyone to feel sorry for him, and he certainly didn't want it to have any affect on the business.

Thoughts on my life with Tom came flooding to me over the ensuing months. When I was young the eight year age difference between us had created a real barrier. I was then much closer to David. He was my mate while big brother Tom was the guy who whacked us. In my mid-teens I decided Tom wasn't so bad after all because he would let me share wine with him over dinner on the nights Mum was out. Mum would leave us a curry to heat up for dinner and Tom believed the best way to cool the heat was to crack a bottle of our Cabinet Claret. Later in life I was closer to him than David, mainly because of the circumstances where I was working alongside Tom in the Hardy's office while David was in the country running our vineyards.

Not surprisingly I began thinking about what I could do for Tom. I think the best thing I did was have him sail *Runaway* across to Hawaii for me so we could compete in the first Clipper Cup series in 1978. In fact it was not *Runaway* he sailed, but *Nyamba*—the same yacht with a different name. While I was in England at the Admiral's Cup there had been some mutterings about the yacht's name and its association with corporate sponsorship, very much a no-no in those days. The rumblings filtered all the way back to Australia until finally Cruising Yacht Club of Australia officials advised me they would protest the name. My protests about their protest fell on deaf ears and the result was that *Runaway* was renamed *Nyamba*. Most people assumed *Nyamba* was Aboriginal for go jump in the lake but in fact it was the Aboriginal name for the area that is now Runaway Bay, Queensland.

Tom's major concern about the cruise to Hawaii was that his cancer may flare up to a degree where he would be useless on the yacht. As it turned out his cancer provided little or no trouble but his crew did. One of them, a Swiss guy, went troppo in the heat while they were sailing through the mid Pacific. Tom finished up having to put him, and another crew member who was a friend, off the yacht at Christmas Island.

Tom's other big problem on the trip was of the four legged variety. *Nyamba* was moored alongside a dock on the western Samoan island of Apia and Tom was having a snooze while the rest of the guys went up town for a drink. Suddenly he was wakened by a strange sensation on his arm. He opened his eyes and was confronted by a large rat moving up his arm and staring him straight in the eye. The rat got as big a shock as Tom did and bolted into the bilge. The solution was to go up town and buy a rat trap. The only style available was a German one, supposedly the Rolls Royce variety. But the rat was too clever for the trap so after days of trying to catch it they had to set sail for Hawaii, rat and all. The destruction the rat was causing on board the yacht was amazing. As well as eating every bit of food it could find it was ripping open cartons of long life milk, which then drained into the bilge. The smell was awful. Every few hours the rat trap would go off with a bang and the crew would rush below to see what they'd caught. For the first two days it turned out to be a false alarm. Then on the third night at sea, while Tom was lying in his bunk, the trap went off once more. The noise was distinctly different and Tom knew he had something. He grabbed his torch, went to the trap and sure enough there was the monster rat—caught by nothing more than its bottom lip. The rat went swimming in the Pacific.

I flew to Honolulu for the regatta. It was wonderful sailing on the beautiful blue waters of Hawaii, where the trade winds never stop blowing. The warmth of the spray on your body was just fantastic.

Nyamba continued to provide the excitement, relaxation and mental stimulus that I felt my life had been lacking for a lot of years. Some people might have called it a second childhood. If that's what it was then all I can say is that it was wonderful and I do not regret one part of it.

Our Sydney to Mooloolaba race on the yacht is one I won't

forget. We were charging north before a howling southerly buster with just a mainsail and poled-out headsail set. It was blowing too hard for us to set a spinnaker. I was off watch about midnight and below deck asleep as we approached Byron Bay on the New South Wales–Queensland border. The boys called me up on deck rather urgently because they couldn't work out what was happening with a very large cargo ship that was approaching us from the north. The ship was literally bearing down on us and every time we changed course to try to avoid it, it also changed course and aimed at us. We started to shine torches on the mainsail to illuminate it so the ship's crew could see us. At one stage it stopped so we tried to get away from it, but it started up again, changed course and aimed straight at us. It was chasing us. We headed inshore and it headed inshore. We headed offshore and it headed offshore, all the time aiming at us and closing on us. Tom Philipson started getting the life jackets ready. Clem Masters, who was navigating, called up the radio relay vessel which was shadowing the race fleet to tell them of our problem. He also tried to call the ship to tell them to stop harassing us. I took over the helm and still we continued on a collision course. To miss the ship at the very last moment we had to suddenly change course and do a complete circle in the southerly gale in the middle of the night. It was really scary stuff because the ship then did a 360 degree turn and came back at us again. We were so close we could have hit it with a rock. In the end we became so concerned Clem prepared to send out a distress call. Suddenly the ship changed course and headed south. We could only resume our course towards Mooloolaba very shaken and completely mystified by the sequence of events.

When we finished in Mooloolaba I told some of the guys from other yachts what had happened. A medico who was among them had sailed up and down the coast for some time. "Oh, that would be drugs," he said.

"What do you mean, drugs?"

"They would have been thinking you were the pick-up boat for a drug drop. They were trying to rendezvous with you."

Tom Philipson chimed in: "Hell, we should have taken the package. We would have been on easy street for the rest of our lives."

Unfortunately I couldn't see the funny side. I immediately became very concerned about what we had seen and decided I didn't want to tell anyone else about it. It wasn't until some time later, when I was at a Wine and Food Association function at Parliament House in Canberra, that I broached the subject with Don Chipp, who was then heavily into the Australian Democrat Party. I told him about our experience and soon after he checked it out. It turned out that our incident coincided with a big surveillance job on the New South Wales north coast which was anticipating a large drug drop from a ship.

After the Sydney–Mooloolaba race we sailed in the Brisbane to Gladstone, Queensland's offshore classic. Clem Masters was our navigator once again and his vast experience in this race contributed to us winning on handicap. The celebration in Gladstone had to be seen to be believed. *Nyamba* became a 42 foot long ashtray—the focal point for a huge party. John Sattler, the famous footballer from South Sydney, and his wife were managing a hotel in Gladstone. I can still see him walking down the dock with a five gallon keg of beer under each arm. He stepped aboard with the kegs and the party started. We plugged up the drains in the cockpit and filled it full of ice to create one of the world's biggest ice buckets.

CHAPTER NINE

Arise Sir James

I FELL IN love in 1979—with a yacht. Its name was *Police Car*, a member of the Australian Admiral's Cup team that year which was owned by West Australian Peter Cantwell. It was a beautiful blue racing boat that had an impact on me something akin to seeing a beautiful woman.

In early 1980 we were sailing *Nyamba* back to Sydney after competing in the Hobart race. When we sailed into Eden we saw *Police Car* anchored in the bay, so we rafted up alongside. I knew she was for sale and after looking over her once more and realising I was the victim of something more than mere infatuation I casually asked the crew how I could get in touch with Peter Cantwell, who was in Singapore at the time. I got his telephone number, went ashore and walked up the hill to the Eden Post Office. I fired my money into the telephone and called the number in Singapore.

"Hi Peter. Jim Hardy here."

"Hi Jim."

"Peter, I would like to buy your yacht."

The negotiations started and before long we agreed on a price. I bought *Police Car*, there and then, over the telephone.

I walked back to the waterfront in a daze—realising the major consequence of my spontaneous urge: "How the hell am I going to pay for this?"

As I climbed back aboard *Nyamba* I decided not to tell anyone about my latest acquisition. But as soon as I was back on the boat

211

when my mate Tom Philipson challenged me.

"Where have you been?"

"Oh, I just went for a walk up town."

"Did you buy *Police Car*?"

I just about choked on my coffee. He had picked it in one. He'd read me like a book.

When we got back to Sydney I put *Nyamba* on the market then made the foolish mistake so many yacht owners make and didn't take the first offer for her, which was something like $75,000. I thought she was worth at least double that because she had cost me over $200,000—the classic example of over capitalisation. I finished up selling *Nyamba* for $35,000 in America three years later. The lesson was there once more for all to see—whatever you are selling is only worth what the market will pay for it, not what you think it is worth. Your first offer is usually your best. Regardless of this, I remained the proud owner of *Police Car* and was destined to enjoy some wonderful racing experiences.

Life at this time seemed to revolve around the theme: Perfect one week, dismal the next. Sadly, my dear mother died in April 1980 aged 87 as a result of bowel cancer, which she contracted about a year earlier. Eileen was 87 years old, or more appropriately, 87 years young. She was an amazing human being who was full of inspiration. So many wonderful memories rush to me when I think back over her incredible life. There were her words, which really mattered—words that came from a caring and loving mother when I was very young, like if I capsized while sailing a Cadet dinghy I was to never leave the boat and try to swim to shore. She absolutely drilled that into me—boats float even when capsized. She told me to always hang on to the boat because people could find a boat but they can rarely find one little head bobbing around in the ocean.

Mum never pushed me in any way, shape or form and always encouraged me. She was a genuine woman with a generous nature. She treated people as she would like them to treat her. Mum also had high values in life and did all she could to impress them upon me. I remember one night Anne, Mum and I had been to a function in Mum's old Daimler. We arrived back at Seacliff and after a while, in fact about twenty minutes later, Anne and I were in the kitchen.

"Where's Mum?"

"I don't know, Jim. I haven't seen her."

I thought: "I bet she is still out in the car."

I went outside to the car and sure enough there was Mum still sitting in the back seat waiting for me to open the car door. She would have sat there all night if she had to.

That was the sort of lesson she taught all of us, a lesson in manners. She never once raised her voice. She just led by example.

Mum always believed that wine was an elixir of life. She often said that if wine had been discovered today it would be considered the greatest drug of all time. She even had us gargle with port wine every time we had a sore throat. Funnily enough I thought every kid gargled with port wine. I don't know if it worked but it certainly made you feel good at school. I remember one morning when I was 12 or 13 and Tom was heading off to university. I was gargling away over the back sink in the house—gargle, gargle, gargle—then spitting it out. It was only Hardy's best, our Gold Label port.

"What are you spitting it out for, Jim?"

"Germs, Tom, germs. I've got a cold."

"Germs. There's enough alcohol in that to kill any germs. Swallow it."

After that I always gargled and swallowed—and always felt much better when I reached school.

Mum also used brandy spirit on any cuts we had. I think it burned the living daylights out of any germs that might have been in the cuts.

Eileen's generosity and feeling towards others resulted in her baking Christmas cakes for all of our branch offices every year. They were huge fruit cakes that had more fruit in them than cake mix. Somehow, no matter what the circumstances, she would overcome hell and high water to get them to the interstate offices in time for their Christmas celebrations.

One night, when I was a teenager, I came home around midnight to find Mum standing in the kitchen looking up at the clock, half mesmerised, with a big Christmas cake in front of her.

"What's the story, Mum?"

"Jim, I am trying to work out what time to put this cake in the oven so that it will be ready at the right time for me to get up and share it and a Christmas drink with the milkman."

A few months later I saw the milkman when he came around to home to collect his money and he told me what happened.

"Did we ever have a Christmas drink! I arrived with the billycan full of milk and your mother was waiting for me. She invited me in and said she'd like to have a Christmas drink with me."

This is apparently how the conversation went:

"But it's four in the morning, Mrs Hardy."

"Yes Mr Crocker, and there's only one thing to drink at this time of day."

"What's that, Mrs Hardy?"

"Brandy and milk! You've got the milk and I've got the brandy."

Mr Crocker said he finished up half full of syrup. The pair of them had enough brandy and milk to empty the billycan.

Mum really enjoyed a drink—but not water. Once I commented that I had never seen her drink a glass of water: "You are right Jim. Water is for radiators." Sometimes she actually drank hot water in the morning before the cup of tea I often made for her. But I really did not ever see her drink a glass of cold water. She would occasionaly drink water with some fresh lemon juice squeezed into it, but never straight water.

It wasn't until her 80th birthday in 1973 that she finally admitted to her age. I had a pretty good idea but it was eventually my birth certificate that gave me the answer. She decided to have an open house for the big day—she even put an advertisement in the local paper inviting everyone in the district. People came from everywhere and one, old Aubrey Brocksopp, the local fisherman, arrived at 11 o'clock in the morning and was still there at midnight. It was at this party we introduced the Eileeen Hardy Bin 80 Claret, a beautiful 1970 McLaren Vale Shiraz. The Eileen Hardy Shiraz and now Chardonnay wines are the top shelf products in our range.

Being 80 presented no barrier to Eileen. She did things how and when she wanted, such as driving up to Sydney by herself in her little Volkswagen to visit Anne and me. She was most indignant when she had to leave Sydney before she really wanted and drive the 1700 kilometres back to Adelaide, just to do a driving test to prove she was OK to be on the road.

The great thing about Mum was that she was a fighter, a survivor. The probate on Dad's estate after he died crucified the family financially, but Mum never gave up. She did everything within her power to give her children the best life humanly possible. At one stage, when things were really grim, she considered selling our home and moving all five of us on board the yacht *Nerida*—which she did not want to sell—and make it the family home.

She retained her fighting spirit and her sense of humour right to the end. While she was in hospital—she was an Anglican in a Catholic hospital—the Sisters asked her when she was last in hospital:

"Oh, I've never been in hospital. My children were born at home. In fact this is the first time I've ever been ill when my mother hasn't been here to look after me!"

The doctors and nurses loved Mum so much she was made an honorary Nun in the Calvary Hospital in Adelaide.

Not long before Mum died I met with Warren Jones, who was a director of Bond Corporation, in Adelaide. He explained that Ben Lexcen had redesigned a part of the underbody of the yacht *Australia* since the 1977 America's Cup challenge and all the signs were that it was a much improved yacht. He asked if I would be interested in steering the boat in the 1980 challenge. Not surprisingly I said it sounded like a good idea.

Their plan was to base the yacht in Sydney after she was rebuilt so we could tune her and train before she was shipped to Newport. We had an extensive series of trials against Gordon Ingate aboard *Gretel II*, which he then owned. That was when I had my first real introduction to young Iain Murray, the hero of eighteen foot skiff sailing and a rising star on the Australian sailing scene. He was invited to steer *Gretel II*.

Our win over him on the day with *Australia* was helped in no small way by a mop handle. Before the race Gordon Ingate had unwittingly left a mop handle below the aft deck and it had jammed in the steering mechanism. It turned out that the yacht steered just fine on one tack, but on the other the mop handle was literally like a spanner in the works and Iain could hardly turn the wheel. Being new to twelve metres' he just thought the steering was extremely stiff.

Australia was shipped to Newport, Rhode Island where we teamed up with the English and began training against their yacht *Lionheart*. Unbeknown to us the English were preparing a secret weapon, a mast with a very flexible top which would give them a ten per cent increase in sail area in their mainsail. In a class like the twelve metre that's a huge increase in sail plan—generating a lot more horsepower. We had beaten *Lionheart* quite comfortably with *Australia* until they

215

produced the bendy mast, then we started struggling, particularly in light airs. Ben Lexcen had seen enough: "We had better copy that, Jim."

"How do we do that?"

"I've got a bloke in Sydney who makes bendy masts for a yacht I've designed. I'll bring him over and we'll build the thing here."

Ben just lived on challenges like that. Next thing he was flat out at the drawing board and at the same time organising for his mast building mate to come to Newport. This was to be his "Top Secret" project for the summer.

About that time John Bertrand arrived on the scene to sail with us because the yachting team had answered Prime Minister Malcolm Fraser's request that Australian Olympians boycott the 1980 Games in Moscow because Russia had invaded Afghanistan. Looking back on it I think it was good all athletes didn't boycott those Games because Australia now remains one of only three countries that has been to every Olympics in the modern era.

One day Ben came to me absolutely furious. He had a newspaper cutting from Australia which said that John Bertrand was flying to Newport to become tactician on *Australia*. I thought Ben was going to explode—he was the tactician and no one had told him he had been sacked. He stormed off in a rage.

The next time I saw Ben he had broken his wrist. "What the hell happened there?" I asked.

"Well, after I read the newspaper article I went back into the office and saw Bertrand's face on the wall so I thumped it as hard as I could. I'd seen blokes do that in the movies so I thought I'd try it myself. I guess I'm no movie star. They never broke their wrist."

John Bertrand really frustrated Ben: "Jim, every time I am with John Bertrand he makes me feel as though I am in an examination. He doesn't seem to realise that I have had only two years at school." Ben, genius that he was, had spent only two years in primary school for his education. John Bertrand came from the other side of the street with degrees from Melbourne's Monash University and MIT in Boston. John was always very factual whereas Benny was very abstract. There was definite friction between them that summer.

WARREN JONES: "It was Alan who was behind the move to replace Ben with John. I had a serious confrontation with Alan

*as Jim and I did not want to disrupt the crew at that late stage.
During this period Jim was the oil on the water. It was only then
that I learnt the saying: 'He who pays the piper calls the tune'.
When I got upset with Alan Jim quoted this to me and said between
us we would convince Alan he was wrong. Thank goodness for
Jim as the matter was resolved and I did not have to carry out
my threat to quit."*

Our first series in the challenger eliminations was against the
Swedes. They looked like they would be easy pickings when we led
2-0 in the best-of-seven series. It all changed in the third race, soon
after we rounded the last mark holding a three minute lead. The
breeze had kicked to around 25 knots so it was quite a fresh beat
to the finish. Ben Lexcen turned to me and said: "Jim, we should
ease up a bit so we don't overload the rig for no reason." He had
no sooner uttered the words when I heard a "click" above my head.
I looked up to see the top part of the mast crumpling and disappearing
over the side of the yacht. I thought: "This is going to be a very
hard race to win." Fortunately, we had a protest to press against
the Swedes, a cut-and-dried port and starboard incident on the starting
line where we held right of way. That night in the protest room
I really fought hard, remembering all the time what had happened
to us after race two of the 1970 America's Cup. We won that protest
and erased the win for the Swedes. But they won the next two races
while we struggled to tune our spare mast. Finally we found form
in the do-or-die fifth race and eliminated them. We were so far ahead
coming up the last beat to the finish in that final race Ben Lexcen
said: "Jim, you can look behind now to see how well we are going."
That was a rare honour for a skipper, being allowed to look behind.

While this series was taking place the bendy mast was being
built in secret, right under American noses in Newport. The final
decision as to whether or not to build it had rested with Alan Bond.
I am pleased to say Alan is a gambler—he was prepared to back
Ben and go for it. We used an old mast from the 1977 campaign
as the bottom section for the new bendy rig, cutting it off where
the forestay was anchored and discarding the top section. The guy
we flew in from Australia fabricated a bendy, fibreglass top which
would be attached to the old aluminium section. The work was done
in an old fisherman's shed on the waterfront. We had to do it all

very secretly because we didn't want to give anything away to the Americans. While our guys worked on the mast, fishermen were coming in to dry their nets. Amazingly, the second day that work was underway one of the fishermen came to me and said: "What you Aussies need to do is make a mast like that English boat has."

"Yeah, that's not a bad idea," I said, leaning on what was the start of the new rig. "Pity we haven't got time to do it."

Breaking the mast while racing the Swedes was an enormous setback for our campaign. Our original plan was to use the new bendy mast in the final challenger elimination series so we could have it fully tuned for the actual Cup match against the Americans. But it wasn't quite ready in time and we weren't prepared to risk it. There had been great debate, in fact an argument, involving John Bertrand and the rest of us, because he didn't want to go for the new mast at all. He thought it was too radical and too much of a risk. Being an old conjurer I supported Ben. If you could pull a rabbit out of a hat then you had to go for it. I think John Bertrand's attitude had been influenced by the fact that he didn't have the benefit of being in Newport to see what a difference the bendy mast made to the performance of the English yacht. When *Australia* and *Lionheart* raced using similar rigs the margin of superiority on our part was quite large. But once they put up the bendy mast on *Lionheart* that yacht suddenly became very competitive. Ben and I were convinced a bendy rig on *Australia* would lift our performance to the same degree as the rig did for *Lionheart*.

The challenger finals were between Australia and the French yacht *France*, skippered by Bruno Trouble, which had beaten the British. We weren't overly concerned about not using the new rig against them because we believed *Australia* was superior even with the conventional rig. But it would have been nice just to have the bendy mast aboard *Australia* so it could be tuned. Fortunately our theories on *Australia* being faster than *France* were correct. We went out and beat them and won the right to challenge America for the America's Cup.

The Sunday following our victory over the French I decided it was appropriate to thank the Almighty (and in doing so hope that he might consider extending my run of good fortune into the America's Cup match) so took myself off to the Episcopalian church in Newport to take communion. At the appropriate time I went forward and took my place, the Vicar then coming along and first giving me the bread. He then went away and came back with the wine. When it came to be my turn to take the wine he offered it to me, then before moving on to the next person, leant forward and whispered into my ear: "Good on you for beating the French." I just about dropped the chalice.

With the French disposed of and the new mast complete the rush was on to get it stepped on *Australia*. But first we had to have it measured by the New York Yacht Club's official measurer to make sure it was legal. We were determined to do everything possible not to let the measurer realise it was a bendy mast, so we painted the top section silver to match the rest of the aluminium and made sure it was lying dead straight in its cradles. He ran the tape measure over the mast and even lifted it to check the weight. He looked along it to satisfy himself that it had no permanent bend in it—which was not allowed under the rules—then checked the centre of gravity. All the time we were holding our breaths, hoping he wouldn't wake up to what we had in store for their Cup defender, Dennis Conner. When the measurements were completed he stamped the mast and announced it was legal. We all looked at each other and gave a sigh of relief.

Soon after sunrise the next morning the entire team assembled at the fisherman's shed, lifted the mast shoulder high and marched it through the streets of Newport to *Australia*'s dock. It looked like the world's biggest human centipede making its way through the town. We spent the entire day rigging the mast then just before sunset put it in place on the yacht. It was then time to let our dockside neighbour Dennis Conner, and the New York Yacht Club, see what we had built in their own backyard. The backstay was hauled on to bend the top of the mast so it arched like a giant fishing rod then a spotlight was aimed at it so it was illuminated for all to see throughout the night.

I couldn't wait to get my hands on the helm the next day and steer the yacht with all that additional horsepower. What an experience it turned out to be. It was as though *Australia* had been fitted with a turbo charger. It made a phenomenal difference to our light wind speed, but we were overpowered when the wind came in. In hindsight it would have been wonderful to have had Ben's upside down wing keel three years earlier. If we had had that keel, with its massive stability factor, on *Australia* in 1980 I don't think the Americans would have seen which way we went.

One thing I didn't like about our yacht was its steering wheels. They were aluminium and bloody cold to hang on to all day long. After much searching I eventually found an old codger in Newport who could sew leather around the entire rim of the wheels—much better for grip and certainly a lot warmer. I took one wheel to him one day and the other wheel the next. The day I walked out of our compound with the second wheel an American heavy from the New York Yacht Club walked up to one of our crew, John "Steamer" Stanley, and made inquiries: "What's the story with Jim Hardy? I noticed yesterday he headed off with the steering wheel in his hand, and he did the same thing again today."

"Jim takes the wheel home each night as a bit of insurance. He's never quite sure who Bondy will have steer the boat the next day, was Steamer's reply."

"Is that right?"

We were to receive a very special guest at our base in Newport before the Cup match—the Prime Minister, Malcolm Fraser. His office had contacted Bondy and said he was keen to sail on the yacht. It was to be a great fillip for the crew. Many people, including me, look back on Malcolm Fraser as the last of the men who wore the office of Prime Minister like a crown. Bob Hawke was the "G'day mate" Prime Minister and the prestige associated with the office seemed to disappear. But when Malcolm Fraser entered a room people would stand up and respect his presence.

For us Malcolm Fraser's presence in Newport presented an unusual problem. He wore size thirteen shoes and no new deck shoes that large could be found. Then someone looked at my feet. Gilbert— my middle name was my nickname—was to be the source for the Prime Minister's shoes.

"Lend us your shoes," was the request from Bondy.

"Who for? What for?"

"The Prime Minister. He's going out on the yacht with you today."

I took them off and started writing my name inside them. I completed "J. Hardy" in one and was writing "J . . ." in the other when Bondy grabbed them: "Give me those shoes. I'll get you some more."

Off went my shoes and they fitted Malcolm like a glove. I was not to see them again. A year later I saw Malcolm's wife, Tammy, at a social function. She remembered the shoes: "Oh Jim, they are the best shoes Malcolm has ever had. He goes trout fishing in them all the time and wears them around the property."

I guess it's not often you get the Prime Minister standing in your shoes.

Another visitor we had in Newport, on my instigation, was the famous Victorian Australian Rules football coach Ron Barassi. I was always a great admirer of his ability to inspire people. Before he arrived I gave each member of the Australia crew a copy of a very stimulating book titled, *The Coach*, which was about him and his efforts. His presence was just fantastic. It gave the crew a real buzz. I will always remember it for one thought he left with me: "The world is really only made up of three classes of people—the people who make things happen, the people who watch things happen, and the people who ask 'what happened?'"

Out on the water we were paying a big price for breaking our mast while racing the Swedes then not having the time to prepare the new rig for racing the French. We were having plenty of teething problems, especially with the track holding the mainsail to the mast pulling off. Had we been able to use this rig against the French we would have eliminated all the bugs and been a far better yacht against America's *Freedom*.

The history of the America's Cup shows we lost the 1980 match 4-1, however in some ways it was closer than the numbers reveal. While I'm not making excuses I can say I believe we performed very well, and given more time with the bendy rig we would have given the Americans a real fright.

There were many memorable moments on the race course. For one race we had a weather forecast for winds of 30 knots so decided discretion was the better part of valour. The bendy rig would be too powerful in those winds so we decided to abandon it for the day and go with the mast in the straight mode. Wouldn't you know it, the 30 knot breeze blew in the harbour in Newport but didn't get to the race course offshore. We led once or twice in that race but didn't win. Had we used the bendy rig we probably would have won. For the next race we went back to the bendy mast for the horsepower we needed and won.

We caught *Freedom* on the last beat to the finish. Dennis Conner was trying to force us out to the right-hand side of the course but we managed to escape his cover and head back towards the centre. Conner stayed on the right-hand side, where he believed the most favourable winds were to be found, but it was getting later and later in the day and, as often happens late in the day in Newport, the breeze moved back towards the left-hand side of the course. Nobody knows to this day what was going on in my mind on that beat to the finish. It all went back to a comment my mother made to our Managing Director, Wayne Jackson, when she was dying in hospital.

"Aunty Eileen, you better get yourself on deck and come over to watch Jim sail in the America's Cup."

"Wayne, I just hope I am up there blowing in the right direction."

So in this particular race I kept saying to myself: "Just head us a bit more, give us a bit more angle in the breeze from the left, Mum." Sure enough the wind started to head us by swinging towards the left. Ben started getting quite excited because Jack Baxter, our navigator, was taking some bearings and we were gaining on *Freedom*.

"If we tack now we would be on a collision course," was Jack's next comment.

I kept saying: "Come on, Mum, head us a bit more. Give us some more breeze from the left."

The wind kept going in our favour so we decided to tack and sail back at *Freedom*. A little more pressure came from the left. What a beauty. We were on port tack and didn't have right of way on what was a collision course.

"We might cross him," Jack Baxter said.

"Come on, Mum. A little more breeze please."

"We're going to cross him."

"Keep it up, Mum. You're doing us proud. Come on, come on, Mum, a bit more pressure."

"We are going to cross him. We are going to cross him."

We were ahead but we were to realise the race was far from over. It was getting towards dark and the next thing I saw was Dennis Conner's crew attaching their navigation lights and turning them on. "Sunset" I thought. "It is time for navigation lights. We must put ours on." Jack Baxter got our port and starboard lights from below and had Scotty McAllister run to the bow and attach them.

Scotty switched them on but they didn't work. He gave them two hard thumps and they still didn't work. Then we couldn't find our stern light and I knew straight away Conner would protest the fact that we did not have our lights set. The thought of that protest was too much for Ben and he lost the plot. He couldn't sit still. He was pacing around the cockpit muttering to himself and putting us all off our game. Scotty went to the bow one more time just before we crossed the finishing line, gave the lights an almighty thump and they came on. He looked down and saw green on the left and red on the right. "I don't think that's quite right," he thought to himself. There was no time to fix it so we crossed the finishing line with our navigation lights back to front. There's a painting in existence today of that finish showing *Australia* with the green light on the port side and no stern light. Conner protested us for not having a stern light but it was thrown out by the New York Yacht Club because they didn't think it was a fair protest.

It blew hard for the next race and we had too much pressure in our rig. Dennis Conner ground over the top of us and sailed away with the America's Cup.

While I was disappointed about losing I was more than pleased to realise I was able to cope and walk away from the match knowing we had given it our best shot. My life had really benefited from that traumatic experience of the 1979 Fastnet race.

WARREN JONES: "We should have won the America's Cup in 1980. In fact we had the tool but not the experience and the know-how to finish the Americans off. We made mistakes which let the Americans off the hook. For example, if we had been better equipped from a resource situation we would never have straightened the mast on the day of the fourth race when the breeze never went above 12 knots. I am confident we would have secured a victory on that day and Jim Hardy would have then gone on and taken the America's Cup before we subsequently did in 1983."

When we finished that final Cup race in 1980 I walked down the deck of Australia and said to John Bertrand: "John, I've had three goes at the America's Cup and haven't been successful. I hope Bondy goes again and gives you a go at the helm because I am out. If he does go again and you get to steer the yacht and there's any way I can help you at all, please yell out."

The next thing a jubilant Alan Bond came aboard *Australia*. He was absolutely ecstatic about what we had achieved. He was incredibly jovial and thrilled by the fact that we had been so competitive. He announced to all on board he would challenge again and invite John Bertrand to be his skipper. It was music to my ears. It was now time for me to watch the America's Cup from the sidelines, and hopefully become a coach.

Not long after I returned from the America's Cup there was another distressing blow for the family when brother Tom died aged 56. The cancer finally caught up with him. He passed away in the same room at our family home in Seacliff where he was born.

Tom had become such a close friend to me. He was the Chairman of the company and had fought hard to keep the family in the business. At times though I think he may have fought too hard to keep the family interest, at the same time trying to ensure that the best people filled positions that became available. He introduced, on his own accord, an employment committee, which we jokingly called the "Nepotism Committee". It was to see that there was no undue preference to relatives. Tom said that if any relative of any employee wanted to work for the company that person had to go through the employment committee. The committee consisted of Tom, our Managing Director Wayne Jackson, and the director responsible for the particular discipline of the company where the vacancy existed. The scheme was really aimed at not having Hardys work for the company unless they were the best qualified for the job. Quite a few Hardys didn't pass the test. My subjective view was that Tom's plan was a very fine, upstanding thing, but from where I stood it had two sides to it. To me, a family member probably has more built-in loyalty and devotion than other people and conversely other people are happier when there's not a family member breathing down their neck. Morally it was a great idea, but I think in a few instances it was used to advantage by the non-family people in the company.

With Tom's passing it was my great honour to take over as Chairman of the company, the sixth in the long history of Thomas Hardy and Sons. I had accepted the helm at a time when it was going from strength to strength.

Among my many first-up tasks in the new role was having to

cope with a very embarrassing situation for our company. The actual start of the problem came before I travelled to Newport, when I launched a book for Australia's first America's Cup challenge skipper, Jock Sturrock, titled *Classic Yachts in Australian Waters*. I was unaware that there was a link between this publication and the subject of a statement Alan Bond made to me while in Newport: "Those boxes of America's Cup port you have brought out in Australia are a howling success." Oddly enough, I didn't know about any America's Cup port we had put on the market. My inquiries back to the office told me that the company had begun distribution of an America's Cup port series that comprised six bottles of our vintage port, each with a different Australian twelve metre on its label. That was fine until immediately after I got home when brother Tom announced: "Jim, we're being sued for one million dollars." It turned out one of our senior staff in Perth had organised for the paintings in Jock Sturrock's book to be copied for the port labels. Then he lifted the associated words for each picture verbatim and used them for the appropriate captions—all without the publisher's permission. As a consequence the publishers were suing Thomas Hardy & Sons for a million. They had us on toast. The books were a limited edition priced at $250 each and there were still 300 unsold. We settled with them on the steps of the court, paying the publishers and Jock what was a considerable amount of money and buying all remaining books. We were taken to the cleaners. I guess we made a slow seller a best seller.

My next big sailing experience was to be at the Congressional Cup in Long Beach, California, one of the world's most prestigious match racing events where racing is one on one. The regatta was not memorable for our results—we finished mid field—but for the fact that Bill Ficker, who was the helmsman of *Intrepid* when we had the very controversial collision in the 1970 America's Cup, was on the Protest Committee. I had always felt in my heart that Bill never believed he would win that protest. I'm convinced he thought it was a real plus for the defence to get that victory in the Protest Room.

At the Congressional Cup I found myself in the Protest Room once more with Bill, but he was on one side of the table and I was on the other. American Dick Deaver claimed I didn't give him the inside running he believed he was entitled to at a mark rounding. It was his word against mine because I didn't have any outside witnesses—or at least I thought that was the case. When final submissions came Bill Ficker, a member of the protest panel, just stunned me. He came forward and said that he had seen the incident. He went out in front of everyone and picked up the two models to explain the incident as he saw it. What was amazing to me was that his hands were shaking noticeably.

"I can tell you that from where I was positioned directly abeam of the two yachts there was no overlap," Ficker told his fellow committee members. His hands were still shaking as he finished his explanation. Case over. We won the protest. But while I knew he was telling the truth I was wondering why he had leapt to my defence.

Dick Deaver and I, who are good mates, shook hands then went out for a beer together.

"Jim, what was the story there? I've never seen Bill Ficker shaking like that. Did you notice how much his hands were shaking?"

"Yes, I did notice that."

"What was wrong with him?"

"I don't know, Dick."

I knew very well. Bill Ficker was telling me he believed he was dead lucky to beat us in that protest in 1970. It was a straight out "thank you".

At the same regatta there was yet another classic example of the communication gap that exists between Australians and Americans. Each of the crews had hostesses allocated to them who would provide lunch each day while we raced and made sure we felt at home. Our hostess was a particularly nice lady and one day, in a move to return some of her hospitality, I asked if she would be my partner at the prize giving the following Saturday night.

"Oh no, Jim, thank you very much. I'm unavailable."

I thought: "A faint heart never won a turkey", so decided to give it another shot the next day.

"This Saturday night. Is there any chance of you not being engaged and joining me?"

"No Jim, I'm committed to attending the trophy presentation."

"But that's what I invited you to yesterday. I wanted you to be my partner for the trophy presentation."

"No Jim. You invited me to something else. You didn't mention the trophy presentation."

"Yes, I mentioned the prize giving."

"That's right. Those were the words. Is that the same thing?"

"Yes, the prize giving is the trophy presentation."

"Oh Jim, they are lovely words. That sounds like Thanksgiving. I'd love to join you."

Yet again I was reminded of George Bernard Shaw's words: "America and England are two great nations kept apart by a common language."

April 1981 saw a very official letter arrive at our home in Manly. It looked just like the one that delivered the news of my OBE award from the Queen some years earlier. This one, however, held an even greater surprise. It was advice from the Governor-General, Sir Zelman Cowan, that I, James Gilbert Hardy, OBE, had been appointed a Knight Bachelor. I was halfway up the stairs to our apartment when I read this and nearly fell all the way back down to the mailbox. I couldn't believe my eyes—Sir James Gilbert Hardy, OBE. The letter also advised me the knighthood was to remain a secret until it was announced in the Queen's Birthday Honours list in June. However, I did tell Anne and her reaction was the same as mine—stunned disbelief. A second letter arrived from the Governor-General's office telling me Sir Zelman Cowan was having an investiture at Government House in Canberra where I could receive my knighthood. I would be entitled to bring three guests. Alternatively, I could go to Buckingham Palace for an investiture by the Queen. My thoughts were: "Sir Zelman Cowan has written me this letter and it has a very strong inference that he would like me to attend his investiture. I'm not sure I want this Hebrew gentleman to complain about this gentile rejecting his invitation and going off to England."

I headed for Government House in Canberra with Anne, our son David and my brother David as my guests for the investiture. Prior to the actual ceremony we had one brief practice session in a back room where I knelt down and was swished around the ears with the sword.

What a special occasion the actual ceremony was—full of pomp and ceremony. It was all quite fantastic, however I was to realise, much to my disappointment, that "Arise Sir James" wasn't part of the proceedings.

The knighthood was awarded for my services to yachting and the community. I guess my charity work over the years and good showing in the 1980 America's Cup and Sydney–Hobart race all contributed. My sailing activities during the preceding twelve months were to contribute to another great honour soon after the knighthood when I was named Australian Yachtsman of the Year.

In receiving the knighthood I was advised I was then entitled to my own coat of arms, and being a traditionalist it didn't take me long to decide it was a good idea to pursue it. But what I thought would be a relatively simple task turned out to be a marathon effort. I wrote to the appropriate authorities in London to get things rolling and they suggested that somewhere, way back in our family history, there would be some form of family crest. I started off looking into the life of a long distant relative, Thomas Masterman Hardy, the Captain of the Victory—he was the guy on the receiving end of Admiral Nelson's order: "Kiss me, Hardy." As soon as Hardy kissed Nelson the Admiral died—good enough reason for a Hardy never to kiss another bloke I guess. I had an artist in Adelaide put my thoughts on paper. The coat of arms I envisaged had on it the Royal Perth Yacht Club and Royal Sydney Yacht Squadron burgees, bunches of cabernet sauvignon grapes, my Deputy Grand Master symbol from Freemasonry as well as other odds and ends. The motto, in Latin, was Anne's contribution. When translated it said: "Manners Maketh the Man". I sent this off to the College of Arms in London for approval, and what I got back was nothing like what I sent. The grapes were just about all that remained. But the end result is quite spectacular with the shield containing the colours of the burgees, a symbolic reference to the sea, the helmet from a suit of armour with open visor, and as its crowning glory a merman, not a mermaid, bearing a trident and, of all things, the America's Cup. The motto remained across the bottom and beneath it the symbols of my OBE and Knight Bachelor awards. It looks terrific, even if I do say so myself, and the wonderful thing is that it can now be handed down through the family. In 1989, when the company honoured me by naming our new release of mid-range champagne, "Sir James", the decision was to put my coat of arms on the label.

If having a knighthood and a coat of arms is supposed to change your attitude towards life then I failed. I always was and always will be the same Jim Hardy. However, if knighthoods were awarded on a points system for efforts within the community then the performance of Sir James Gilbert Hardy, OBE, and his crew in the Brisbane–Gladstone race, or more specifically, in Gladstone itself, the year after the knighthood would probably have seen me score nil. It all started when I had well-known Brisbane sailing identities Peter and Greg Cavill sail *Police Car* up to Brisbane for me so we could sail in the Gladstone race. When they arrived in their home port Peter decided the crew should follow the trend set in the previous Sydney-Hobart race and have uniforms—police uniforms! The New South Wales Water Police, who were good mates, had given everyone on the crew police shirts for the Hobart race as a goodwill gesture. We thought it was great because the dear old police force in this country doesn't have a lot of friends. In *Police Car* they had a friendly and successful yacht that they could associate with. Interestingly, the original owner, Peter Cantwell, named the yacht *Police Car* because "no one passes a police car".

Using his contacts in Brisbane—his father ran the famous Breakfast Creek Hotel—Peter went out and procured ten Queensland Police Force shirts, complete with badges.

The start of the race was fine. We were the centre of attention with all ten of us dressed in our police shirts. My captain's cap was a New South Wales Police cap. As always, when you have a good yacht and a good crew you tend to enjoy yourself, and this race was no exception with *Police Car* performing like its land-based equivalent does with all lights flashing. There were plenty of laughs, especially when Clem Masters produced his famous breakfast, Moreton Bay Porridge—rum and milk. Clem, a great sailor in his own right, was always full of good times and good stories. At one stage, as we headed up the coast, he told us about a Gladstone race he had enjoyed while sailing his own yacht a few years earlier. His crew comprised mainly enthusiastic young dinghy sailors who were out to enjoy their very first big ocean race. Seeing the opportunity for a bit of a practical joke Clem took aboard a few empty dog food tins in his kit bag. It was pretty rough over one stretch of the course and the youngsters were starting to turn a whiter shade of pale. Clem seized on the opportunity and casually went below after announcing he would prepare a meal. He turned on the stove and made the appropriate noises in the galley then handed up a couple of the empty dog food tins to one of the youngsters in the cockpit: "Here, throw these over the side," he said. A few minutes later Clem appeared on deck: "The stew's ready. Who's for some?" There was a chorus of "No thanks. No thanks," from the crew.

Clem sat there and ate what the youngsters thought was dog food. It was proper stew.

"This is great," he said, slurping into it. "If I'd known you blokes were off your food I would have only cooked for myself."

When we sailed *Police Car* into Gladstone we were more than pleased to learn we had won our division in the race, so I asked the boys to wear their police shirts for the trophy presentation when it was held the next morning. They all agreed. My mistake was that I should have added that after the presentation they were to take them off. The sequels were something else.

Immediately after the presentation I was walking up the main street of Gladstone wearing my New South Wales Police cap and my Queensland police shirt when two charming old ladies stopped me.

"Excuse us, Officer. Is the Harbour Carnival coming this way tomorrow morning?"

"Oh look ladies, I don't know. I'm from New South Wales."

They kept looking at the Queensland Police shoulder badges on the shirt, totally confused. They toddled off completely baffled.

I then walked into a Chinese restaurant to organise a dinner for the crew. The little Chinaman, on sighting me in full regalia, went white. What did the police want with him? He couldn't be helpful enough. Dinner was booked—any table I wanted. I went back to the yacht club to advise the crew of the venue. Two of them, still wearing their police shirts, elected to stay at the bar instead of joining us for dinner.

The rest of the day and night saw much mirth and merriment.

The next morning—we were all living aboard the yacht—we were down in the cabin thinking about getting breakfast, when suddenly there was an almighty crash on the deck. Then there was an equally frightening crash. Then more. Seconds later we knew what had caused the noise. I looked out through the gap in the companionway at the rear of the cabin to see dark blue trousers and thick soled, heavily polished, black shoes. The police!

"Who's in charge of this vessel?" a voice boomed into the cabin.

Six of the crew, who had been sitting around the cabin drinking coffee with me, scurried everywhere like cockroaches do in a kitchen when you turn a light on. I don't know where they went but they vanished.

I struggled up onto the deck to confront the constabulary, realising straight away I'd made a huge mistake. I had slept in my Queensland Police Force shirt and was still wearing it. It wasn't a good look. There were six burly police around me—all glaring and looking very official.

"Oh, uhm, good morning office—"

"CROWN SERGEANT!"

"Oh, sorry . . . Crown Sergeant."

"There is going to be police action and civil action. Your crew has made a mockery of my station."

"What have we done that is so wrong, Sir?"

"Look at that sign on the deck for a start."

My eyes swept forward and locked on to a large "Road Closed" sign, complete with flashing lights.

"Yes officer, sorry, Crown Sergeant. I saw that when I came aboard last night. I didn't think it was very funny. I was going to have the crew remove it first thing this morning."

After a thorough dressing down by the Crown Sergeant he and his men departed. I was still somewhat confused about what had happened, but I decided it was best I didn't ask any additional questions.

About two hours later I was up at the hotel in Gladstone where crews in the race were gathering to share a brewery's gesture of eleven hundred beers at 11 o'clock. I noticed that one of the police officers who had been with the Crown Sergeant on the yacht was there. He seemed a nice bloke so I thought I should strike up a conversation. I was then dressed in street clothes and said, jokingly: "You're not masquerading as a policeman in that uniform, are you?"

Oops. He didn't even crack a smile—then I realised why. The big Crown Sergeant was right behind me. He bawled me out again.

"Think you're funny, eh? You mob from down south think you're so smart."

"Look, Crown Sergeant, before you take me off to jail can you enlighten me as to what my crew has done to upset you so much."

"Many things. Many things."

"Such as?"

"Well, for one, there was a skirmish at the yacht club last night and they phoned me for help. I sent down two men to quieten the problem and while they were there in the thick of it, trying to get things under control, there were uniformed men at the bar who were more of a hindrance than a help. The fact that they just stood there drinking and shouting 'book him Danno, book him' instead of rendering assistance did nothing to help my men execute their work."

"This guy thinks my boys are off-duty police," I thought to myself. "I'll say no more."

"And that's not all," the Crown Sergeant continued. "Another man dressed as a police officer stopped a young lady in a small car at one o'clock this morning and demanded to see her driving licence. She told him she thought he'd been drinking and he responded 'That's none of your business.' That's not good for our image around here. You'll be hearing more about all this."

It was obvious the scene was getting very heavy. It was time for damage control. I contacted the local Member of Parliament, thinking apologies through that channel would be a good start. He arranged to meet us at the yacht club at 3 o'clock that afternoon. We waited—4 o'clock, 5 o'clock—by 6 o'clock the Bundaberg Rum and cokes had taken a hold and we were all over the moon again. He finally called to say he couldn't make it. He would see us on the yacht at 7 o'clock the next morning.

The local member did know of our predicament and the problems our shirts had created. "I have been in touch with the office of the Police Commissioner, Terence Lewis, and had it confirmed you were given the shirts—but only for ceremonial purposes." We immediately started a systematic series of apologies and finally managed to regain some semblance of credibility in the town.

It wasn't until some months later that I was to realise the complete scale of events involving my crew in Gladstone. I then understood why we hadn't been a hit with the local police. Each year the highlight of the Harbour Festival, which is staged when the race yachts arrive at Easter, is a parade down the main street of Gladstone to the waterfront. It turned out that two of my crew dressed in their police shirts stood in the middle of the street and redirected the parade, including all the decorated floats, straight up a blind alley. No wonder we were unpopular.

While I was gaining great pleasure racing *Police Car* I remained a fleet owner. *Nyamba* had become an albatross around my neck because no one in Australia wanted to buy her. My only alternative was to have her sailed to America and hope there was a market there. En route *Nyamba* contested the Clipper Cup series in Hawaii with son David in the crew. It was a great experience for a young man. After racing was completed *Nyamba* set sail for San Diego, where she was to go on the market. I was to soon realise that there was no action in that city so I decided that campaigning the yacht in America's major offshore championship, the Southern Ocean Racing Conference (SORC) out of Florida, might generate some interest and provide some pleasure. *Nyamba*, complete with a large Australian flag painted proudly on her hull, was trucked across America to St Petersburg for the start of the regatta.

St Petersburg was to present a new face of America to me, one of a huge, very slow-moving retirement village. I had never seen so many old people in one place in my life, and said so to one of the members of the yacht club: "No Jim, you are wrong," he told me. "The old people are in Tampa. Their parents live here in St Petersburg." He had further comment: "Y'know, the airlines offer special deals to the old folk from up north who want to come to St Petersburg for the winter—a ticket down and freight back!"

The exercise of having the Australian flag emblazoned on *Nyamba* for the SORC was to provide a real education for me. I was a proud admirer of the Australian flag—I just loved it when we wore our sailing sweaters during the 1970 America's Cup campaign that had the Australian flag and "Gretel II" embroidered on them. I decided the crew for the SORC would have similar sweaters to match the flag on the hull.

After we had sailed in three races an Englishman who had been watching his son compete came up to me: "I've spent the past week looking at this flag," he said, pointing to the one on my sweater. "I know it is British, but I can't work out where it is from."

"It's not British, it's Australian," I announced very positively.

"Oh, Australian is it."

That was enough for me. It brought to the surface a belief I'd been nurturing in recent years—we really kid ourselves about our international identity. We live on an island that is virtually untouched by the rest of the world, something we really value. At the same time we think the flag is very important to us, but internationally it is very confusing. While we sit there being justifiably proud of our country the rest of the world hasn't got a clue it is our flag when they see it. We do not have our own identity through the current flag. As far as Jim Hardy is concerned we should follow the lead of the Canadians and create a flag that says, very boldly and proudly, "Australia".

The guy's comments hit me where it hurt and I decided to do something about it, immediately. I would have a flag made with a kangaroo on it. I couldn't find a suitable photograph or drawing of a kangaroo anywhere, then suddenly realised that local coin collectors would have an Australian penny in their collections. The penny had a great outline of a kangaroo on the back. Sure enough I found a penny and had the flag made. From that moment on everyone in the regatta and around the waterfront knew we were from Australia. Hospitality came from every direction and free drinks flowed—all because of a flag.

When I arrived back in Sydney I was sufficiently fired up on the subject of the flag to accept the position of Chairman of Ausflag, a public committee formed in Sydney by an old acquaintance from Adelaide, Chris Hurford. Its charter was to look into three aspects of our national and international identity, the national anthem, Australia's colours and the Australian flag. My suggestion on the flag was that we should look at the Canadian example. I noted with interest that of the 66 countries in the Commonwealth Games, about 60 had their own flags, flags that didn't say "British". Australia wasn't one of those 60. Every municipality in England has a defaced blue ensign that relates to their region—and that's all our flag is, a defaced blue ensign.

It didn't take long for me to know what a hornet's nest the whole issue of the Australian flag was in our community. The people were very clearly divided into those for the flag and those for a new one. It was an emotive issue, to say the least, so emotive in fact that I had no choice but to resign from the position of Chairman of Ausflag. That decision came as a direct result of an incident involving one of Hardy's salesmen in a remote town in western New South Wales. He had gone into a Returned Services League club looking for his usual order when an old Digger, a war veteran, came running at him with a bayonet on the end of a vintage 303 calibre rifle.

"Get out of here. Get out of here," the old Digger shouted, waving the bayonet at our man.

"What the hell's going on?" our man asked.

"Your boss—he's that Jim Hardy who wants to change our flag, isn't he?"

"Well, yes."

"I fought for that flag and so did all my mates. Now you get out of here. We'll never stock Hardy's wines again."

That was just one of many incidents that led to the Hardy's Board coming to me and saying: "Jim, you might have personal views about the flag, but it is now really hurting our business." So I resigned as Chairman of Ausflag—but I remained a member of the organisation. I still say we don't need to quit the monarchy, but we do need a new flag.

On the subject of business, it was around this time that the Wine and Brandy Association was to wind up its activities. The Association came to an end after 100 years as a direct result of the influence of the Trade Practices Act on the industry. Deeta Colvin, who was the secretary of the Association, organised a huge wake around our offices at the Showground. The theme was appropriate, with everyone dressed in black. There was even a hearse and coffin. As President of the Association I landed at the Showground by helicopter. Deeta decided on a spectacular finale for the party, one using a stuntman. Out of the blue came an almighty explosion in the middle of the showground arena and a coffin that was lying there blew to pieces. A body went hurtling through the air and thumped onto the ground. What a great stunt, everyone thought. But then the body, the stuntman, didn't move. People rushed over and finally he staggered to his feet, very shaken. It turned out he'd overdone the explosives in the coffin and just about killed himself. If nothing else it was an impressive way to end the Wine and Brandy Association.

Hardy's was continuing with its impressive expansion. Rhinecastle Wines, which had been owned by the Sydney-based Walker family of Johnny Walker bistros fame, was up for sale and we decided to bring it into our fold. Rhinecastle was strong in Victoria and New South Wales, particularly in the area of restaurants, and that appealed to us. It brought with it the national distribution of Redman's and Chateau Tahbilk labels, and it was a purchase that plugged another gap in the market for our company.

The Board of Hardy's decided it would be in the best interests of the company to then create two divisions, one handling all non-Hardy's labels, like Houghton's, Redman's, Chateau Tahbilk and Rhinecastle, which would be distributed under the banner of Rhinecastle Wines.

Thomas Hardy & Sons would handle all other products.

Within twelve months of that takeover we had added Chateau Reynella to our stable. It was a double-edged gain because it came at a time when we needed to expand our head office at Mile End. Over the years we had bought the properties adjacent to our premises until we owned virtually the entire block. Some of the houses were accommodating different sections of the business, like the export division which was now twenty per cent of our business. It wasn't what you would call efficient, so we decided to rebuild and get all departments under one roof. Consideration was given to moving the entire operation out to McLaren Vale, where our old winery was situated. But while there was plenty of land available there it was 30 kilometres from the city and we thought the distance was a negative for such a move. Chateau Reynella, which was half the distance from Adelaide, was another alternative. After much consideration we decided to buy Chateau Reynella from Rothmans of Paul Mall and relocate our head office at that property.

With the purchase finalised Thomas Hardy and Sons had all but completed a full circle. This was the property where my great grandfather, our founder Thomas Hardy, took his first job, with John Reynell, when he arrived in Australia in August 1850.

Our plans for the establishment of our new headquarters at Chateau Reynella involved taking the old family homestead back to its original condition, with beautiful furnishings. The chateau, which had been a winery, was made a working office and we built a huge new bottling hall on the property. We were fortunate enough to be able to sell about half the vineyard area on the property, which we didn't need, for around five million dollars. The sale of this land for housing certainly helped offset the development and restoration costs we had faced.

In those years it seemed that everywhere I turned there were offers and opportunities. The then Premier of South Australia, David Tonkin, asked me to be the Chairman of a symposium in London aimed at creating an awareness of South Australia's resources. I was to act as a Master of Ceremonies as much as a chairman, introducing the speakers and outlining their respective industries. It was an enlightening and very educational experience where I also learned a hell of a lot about just how vast and dynamic the resources of my home state really were. For example, the Roxby Downs project was the biggest single mineral discovery this century which had no surface expression—meaning there was no evidence whatsoever on the surface of the land to indicate the existence of the minerals below. The discovery was a great achievement by the geologists. They found copper, uranium, gold and other minerals in a deposit the size of the city of Adelaide, which is a mile square. Opportunities like this symposium always led to me meeting interesting people and gave me the chance to spread the word about Hardy's wines.

My travels were diverse and different—from London to Hawaii and across the length and breadth of Australia. The trip to Hawaii allowed me to continue my wonderful love affair with *Police Car* and become famous for my pink erection—mast erection, that is. With the strong and steady trade winds blowing for the Pan Am Clipper Cup series *Police Car* was right in her element. For me it was just the best sailing I'd enjoyed in years—the sun was warm on your back, the wind never stopped blowing and the seas were big, blue and beautiful.

After a good win in the first race it was obvious we had the potential to win the series. One hundred yards from the finish in the second race we again had most of our opposition under control. One more tack and we were across the line. We were sailing off Diamond Head and *Police Car* lifted over a really big, square sea which didn't have a back to it. Our blue-hulled girl burst through the top of the wave and speared out into mid air, then came crashing down into the trough that followed. Crash! Crack!

"What a bugger," I said looking aloft and not wanting to see what my eyes were recording. Our bird had a broken wing. Down came a cloud of sails, twisted aluminium and metal rigging. The moment it happened I could see Alan Payne's finger running over a photograph of the yacht I had shown him months earlier, his eyes sensing a hard spot, an uneven bend, in the section exactly where the mast broke. In a split second we had gone from being cock of the roost to a feather duster. The crew fumed and swore as they scrambled to unravel the wreckage. They realised their sailing holiday in Honolulu would now be spent watching the rest of the fleet race while they sat on the deck at the yacht club.

We set our kangaroo battle flag upside down to symbolise our exit from the series. Then, as we motored back to the dock and consoled ourselves with a few beers, it became apparent that with some extreme levels of co-ordination and effort we might be able to get a rig back into the boat for at least some of the remaining races.

The next few hours revealed what desire and determination can achieve. The crew created a plan and set about finding a suitable replacement aluminium extrusion in Sydney, air freighting it to Honolulu, commandeering a mast maker's facility and establishing a work schedule. Fortunately the yacht's designer, Ed Dubois, was in Hawaii from England. *Police Car*'s chart table became his design office, where he sketched out plans and a step-by-step set of instructions for the creation of the best possible rig in the shortest possible time.

Incredibly, the whole program came together and after three days of work around the clock the mast was all but ready. We looked at Ed's fourteenth and final instruction on his job list. It read: "Paint mast pink if time permits." In England that meant pink aluminium primer, but in Honolulu no such pink primer existed. There was an opportunity for some artistic licence.

"What colour pink do you want?" asked Timmy Rhea, the owner of the rigging shop where we were working.

"That colour," I said, grabbing him on the nipple.

He scurried into his paint locker and emerged with a can of shocking pink enamel. Out came the brushes and the bottom half of the mast was painted pink. When we stepped it back in the yacht we were the talk of the town. If nothing else it certainly made the yacht very easy to find among the forest of masts at the dock.

Away and at home I was doing more and more of my own thing socially, primarily because my emotions towards Anne were being eroded. I was being continually confronted by frustrations which, after years of endeavour, were becoming too hard to handle. The more I tried to help Anne the worse things became and it wasn't until she was in such a state where she virtually could not move across the room that she would surrender and cry for help. Then it was time for hospital once more, recovery and then the resumption of the entire cycle again. David decided it was time to pull up his stumps and move out of home. First up he shared a house with a mate in nearby Seaforth. Later he met and married a delightful American girl, Juliet.

I was always receiving invitations to attend social and charity functions across Australia. One such invitation was to the opening of the Adelaide Hilton hotel in November 1982. The man behind that invitation was Roger Lloyd, the manager of the advertising agency which handled the Hardy's account and son of our local pastor, Reverend Lloyd. I had known Roger since before he went to school. In fact, I guided him to school on his very first day. Barry Crocker, who I knew, was the entertainer for this spectacular evening and he had a delightful partner on stage, a blonde lady, Joan McInnes, who sang with him. She knocked me off my feet. "Boy oh boy, what a wonderful woman she appears to be," were my thoughts. While I didn't meet her that night I knew I had fallen in love with her. Her impact on me was indelible but it would be some four years before I would finally meet her.

While my life has had its share of happiness and sorrow I have always experienced deep-seated grief for the plight of those on this earth who are fighting to merely stay alive. In recent years I have watched with considerable sadness the senseless slaughter that has taken place in what was Yugoslavia. I carry wonderful memories of that country, especially of the warm and very friendly people living along the magnificent Dalmatian coastline on the Adriatic Sea. It took an invitation to a regatta organised by the Dalmatian Tourist organisation in 1982 for me to firstly appreciate a beautiful and relatively unspoiled part of this world and discover a new level of pleasure in sailing competition. The authorities invited sailors from fourteen countries to contest the Dalmatia Cup and I was the representative from Australia. They asked me to take another yachtsman and two sailing journalists as my crew. I invited the three Roberts, journalists Rob Mundle and Bob Ross along with Robbie Brown, a sailing mate from the America's Cup and Admiral's Cup. Our enthusiasm for the event was quickly frustrated when the Yugoslav Airlines plane due to carry us to Belgrade then on to Split expired before it reached Sydney. We had two options: catch a later flight and miss the first race or not go at all. The vote was to go.

We arrived in Split on the Dalmatian coast—which seemed like the Riviera compared to Belgrade—and caught a ferry across to the wonderful little port of Hvar on an adjacent island. The competing yachts, including the one we would race, were tied to the dock but the competitors were nowhere to be seen. We then realised they were at a reception in an old castle on a hilltop hundreds of feet above us. Not being ones to miss a party we trudged through the bush up the hill until we found the party. What a reception we received.

That was the start of the most fun-filled regatta I had ever experienced. Nothing was ever taken too seriously, especially when it came to the racing. The organisers insisted we had a good time, and we made sure we did. If ever things became anything like serious on the yacht as we raced from island to island the cork would immediately come out of a delightful bottle of local red wine and the frayed nerves would be soothed. It was the first time I had done a regatta like this and when it ended I realised it was one side of the sport I had really missed. It was a wonderful feeling to be really enjoying racing where there wasn't a Sir Frank Packer or an Alan Bond insisting you perform, just organisers insisting you had a good time. Did I say perform? Well, we certainly did that, but not so much on the race course. The Dalmatians had never previously had a knight in their presence and they didn't know quite how to handle it. To them I was "Sir Hardy". It was a situation that my crew exploited in the name of fun from time to time. For example, every time we were in a bus on a guided tour and it stopped for us to take in the scenery my crew insisted everyone remained seated until I, Knight Bachelor, a Knight of the Realm, a man the Queen of England could call to her side at any time, had alighted. The procedure was for the crew to go to the front of the bus and form an arch with their arms for me to walk under as I got off the bus. Our hosts were very impressed by what was obviously a tradition for all knights in Australia.

The hospitality during this week of sailing seemed endless. It was tougher trying to survive the round of parties and sightseeing than it was to race. At one very big reception we were treated to on the magnificent island of Korcula, folk dancing and singing were highlights. It was quite serious stuff for the people of the village as they entertained us under the gaze of burly uniformed military officials who sat all but motionless on a stage at the front of the hall. There was plenty of food and plenty of drink for all to enjoy, so much so that as the night wore on things loosened up and we decided we should show our appreciation to our hosts with the presentation of an Australian folk song and dance. We chose that famous old rugby song "Old MacDonald had a Farm". For those who don't know, it is a song that has actions to match the words where Old MacDonald has things like pullets, rams and turkeys on his farm.

240

It gets a bit naughty towards the end but it never fails to raise a huge response from a crowd. So there we were, up on the tables, acting out our folk song and dance. Well, we brought the house down, the actions alone being enough to bring a smirk to the face of even the most serious of the officials on the stage. It was like Charlie Chaplin revisited—you don't need any language to laugh at him. Later one of the officials came up to me and said in fractured English: "I did not understand words but you very funny."

What fascinated me most when sailing along the coastline and through the islands off the Dalmatian coast was to see the healthy growth of vines and stone fruit trees, like olives. The place looked like a giant rock farm, but the soil that is there must be very rich in all of the nutrients and trace elements. In Australia we so often have to add this, and that and something else to get the soil structure correct for growing things. But over there the vines looked so healthy yet they were growing out of what looked like rock. It was then obvious why some people referred to the grapevine as the "Mediterranean weed".

"On to Dubrovnik" was our call, the final port in this delightful regatta. The end was as good as the start, with all crews and many locals gathered aboard the racing yachts on the waterfront of what is the largest remaining full walled city in the world. We were sitting on our yachts just enveloped by a spectacular piece of the world's history. How sad it was to be at home some years later and to see television pictures showing the relentless bombardment of Dubrovnik from the hills above.

While sailing was consuming most of my sporting life my interest in Australian football remained as high as ever. About this time back in Sydney I was approached by Dr Allen Aylett, a dentist and more importantly the President of the Victorian Football League (VFL). He was also a fellow Trustee with me on the Rothmans Sports Foundation. He asked if I would be interested in being involved with the Sydney Football League, which was part of the New South Wales Football League. The desire of the Victorian Football League was to appoint me President of both groups and a Director of the Sydney Swans. I gladly accepted.

The VFL had decided to transfer the South Melbourne club, which had been struggling in many ways, to Sydney and have it become the Swans. I thought it would be a nice way for me to get closer to the game. I had missed my close association with Australian football while I lived in Sydney. My favourite team, Sturt, in Adelaide, had done marvellously well, winning six premierships. But all the time I had been in Sydney and not able to follow them the way I would have liked.

Had I realised what I was letting myself in for in becoming involved with the transfer of South Melbourne to Sydney I would have had second thoughts. There were times, especially in the very early days, when I wished I had been someone else, somewhere else, and hadn't been part of it. A couple of the meetings of the South Melbourne Club at the headquarters at Albert Park Lake in Melbourne were more trying than any other meeting I had experienced in all my life. We were confronted by a large group of supporters who had formed under the banner of: "Keep South Melbourne in South Melbourne", and it was not a pleasant confrontation. I remember one old Digger who came up to me after one meeting in tears: "How can you do this?" he cried, tears streaming down his rugged old cheeks. "My grandfather, my father and I all played for this club."

All I could say under my breath was: "Please don't do this again, Melbourne. If a club can't make it, let it merge or die in peace." To see the effect the decision to transfer the club to Sydney was having on the emotions of the long-time supporters of the club was something I never wanted to experience again.

Trying to breath a new lease of life into a dying club by transferring it from South Melbourne to Sydney did more harm than good. The move got the Sydney Swans off on the wrong track in the eyes of the vital ingredient in the game, the supporters. The VFL should have established a completely new club in Sydney, largely because the players who would have joined would have had their change of allegiance to Sydney on their own shoulders. If they had left another club for Sydney, just as others did later to join Brisbane, they would have to cop it sweet with supporters of the clubs they left. The way South Melbourne was transferred to Sydney made us look like robbers—we had robbed South Melbourne of its heart, its football club.

CHAPTER TEN

How Sweet It Is

I CONSIDERED IT a great honour when Warren Jones asked me on behalf of Alan Bond to become a Director of his 1983 America's Cup campaign. Over the years, I have grown to like Alan and admired a lot that he's done. However, I must say I was very disappointed by the comments attributed to him about his senior man in Bond Corporation, Peter Beckwith, after Peter died. It was the period when Bondy's star was really beginning to fall out of the sky and for him to go on record and lay much of the blame for the company's downfall on a man who had departed this earth was, to me, a low point in Alan's life. As it was reported, Alan just tipped the bucket all over Peter Beckwith.

I had always found Alan very friendly, but his attention span on any subject that he wasn't intensely interested in was very brief. Our relationship, even during the America's Cup campaigns, was more like: "G'day, Alan"—"G'day, Jim". For him the America's Cup was just another project, and certainly not the most important thing in his life. He left the challenge in Warren Jones' very capable hands. Alan was far more interested in his business and making maximum dollars. He was a fighter, in the America's Cup and in business, right to the end when his financial bubble finally burst. When things were really starting to look grim around 1990 I called Warren Jones— who was then the boss of Bondy's Channel Nine Television network— to ask how things were really going for the Bond empire.

"Warren, just don't let the bastards wear you down."

"We'll try not to, Jim."

"How will you go? Will Bond Corp. get out of it?"

"Jim, it's like climbing Mount Everest backwards wearing thongs. It can be done, but I don't think we'll be able to make it."

Over the years when Alan and I met on a one-on-one basis I found him very stimulating and very pleasant company. Unfortunately that experience didn't come around too often because his mind was consumed by so many other matters.

One of my favourite memories of Alan came during the early stages of the 1980 campaign. He invited me to fly to Perth to attend a special meeting of the Perth Trotting Association and to also join in some America's Cup fund-raising activities. I stayed at his home at Dalkeith for the weekend.

As I arrived in his driveway by taxi on the Friday evening I was immediately struck by the assembled toys. There was a twenty foot speedboat on a trailer hooked up to a four-wheel drive, a BMW and then Bondy's big, grey Rolls Royce.

The next morning Alan decided I should have a car so I could make my own way around Perth. "We've got a few cars down below. Craig will find one for you." Craig, Alan's son, then escorted me downstairs into what was another world. This particular part of the house had been created to look like a Roman bath, with marble and arches everywhere.

"This is a great area for parties, Jim. I just put the hose over it in the morning to clean it out."

"That's logical, Craig."

We then walked out to the back of the Roman bath into the car parking area, and I honestly thought I'd walked into a car dealer's yard. I literally took a step back to take it all in. There was a green Jensen Interceptor, a big Porsche which Craig promptly jumped in and started. Next to it was a yellow Rolls Royce Corniche, another speedboat—this one with skis hanging out of the back—a Triumph Stag under cover which I assumed belonged to Alan's horse-loving daughter Susan, and next to it a very old MG TC which had a flat rear tyre. Finally, there in all its crowning glory, was a brand new, gleaming black Rolls Royce. Phew!

Craig extracted himself from the Porsche, which was idling away and emitting a very throaty note through the exhaust. He told me it was my car for the weekend. I drove away from the house and down the Stirling Highway, heading for the Myer Store in Fremantle where we had to autograph posters and shirts to raise funds for the 1980 campaign. There seemed to be some disparity in the entire set of circumstances. There I was helping to sell posters that contributed one dollar in profit to Bondy's 1980 Cup campaign while his Porsche sat outside. But I still had no hesitation in accepting his offer to become a Director of the *Australia II* challenge for 1983.

My first involvement in the 1983 campaign came when I received a telephone call from Ben Lexcen, inviting me to his home as soon as possible. I detected a sense of urgency in his voice. When I arrived at his house in Seaforth, on the shores of Sydney's Middle Harbour, Ben was beaming. A smile that spread right across his friendly face. We went down to his design office on the lower level, where he unrolled a large sheet of paper on the drawing board.

"Jim, I'm going to show you something now and I don't want you to tell anyone. What do you think of this? It's the yacht we have designed for the Victorian syndicate."

My eyes scanned over the easy flowing lines of an America's Cup twelve metre class yacht.

"That's a beautiful looking yacht, Ben."

It looked like a logical development of *Australia*, the yacht I sailed in 1980. Then, while I continued to consider and appreciate the modifications he had made to that previous design, he unrolled another sheet of paper over the top. As he did I sensed something different about Ben. Suddenly he was bubbling—he was like a little boy about to show you the biggest and best toy he had received for Christmas.

"Now have a look at this."

"Jeeezus, that's different," was my only comment. After that I was lost for words. I was obviously looking at something resembling the design for a twelve metre—but it was radical. The keel looked to be upside down and huge wings were attached to the bottom of it. This incredible design appeared to have a lot more speed inhibiting wetted surface than other twelve metres. "Why?" I asked myself. Over the years keels had been getting smaller and thinner, all in the quest for less drag, less wetted surface and more speed. Here was Ben at the other end of the rainbow—going the other way. I was trying to be as polite as I could, knowing that over the years Ben had gone off on some amazing tangents with yacht design. I couldn't understand why he would design a yacht that would need to drag wings around on the bottom of the keel, especially when sailing downwind.

I began to unravel the maze of different features of this design. It started to become apparent that Ben had really done his homework. He had attacked the twelve metre class America's Cup design rule from a completely new angle. He had created the lightest and smallest twelve metre in the history of the Cup, which was in keeping with his theory that steamrollers were the only things on earth where weight was an advantage. It all started to make sense. By having the keel upside down and fitted with the wings there was an enormous concentration of ballast where it was most useful, down low. That would make this yacht far more stable than other twelve metres. And because the yacht was so light and had minimum waterline length it could carry an enormous amount of sail. That meant it had the power to drag the wings downwind and still be fast. I looked at Benny and smiled. He knew I had realised where he was coming from. He was off the planet with enthusiasm.

"This thing is going to get to the windward mark three minutes ahead of anything else, Jim. There will be a big reduction in leeway. The keel is really efficient."

It was typical Ben. His numbers and his calculations were somewhere between the design testing tank and reality. But the concept was stunning.

He had decided to experiment with wings on the tip of a keel while he was tank-testing models of his America's Cup designs at a facility in Holland. While there he spotted a group from one of Europe's leading aircraft manufacturers experimenting with endplates, or winglets, on the ends of conventional wings to improve efficiency. Ben, in his inimitable style, leapt into research on endplates and winglets at 100 miles an hour. This winglet idea was right up his alley because more than twenty years earlier he had experimented with wings on the tip of the centreboard in an eighteen foot skiff he was racing. This time around, armed with the latest computer technology and twenty years in the design business, he started coming up with some amazing answers. After a short while he realised the upside down keel with wings was the way to go.

In late 1982 *Australia II* was launched with a veil of secrecy surrounding her underbody. Very few people knew just what the secret appendage was hanging from the bottom of the hull. Others could only speculate. The majority believed the cover up was just a bid by Bondy to psyche the Americans. I was in Fremantle soon after the boat was launched and was invited by Warren Jones to take it for a sail and give the team my thoughts on how it performed. What a stunning experience that was. There was a moderate south-easterly blowing and *Australia II* quickly showed she was unbelievably lively, and very easy to manoeuvre. With the shortest part of the keel at the hull, instead of its base, the boat would spin as soon as the helm was turned. But all this liveliness and huge concentration of lead down low made it difficult to sail downwind. It bounced around so much—like a cork on a rough sea—it was difficult to keep pressure in the sails, especially the spinnaker. It was the stability the yacht had when sailing upwind that impressed me greatly. It was difficult to comprehend—having the wind in your face telling you the yacht should be heeled around twenty degrees while it was almost upright. I can say in all honesty that when I came ashore after that outing I knew we had the yacht with the potential to win the America's Cup. The most pertinent comment I could make in the debrief was that skipper John Bertrand had one heck of a job ahead of him learning how to handle a yacht that was so different to any other.

My next involvement came a month or two later when Warren Jones invited me to Melbourne to be part of an intensive training session. The Victorian syndicate that had built Ben's original design and named it *Challenge 12* had collapsed and I was needed to sail that yacht against *Australia II* in trials on Port Phillip. John Bertrand had organised housing for the team in an old Customs building in Williamstown. It was a great move on his part at that early stage of the campaign—getting the entire team used to the lifestyle and to the way things were going to be in Newport, Rhode Island.

On the water John was quickly becoming disillusioned with *Australia II* as we often beat him with the far more conservative *Challenge*. What he didn't realise was the yacht wasn't the problem. The problem was that he just couldn't steer it. *Australia II* was a very different yacht and he was struggling with it. I certainly had no intention of going slow and easing the pressure *Challenge 12* was applying.

Halfway through the trials we had two really good wins over *Australia II*. Then for the third and final race on the day John set a brand new headsail on *Australia II*, the likes of which had never been seen before. The crew named it the Shogun jib because there was some resemblance to the rising sun with the way the panels radiated out of one corner of the sail and met with the vertical panels. This sail reflected the creative genius of the syndicate's sailmaker, Tom Schnackenberg. Once the jib was set it was the last we saw of *Australia II*. It was a breakthrough sail and for us shogun meant sayonara. *Australia II* blew us off the face of the earth. It was a turning point in the Bond campaign because the sail gave the yacht the power it needed to harness the power the keel could generate. *Australia II* was a different yacht from that day on.

One day towards the end of the trials in Melbourne Alan Bond returned to our camp one day to report on the latest developments in his bid to find someone to take over the Victorian syndicate.

"I had lunch today with a chap named Richard Pratt and I think he might take over the syndicate."

"Richard Pratt. Has he got enough money to go through with it?" I asked Alan.

"Jim, I've got a lot of paper money. He's got real money."

When we completed the session on Port Phillip I came away saying to myself: "We are going to win the America's Cup with *Australia II*." To see it sail in a fresh breeze on the bay and thrash *Challenge 12* and *Gretel II*, which was also there, left me convinced we had the yacht for the job. The two other yachts lay on their sides and copped a soaking while *Australia II* stood up like a honeymoon erection and powered ahead. John Bertrand was gaining his confidence while Ben Lexcen was over the moon with excitement.

With Australia having 21 years of America's Cup challenge experience, and this being Bondy's fourth effort, we had the benefit of great experience in the Cup arena. I did everything I could to encourage Warren Jones to go to Newport with the minimum number of people. Back in 1967 the *Dame Pattie* challenge fell apart because there were too many people involved. There were also too many people involved with Bondy's 1974 challenge. It was agreed that we would go with the smallest team possible. If any additional people were needed they could be flown in at a later date. The other great asset for the team was having Warren Jones as manager, Mr 100 per cent, who led by example. If Warren had to simultaneously stop an avalanche and repel invaders, he would.

My role in the challenge was that of reserve helmsman and observer. Each day I would go out on *Australia II*'s tender boat, *Black Swan*, armed with a notebook and binoculars to watch everything the boys did, be it a race or just a practice day. Every evening there was a debriefing involving John Bertrand, Warren Jones, Ben Lexcen, John Longley, me and Bondy, if he was on the scene. It was a very valuable brains trust for the campaign.

The Australian sense of humour and our penchant for nicknames and rhyming slang got some of our opposition offside very early in the summer. One day Warren was confronted at our dock by Comandante Gianfranco Alberini, the head of Italy's Yacht Club Costa Smeralda syndicate, with an official complaint. The Commandante handed Warren a letter complaining about the crew of *Australia II* referring to his crew on *Azzurra* as the "Dapto Dogs".

"Warren, I do not understand what is a 'Dapto', or what 'Dapto Dogs' refers to, but I can tell you it is disparaging to my team. Would you please tell your crew to refrain from referring to my team as the 'Daptos' or the 'Dapto dogs'."

"Dapto Dogs", which was abbreviated to "Daptos", was rhyming slang, which was rife among the Australians in Newport that year. No one seemed to want to refer to them as the Italians, and certainly no one wanted to call them "the wogs". So "Dapto dogs" it was. In the same light that year the Canadians were referred to as "the seal bashers" and the British the "soap dodgers". It was harmless fun among the crew. But the Italians really took it to heart.

Warren took Comandante Alberini's complaint on board and the next morning at breakfast, poker faced, he advised the crew they were to no longer refer to the Italians as the "Daptos" because it was upsetting them. You can guess what effect that had on the crew. It was "Daptos" forever.

The one thing that continually impressed me about the *Australia II* team was the professionalism and tightness they held as a team. They were men on a mission who found their fun within the camp and not outside. In previous challenges the fun factor took in places like the Candy Store and the Black Pearl, two of the better bars and restaurants on the waterfront. On top of that there was the entire social scene in Newport during the Cup summer. The stories from that scene are legendary—you could write three books just on the social activities of Newport—the scandals, the parties, the gossip.

But this time around there was total dedication. The entire team would be in bed before 10 o'clock every night as everyone knew plenty of sleep was an important factor in the campaign. Their heads were absolutely in the right place—to a degree where outsiders might have seen it as arrogance. It was as though the team was surrounded by armour plate. The only bloke outside the plating was Warren Jones, who was fighting the New York Yacht Club and their challenges as to the legality of *Australia II*'s keel. Winning that fight—which was well documented at the time—was a huge turning point for our challenge. Watching it all unfold from the inside was even more interesting. Warren was handling the entire episode very well, but Bondy was getting jumpy. One day Bondy blew back into Newport fresh from a deal in London with both guns blazing. He walked into our office at our compound on the waterfront and started giving Warren a massive serve on what should happen and shouldn't happen over the entire keel issue with the New York Yacht Club. He was firing from the hip without having the facts at his disposal. Warren just stood up and strolled out of the office while Alan was in mid sentence. It was gutsy stuff. Next thing Bondy chased Warren like a puppy following its owner.

"What's wrong, Warren? Why won't you speak to me?"

"I won't speak to you until you come down out of the clouds and get back on the rails with me right here."

"OK. I'm sorry, Warren."

The saddest part about all the drama with the New York Yacht Club was the effect it was having on Ben. He just couldn't cope with being labelled a cheat by the Americans. When the Americans went to maximum heat with their challenge on the legality of the keel it all became too much and he suffered a mild heart attack. He spent quite a few days in hospital in Newport. If there was a plus side to this it was that it further firmed our resolve to go out and take the Cup. Benny had always said he wanted to win the America's Cup just to put it out of its misery—he once wanted to put it under a steamroller and turn it into the America's Plate. We were then more determined than ever to make it happen.

John Bertrand was another contender for medical attention in the lead up to the Cup match when he pinched a nerve in his neck while playing volleyball one morning with the rest of the crew. That led to me steering the boat in eleven of the races in the Challenger

Selection series, an experience that gave me a better handle on how things were going with the boat. We won ten of the eleven contests and the one impression I came away with was that the yacht was very vulnerable when running straight downwind under spinnaker. John was then the manager of the North sailmaking business in Melbourne and, not surprisingly, he was looking at his long-term future in wanting an entire North Sails wardrobe on *Australia II*. But I saw the North spinnakers as a real problem and told both John and Warren just that. The sails weren't stable enough to hold the wind when the water surface was choppy.

"Warren, if we persist with the North spinnakers we are in trouble. You have a guy in the crew who knows more about making fast spinnakers than everyone else in Australia—Hughie Treharne."

My assessment was that Tom Schnackenberg was doing a great job with the fore and aft sails, the mainsails and jibs, but the spinnakers scared him. Warren and Alan agreed Hughie should be given the spinnaker development program. John, realising the forces were against him, went very quiet on the spinnaker agenda. In the early stages of the new program there was quite a bit of tension between John and Hugh, who was also sailing on the yacht as tactician. Tom Schnackenburg complained about Hugh's involvement first up, but I could tell when he was complaining that his heart wasn't in it. Tom was also a North Sails loft boss in New Zealand so had to be seen to be doing the right thing by supporting another North loft sailmaker in John Bertrand. All I can say is that it was a proud moment for me when *Australia II* breezed past Dennis Conner's *Liberty* on the run to the last mark in the final race of the America's Cup with a Hugh Treharne spinnaker set.

Everything turned out for the better as the summer progressed. John was having the mainsail and jibs changed just about every day, and this kept "Schnacks" and his team working all but around the clock. They would have been over-pressed had they worked on the spinnakers as well. Altering the sails each day had become a cloak and dagger affair. Bondy was insisting that nothing on the boat should be altered, especially the sails, but he wasn't a sailmaker and the guys knew what was needed. They just kept telling Bondy the sails hadn't been changed, that they were really happy with the shapes. Bondy would have been irate if he had known how often they were being altered.

In the lead up to the America's Cup match a tug of war developed between Alan Bond and my friend Dennis O'Neill. Dennis was in Cowes, England with his ocean-racing yacht *Bondi Tram*, a member of the Australian team challenging for the Admiral's Cup. Hugh Treharne was originally scheduled to race as tactician and helmsman with Dennis, but Bondy wouldn't let him go. I suggested to Alan that Hugh could go over to do the first four Cup races and I could relieve him and do the final events, including the long one, the Fastnet race. That way Hugh would only be away from *Australia II* for a few days and everyone would be happy. Bondy called Dennis, the deal was done.

"I'll get you a ticket on the Concorde," were Alan's parting words to me. I couldn't believe my ears.

Soon after I was on the train from Newport to New York and then aboard the Concorde. What a ride. After take-off our very English-sounding captain came on the microphone. He explained that he was celebrating twenty years "in supersonic transport".

"The speed of the machine is displayed on the Mach digital speed print out positioned on the forward bulkhead," the captain said. "I'd like to explain that just as we approach the speed of sound, Mach One, the engines have to get a recharge to push the machine through the sound barrier. It will feel like changing gears in an automatic car. There will be a little bit of buffeting as we push through the sound barrier."

I sat back in my seat, glass of champagne in hand, watching the numbers rise—0.94, .95, .96, .97, .98, .99, Mach One. And just as the captain described, there was a sensation similar to an automatic car changing gears and a slight buffeting. The numbers kept going up until we were travelling at almost twice the speed of sound. I kept sipping and enjoying my champagne.

Three hours later, it seemed like around the time it normally took me to fly from Adelaide to Sydney, we were descending into London's Heathrow Airport. It was all just mind boggling. The attitude of the Concorde as it came in to land was quite amazing, the front of the plane pointing way up in the air with the nose drooping down so the pilot could see the ground. It reminded me of how a pelican looks when it comes in to land with its feet stuck out in front. The Concorde was a beautiful bird—an amazing machine.

I made my way straight down to Southampton, then across the

Solent by ferry to Cowes where I found Dennis and the rest of the team. Dennis, approaching 50 and a bachelor, was—and still is—one of the most liked guys on the Australian sailing scene. He wasn't short of a dollar, knew how to have a good time, and was always attracted to young and pretty ladies. Accordingly, I wasn't surprised by his opening comments to me when I arrived.

"Jim, I'm in love."

"Dennis, I've known you for a long time and you've been in love a lot of times."

"But this is it, Jim. This is the real thing. Charlotte is her name. She's b-b-b-beautiful."

Dennis started stuttering and I immediately knew he was really excited.

"I don't think I'll do the Fastnet race, Jim. You'll have to take the yacht because I'm going to marry this girl. I need to make plans."

"Come on, Dennis. You've been going to marry lots of girls."

"No, believe me, Jim. This really is the one."

I soon met Charlotte, a really down-to-earth, super English girl who was totally unpretentious despite having connections in all the right areas, including the Royal Family and Princess Di. The end result was that I sailed in the Fastnet race, Australia didn't win the Admiral's Cup, and Dennis stayed ashore and got his girl. The fact that Dennis did go on and marry Charlotte and have lovely children was the highlight of the regatta for me. With the racing complete I was headed back across the Atlantic to New York and Newport—a jumbo jet, not the Concorde.

Things were getting better and better for *Australia II* until our bowman, Scotty McAllister, broke his arm. It was a horrible accident. He was at the top of the mast when what we call the crane, an aluminium strut extending back from the masthead, buckled, snapped his arm and trapped him. With Scotty in hospital we had to find a replacement. My suggestion was young Greg Cavill, from Brisbane, who had sailed with me on *Police Car* and *Nyamba*—he was in Newport sailing as bowman on Syd Fischer's challenge contender *Advance*.

Greg's name went up for consideration alongside that of Damian Fewster's, who had been sailing on the bow of the Victorian yacht *Challenge 12*. The selection was made easy when Greg Cavill was wheeled into the bed alongside Scotty McAllister in hospital. He'd gone over the handlebars of his little moped and put his face into the pavement while riding along a street in Newport. So Damian, or "Knuckle", got the job. He turned out to be a great sailor and a terrific human being—a very funny young man who was also extremely genuine in every way. Ironically, after taking on the job of bowman he went on to meet Alan Bond's daughter Jodie. Love and marriage were to follow.

There was another problem with the crew structure on *Australia II*. John was having difficulty getting his orders heard by the guys on the foredeck. I suggested he put John "Chink" Longley—a big, very fit, former school teacher—in the crew to operate the coffee grinder winches. He had been a member of all Alan Bond's previous America's Cup crews but this time around he was Shore Manager for the syndicate. John picked up on the suggestion, put Chink in the crew and solved the problem. However, that development led to what I saw as a wrong move with the crew structure. Because he didn't know Damian Fewster, John didn't have enough confidence in the youngster to have him call the time and distance as *Australia II* approached the starting line. It's a very important part of the starting procedure on the yacht where the man on the bow advises the helmsman the time and distance the bow of the yacht is from the starting line. Instead, John gave Chink the job in the pre-start manoeuvres. I saw it as a mistake because Chink hadn't sailed on the bow for a few years. He was a bit out of touch. My beliefs were confirmed when Chink gave John a couple of bum steers in the actual America's Cup races and *Australia II* broke the start. John would have been better off encouraging Knuckle and fitting him into the role on *Australia II* that he had already played aboard *Challenge 12*.

What I was doing for John was being a coach. It was something I felt I had always missed when I had been in his position as helmsman for the America's Cup. We did have a team coach in Californian Rod Davis in 1980, and he did a great job. But I always thought it would be good to have someone I could talk to about how I was sailing the boat and to bounce ideas off. So every morning, while the rest of the team were off doing their run, John and I would go through our own exercise program on the verandah at the crew house and chat about what I had observed from *Black Swan* the previous day. Along with the spinnaker problems I had also noticed that *Australia II* appeared to be sailing better when each headsail she was using was near the top of its wind range—when the sail was getting close to being changed for a stronger one the yacht was really performing. *Australia II* seemed to be enjoying the increase in pressure when the keel was put under more load and the yacht developed a little more angle of heel. We talked about it and John did some experimenting. The theory worked so he re-rated every one of the sails in the wardrobe up to a higher wind range. *Australia II* was a better yacht as a result of the change.

The team spirit among the entire *Australia II* squad in Newport was the best I had experienced in any America's Cup campaign. There was a wonderful attitude and atmosphere, from Alan Bond, Warren Jones and John Bertrand through to the youngest of the sailmakers and the girls in the office. They were there for a common goal and could not be distracted from it. The team had its share of colourful characters, like former Royal Perth Commodore and architect John Fitzhardinge, but none more so than Newton "Newty" Roberts. He was an absolute gem—a returned World War II man, one time Alderman of Bunbury in Western Australia and a very successful businessman. He was a short, stocky man with thin grey hair swept back above a cherubic face which oozed personality and mischief. Newty's job was that of deckhand aboard *Black Swan*, a role he had played in all of Alan Bond's Cup challenges. His other role was that of team practical joker. One day during our preparations for the Cup we were off Newport with *Australia II* and *Black Swan* waiting for the wind to arrive so we could begin sailing. We waited for hours and the day got hotter and hotter until eventually just about everyone went swimming, except for me. I don't like being cold and the water out there was so cold blokes got lumps under their ears. That wasn't for me. Bondy was among the group swimming around, all giving me a hard time about not diving in. They kept chiding me until finally I could take it no more. No one had swimming costumes with them so it was everyone in the nude. I stripped down, left my underpants on the aft deck of *Black Swan* then dived in. When I climbed back onto *Black Swan* Newty Roberts was standing there with an awful look on his face: "Everybody's disgusted with you, Jim. Have a look there."

I looked down and there in my white underpants was a terrible brown mess. Everyone was bagging me while I hastily tried to explain my way around something I knew nothing about. It turned out Newty had put a Snickers chocolate bar in my underpants, and the screaming

255

heat of the sun had melted it to the stage where it resembled something just awful.

While our team retained its sense of humour, the officials of the New York Yacht Club were starting to lose theirs. It didn't take a lot of intelligence to realise that our "little white pointer with its wonder keel from Australia" was shaping up as the strongest foreign contender seen in the 132 year history of the contest. Their challenges to the legality of the keel on *Australia II*—they were saying Ben didn't design it so therefore it was illegal—had reached the stage where they were beginning to reveal a win-at-all-costs attitude. I didn't like what they were doing or saying, however my previous Cup experiences told me that what I was seeing was the norm for the NYYC. As always the Americans were playing hard ball, but this year, for the first time, they had someone throwing a harder ball back at them and they didn't like it. They were being beaten at their own game.

The NYYC had its own share of friction among the contenders in their selection trials. One day I spotted three measurement marks on the hull of Dennis Conner's *Liberty* where every other yacht in Newport had one. What it meant was that Dennis was in effect racing three boats because he could change the displacement to which-ever mark he chose to suit the weather conditions. When his rivals from the *Defender* and *Courageous* syndicates realised what he was doing they challenged the New York Yacht Club, saying that Conner was gaining an unfair advantage. They asked why their syndicates hadn't been informed of what Conner was doing so they could have adopted the same system. The response from the New York Yacht Club reflected the often strange attitudes that came from within its walls—they hadn't told the other defence contenders "because they didn't ask".

Fortunately the *Australia II* team hierarchy had seen all these antics before and were ready for any shot the NYYC wanted to make. We had seen *Intrepid* allowed to race what they considered to be a legitimate twelve metre in the 1970 America's Cup when in fact it was illegal because the waterline length measurement was wrong. Then after the 1974 America's Cup we were to learn that *Courageous* was not a legal twelve metre because it was underweight. When I broached that particular subject with Bus Mosbacher, of the New York Yacht Club, he once again showed how the New York Yacht

Club always managed to have what you might call answers of convenience. "Yes, that's right, Jim, when we did weigh *Courageous* after the Cup she was too light. But I might remind you that we never weighed *Southern Cross* after the Cup."

What could I say but "fair enough". There it was yet again, an admission that their boat was illegal, but how could we prove to them in the end that our boat wasn't illegal. We all knew that *Southern Cross* was a legitimate twelve metre, but as far as the Americans were concerned it hadn't been weighed but had been accepted as legal. The insinuation that our yacht may also have been illegal was enough, in their minds, to clear their conscience and wriggle out of another tight corner.

The drama over our concealed keel on *Australia II* reached new heights early one morning not long before the Cup match. Soon after 6 o'clock, while the team was out on the morning run, I took a telephone call from our dock security man. He had spotted two divers with cameras swimming under the yacht. Our tender boat driver, Phil Judge, dived into the harbour and caught one of them. I told Warren Jones as soon as he returned from the run and he took off like a rocket for the dock. There he decided to have charges pressed on the diver, a Canadian, because he wanted to send out a warning to everyone else—when it came to trying to spy on *Australia II*'s keel we would pull out the heavy artillery. Warren said it turned into a scene straight out of Hollywood when he told the police to charge the guy. The police just marched in, handcuffed him, and marched him away as though they had captured America's most wanted. The poor bloke finished up going to court that day still dressed in his wet suit.

When *Challenge 12* was eliminated from the Challenger Selection series the syndicate boss, Dick Pratt, very graciously put the yacht and all its equipment at Alan Bond's disposal. It became *Australia II*'s trial horse right up to the Cup and then was used as a warm-up boat before the actual Cup races. I was given the job of helmsman and took Iain Murray and many of the crew from Syd Fischer's *Advance*, which had also been eliminated, with me. It was a grand gesture by Dick Pratt, one which he felt Alan Bond didn't recognise appropriately when *Australia II* won the America's Cup. Right up until *Challenge 12* was eliminated there was intense rivalry between the Melbourne-based crew and the *Australia II* team. I got a great laugh out of it all in the early stages of the campaign when I heard that Dick Pratt had announced to his team that he didn't want any Hardy's wines in their camp because Jim Hardy was a member of the *Australia II* team. As a result of this directive his team decided they would drink only Houghton's wines, from Western Australia. What they didn't realise was that Houghton's was a wholly owned subsidiary of Hardy's.

Australia II's impressive sweep of the challenger elimination series did not, I am pleased to say, generate any air of over-confidence among the crew on the eve of the America's Cup. They were showing the real benefit of Australia's considerable experience in challenging for the America's Cup. On the morning of the first race the entire attitude among the team was that it was "just another day at the office". There was probably a little more tension in the air but they were all being very professional about the task that lay ahead.

After breakfast I headed for the dock and linked up with Iain Murray and his crew to prepare *Challenge 12* for the pre-race warm up session with *Australia II*. The procedure that day and for all remaining race days was that after the warm up session I would transfer to *Black Swan*, *Australia II*'s tender, to watch the race with Alan Bond, Ben Lexcen, Warren Jones, and the crew reserves.

We lost any chance we had of winning the first race when the steering system collapsed while under maximum load as we rounded the final mark right on *Liberty*'s stern. That brought another clash between John Bertrand and Ben Lexcen, with John saying Ben's engineering on the boat was wrong. For me it was probably as much John's fault as anyone else's. He was the only man with all the engineering degrees and he was the one, as skipper of the yacht, who should have gone over it with a fine tooth comb. He may have spotted the design weakness.

We had another structural failure in race two when the top of the mainsail ripped apart. Once again *Australia II* had shown she had the speed to win the America's Cup, but at the end of the day the score was America two, Australia nil. For me it was dejá vu. I had seen it all before, and once again tension was creeping into the camp.

The tension disappeared and unfortunately was replaced with cockiness when *Australia II* next went out and established a huge lead in light weather, but then ran out of time and saw the race postponed. The next day, when that race was resailed, we won convincingly. I think after those efforts many of the crew thought we had the Cup as good as won. They quickly changed their minds when Dennis Conner handed out a sailing lesson and beat them in convincing fashion in the fourth race, sailing what I believed was a slower boat.

The Americans, with a score of 3-1 in the best of seven series, then became convinced they were going to win the Cup. They actually began planning a huge celebration for the completion of the next race, which they expected to be the last. On the morning of that race I could only say to myself: "Holy Moses, here we are down 3-1 and standing on the cliff edge once again." That thought had been playing on my mind all night and I kept wondering what I could do to contribute. I came up with an analysis of the situation that I passed on to John Bertrand while we did our exercises on the verandah of the crew house.

"Nothing has changed from yesterday morning, John."

"What do you mean, Jim?"

"Well, yesterday morning when you left here you had to win three races to win the America's Cup—and you still have to win three races. So nothing is different."

I sensed an immediate change of attitude in John.

While I was concerned about the situation, Alan Bond was darker than pitch. When we returned to the dock after losing the fourth race you could see he was thinking: "Here we go again. I've seen all this before. We've blown the America's Cup."

On the morning of that crucial fifth race Alan broke with tradition and joined us for breakfast. There he gave one of the best motivational speeches I have heard from any man. He hammered away at the guys, convincing them they were the best in the world. He left them in no doubt that he was convinced they would win the Cup. I could only sit back and appreciate what an amazing man Alan Bond really was. The previous night when I saw him leaving *Black Swan* he was a downtrodden man, yet there at that breakfast he was taking up the challenge and lifting the morale of his troops. It led me to understand how he lifted his company directors back on to their feet when they believed all was lost for Bond Corporation back in 1974. One day he would be in America with us while we prepared for the America's Cup and the next day he was back in

Australia battling to save his company. His directors would tell him that it was all over, that his house of cards had collapsed and the company was finished. Bondy refused to accept that, telling his directors that it was all a figment of their imaginations, that it wasn't all lost and that they should lift their game. We all know now Alan Bond saved his company that year.

Back in 1974 I saw another interesting side to Bondy's character. The Rolex watch company had presented the American crew defending the Cup with watches, but Alan hadn't accepted them for our crew. When I told him the boys thought they deserved the watches he said to me: "If that's the way they feel tell them that I'll replace them with the *Gretel II* crew." The crew didn't like the news, but accepted the umpire's decision and forgot about the watches. Next thing an advertisement appeared in a large American magazine saying that if you raced in the America's Cup you would wear a Rolex. It had a photograph of me wearing a Rolex. Bondy got the lawyers on to it straight away, taking Rolex to court on the grounds that his crew weren't wearing Rolex watches. On the steps of the court the Rolex company settled and supplied 60 watches. The crew was happy.

Alan decided to reject the watch offer again in 1983, this time electing to give each member of the crew a specially struck Bermudian America's Cup gold coin valued at $1500, together with a personal note to each team member. He was saying in effect that if the guys wanted they could sell the coins and go out and buy their own Rolex.

The start of race five was a total disaster for *Australia II*, with the time and distance calls from the bow being off target and the yacht breaking through the start line before the gun. *Australia II* set out thirty seconds behind *Liberty*. It was an unforced error and while everyone on *Black Swan* believed they were watching a dying swan, the feeling on board the yacht was worse. John Bertrand was a beaten man and threw his hands in the air in disgust. As far as he was concerned it was all over. *Australia II* wasn't going to win the Cup and all his dreams for the future had sunk in the waters around him. Colin Beashel, who was working the mainsheet, flew at him: "How 'bout thinking about the rest of us and not about yourself. We're all in this together. We've got to get this show back on the road." John settled down, got on with the job and through an exceptional effort on everyone's part, *Australia II* won and took the score to 3-2.

I considered the next race the best of the entire summer in Newport, but it also brought one of the worst displays of sportsmanship I had ever witnessed in a yacht race. With *Australia II* leading at the second last mark Dennis Conner literally sailed *Liberty* off the course and tried to collide with our yacht. He was obviously hoping he could be involved in a collision and win the race on a protest. He didn't change course once to try to engage *Australia II*, but three times. I was furious and let the race committee from the New York Yacht Club, who were right alongside us on their boat, *Fox Hunter*, know it. I was screaming and yelling at the Commodore, Bob McCullogh: "That's the worst display of sportsmanship I have ever seen. It's a disgrace." I was still fuming when Benny Lexcen came up and put an arm on my shoulder: "I didn't think knights were supposed to lose their temper, Jim." While I was shouting at the race committee our boys on the yacht were also using the world's most colourful language to leave Dennis and his crew in no doubt how they felt about the move. Fortunately they didn't lose the plot, sailed brilliantly and won in fine style. The Americans were rocked to their keel bolts. With the score at 3-3 the America's Cup match was then down to just one race. The longest winning streak in the history of sport, not just sailing, was in danger of being broken. America had not surrendered the Cup since it was first won in England way back in 1851.

Just about every move in the war of nerves, the psychological battle between the Americans and the Australians, had been made. If I had to give a score on the morning of that final race then our guys were well ahead on points. They had copped every piece of flak the Americans could hurl at them and returned it in considerably larger doses. The way in which Warren Jones handled the sometimes ruthless, almost gutter level, tactics from the New York Yacht Club over the keel, and at the same time still manage the team, was remarkable.

The world knows what happened in that historic final race, but I can tell you there were some long faces and very depressed people aboard *Black Swan* when *Australia II* trailed *Liberty* by around two minutes halfway through the race. Bondy was beginning to wonder what he had to do to win the Cup, Benny could hardly watch, and Warren just sat there putting on a brave face, trying to be as positive as he could when everything seemed to be collapsing around him.

"Heck, we can't be like this for the rest of the day," I thought.

"Alan, don't worry about this," I said, patting him on the back. "We'll run him down under spinnaker and nail him before the last mark. We'll go on and win the America's Cup."

"Ah, come off it, Jim."

"Trust me."

I was flying a kite and revealing a dream I desperately wanted to come true.

When the two yachts came around the second last mark and set spinnakers, *Liberty* was 57 seconds in front. We decided we wouldn't watch the yachts but concentrate on the computer screen aboard *Black Swan*, where we could call up through the telemetry any one of 60 functions from the computer aboard *Australia II*. We concentrated on wind angle and wind speed, which were critical for her to gain on *Liberty*. As we watched the numbers bleeping away on the screen excitement began to mount. The wind velocity was starting to increase in *Australia II*'s favour. Conner had elected to sail down the left-hand side of the run and not cover *Australia II*, which had gone out to the right. The wind angle was slowly changing— 205 degrees, 210, 215 and all the way to 225 degrees. At the same time *Australia II* was sailing into stronger wind—more pressure meant more speed.

"Jeeezus, if this keeps up we'll cross ahead of them when we gybe," someone said, peering at the screen.

Everyone on board *Black Swan* was trying to keep the lid on their excitement. We'd seen races won and lost before. There was still a long way to go. The two yachts approached each other from opposite gybes. *Australia II* looked to be in front. Closer, closer. YES, YES, YES—AUSTRALIA II WAS IN FRONT! Can they hang on? What can go wrong?

I made a terrible mistake while watching the final upwind leg to the finish. I noticed Kenny Judge, who was trimming the jib on the starboard side of the boat, was not doing a very good job when *Australia II* came out of a tack. Instead of easing the sail around and trimming it to the course being steered by Bertrand he would religiously pull the sail in until it was eighteen inches or so off the end of the mast spreader and hold it there. At the same time Bertrand wasn't exactly making Ken's job easy. The pressure was obviously getting to him because he was coming out of the tacks quite erratically, trying to cover *Liberty*. But Skip Lissiman, the jib trimmer on the other side of the boat, was doing a great job and reading John's new course after each tack very well. It was the difference between a natural sailor and a numbers sailor. I told Benny what I was observing and he watched it all for a few minutes, then erupted. He went absolutely bananas, shouting that we were going to lose the tacking duel Conner had started as his last ditch bid to regain the lead. He was jumping up and down on the deck of *Black Swan* and charging around like a caged bull. "Calm down, Benny."

No one aboard *Black Swan* was game to say we were going to win the Cup, not even when it was obvious to the rest of the world it was ours. But when the gun went off the shouting, screaming, hugging and back slapping was everything you could dream of. For me it was as though I had steered the yacht. I knew the level of euphoria I was experiencing could not be bettered. Everyone who had been involved with this challenge, like sailmaker Tom Schnackenberg, maintenance man Ken Beashel, Newty Roberts, the riggers, the sailmakers, the office staff, had all contributed to the magnificent victory. This was a real team win that reminded me of the old adage: "You never know which piece of coal makes the whistle blow."

As soon as *Australia II* crossed the line Coast Guard patrol boats came from every direction to form a security circle around her. We clambered onto our rubber duck support boat and raced across to go aboard and congratulate the guys. Bondy was beaming, the crew were shaking their heads in disbelief. They were still coming to grips with how it felt to be the first people to get to the top of sailing's Mount Everest. The ride into the dock, as darkness descended on Newport, was something I'll never forget. It was better than I could have ever imagined—sirens, horns, cheering, trumpets, whistles, ships horns, kangaroo flags, banners, Australian flags and, flashing lights. There were incredible scenes of elation all around us.

We arrived back at the dock to be greeted by hundreds of people making up a huge reception. Champagne was going through the air as though it was coming from fire hoses. When it came time to lift the yacht from the water I noticed the large plastic skirt that had shrouded the keel since the day it was launched was in place. I went straight to Alan Bond: "Bondy, you have to show the keel."

"Oh, I couldn't do that, Jim."

"Why not?"

"It would be showing off."

They were strange words coming from Alan Bond. It was another example of the incredible mixture of the man. I couldn't believe he was concerned about showing off. Rupert Murdoch, whom I had known since I was a young lad in Seacliff, was with us on the aft deck of Black Swan, so I went to him to repeat what Bondy had said.

"I'll fix that, Jim."

He went straight to Alan and spoke with him. The look on Alan's face was one of relief. You could almost see the pressure being transferred—from a situation where he feared he would be seen to be a show off to one where the people were demanding to see the keel. The chant went up: "Show us the keel. Show us the keel."

With that Bondy, showman that he is, stood on the back of Black Swan and, with a gesture that would have done the conductor of the Boston Philharmonic Orchestra proud, shouted: "Show them the keel." He was so obviously happy about being able to share his moment and his secret with the world.

Up came the yacht and slowly the keel emerged from the waters of Newport Harbour. Suddenly people in canoes and small boats were swarming around it, kissing it, hugging it, even using the wings to stand their drinks on. It was a sensational scene that will remain with me forever.

At that stage Dennis Conner came aboard Black Swan. He knew me as well as he knew anyone else on the boat so claimed me for moral support.

"Jim, I can't sail any better than that," he said as tears started rolling down his cheeks. My only thought was: "I don't feel sorry for you, Dennis. I'm not going to say bad luck to you, Dennis." Instead I put my arm up and patted him on the shoulder.

"Dennis, I know how you feel."

And I did know how he felt. Sure, I'd never won the America's Cup, but I'd lost it three times and once or twice thought I might have had a real chance of winning.

After not being impressed by Dennis's blatant attempt to collide with Australia II in the sixth race, my feeling for him went even lower when he didn't turn up the next day for the presentation of the Cup to the Royal Perth Yacht Club. He then didn't join his crew and the *Australia II* team when they were invited to a reception at the White House by President Reagan. He might have had an excuse in his own mind, but when you turn your back on something you've lost after being beaten by a better team, it doesn't sit well with me. Also, you would think the President of the United States and the presentation of the America's Cup would rank above all else. Obviously not so with Dennis. I considered it bad sportsmanship on his part. His absence yet again reminded me how my mother had chastised me for displaying what she saw as bad sportsmanship back in 1950 when I was thirty minutes late for the presentation of the Stonehaven Cup in Perth.

While the parties raged around Newport the night after we won our team retired to the crew house for an early night. They reminded me of a team of commandos who had penetrated enemy lines and carried out a highly successful mission. It was as though they had returned to their own lines, where a hero's welcome awaited them. But for the entire mission the commandos had lived on their wits and their will to succeed. Adrenalin had kept them going. When they returned to their base they were so physically and emotionally drained they could not comprehend the adulation being heaped on them. The *Australia II* team were Australia's sailing commandos.

My closing memory of the America's Cup in 1983 involved what we called the Red Card. Throughout the entire campaign anyone who was considered by other team members to have thrown a temper tantrum, botched their job on the yacht or been caught doing something they shouldn't have been doing was given the Red Card. The recipient had to wear it on a string around his neck until someone else in the team was deemed to have broken the unwritten rules. I received the Red Card for my outburst at Commodore McCullogh and the New York Yacht Club Race Committee after Dennis Conner tried to put *Liberty* on a collision course with *Australia II*. I was concerned that I would be the last holder of the card because it was so late in the campaign. Fortunately, a spectacular act by Warren Jones saved me from the dubious honour of having the Red Card for life.

At the end of the America's Cup campaign none other than Gordon Ingate, supposedly Australian to his boot laces and a twelve metre yacht campaigner from way back, walked through *Australia II*'s dock wearing a New York Yacht Club straw boater, complete with a band in the club's colours. Warren Jones, who had spent the entire summer fighting with the New York Yacht Club, saw red. He couldn't believe an Australian would be parading around in a hat like that. He charged up to Ingate, ripped the hat off his head, threw it in a puddle, then jumped up and down on it like a child throwing a tantrum.

While Warren's act saw the Red Card lifted from my shoulders and placed around his neck by the team the next day, I saw his antics as a fitting end to the 1983 America's Cup match.

266

CHAPTER ELEVEN

Now You See It, Now You Don't

WHILE *AUSTRALIA II* carved across the waters of the Atlantic Ocean off Newport and sailed on to a superb victory in the America's Cup, part of my mind had been elsewhere. It was with Anne.

She had been in Newport with me all summer and seemed to be enjoying herself until her health deteriorated. Her problem had finally got the better of her and she had been admitted to the highly specialised care of the Edgehill Hospital.

For me it was as though she had been committed to a prison. Her treatment was so intense that I was only permitted to see her on weekends. Matters were made worse by the fact that each day, as we sailed out of, then returned to, Newport Harbour, we would sail past Edgehill Hospital and its sprawling grounds.

Anne had been unbelievably loyal to me that summer—almost too loyal for her own good. I believe her loyalty, which was almost fanatical at times, accelerated the deterioration in her health.

When *Australia II* was shaping up as the likely winner of the America's Cup, Anne found it hard to accept that I wasn't the helmsman. She had followed me through all my Cup campaigns over the last 23 years and knew how keen I was to win. Now, finally, here was the yacht likely to win and I wasn't on it.

I was more than happy in the role I had with the syndicate, knowing that being an observer and a coach for John Bertrand was the most valuable contribution I could make. John went on record and said nobody in the team wanted to win the America's Cup more than Jim Hardy.

Anne had been away visiting some dear friends of ours in Boston not long before the actual Cup match when she collapsed. It was another close friend, Dr Robin Wallace, an English doctor who was also the secretary of the 12-Metre Class Association, who called me to say Anne was in need of the best treatment available. Edgehill it was.

Sadly, in so many ways, her confinement meant I had to farewell the rest of the *Australia II* team in Newport as they headed home to a hero's welcome across Australia. I would have given just about anything to be with them, especially for the big reception in Perth, but Anne's treatment wasn't complete and it was more important that I stay with her.

With the Australians gone Newport became something like a morgue overnight and as I was unable to visit Anne during the week I decided to travel across America promoting our wines and at the same time visiting friends. On weekends I would return to Newport. One of my favourite episodes then was my visit to the legendary Fort Worth Boat Club in Texas, where I am a member. I received one of the warmest welcomes I'd experienced anywhere in the world. It was there that a chap from San Diego gave me yet another insight into Dennis Conner: "He's our incoming Commodore at San Diego Yacht Club and I've known him all my life. I can tell you Dennis Conner's ego is so immense he's happy he's the first American to lose the America's Cup." On reflection I think he was right. With no disrespect to Dennis, I think he very cleverly applies his ego as a tool. He reminded me of John Cuneo, who used his fastidious attention to detail to frighten his competition.

Just before Anne was due to leave hospital I was counselled by the staff so I could help her continue on her road to recovery. One of the counsellors really opened my eyes as to what was happening: "You are in effect going to see your wife for the first time when she is completely sober. And she is going to see you for the first time when she is completely sober. These are going to be two very different people. It will be a major problem for you. You must also remember this is not your problem, it is her problem. Should she go downhill again no amount of cajoling on your part will help her. She is only going to be able to help herself." It was suggested we find a clinic in Sydney to help Anne continue with her treatment and, with the assistance of the doctors at Edgehill, appropriate arrangements were made.

Each weekend when I had visited Anne in Edgehill I was impressed with the improvement in her condition. When it came time to fly back to Australia she was better than at any time I could remember. I was feeling very proud of her. We were both determined to keep the treatment going, so as soon as we arrived back in Sydney we visited the clinic. Not long after we started our first interview with a counsellor, a young fellow was literally dragged into the clinic kicking and screaming. He was uncontrollable. Anne turned to me and said: "I don't need this. I don't need this place. We're leaving."

"You do need it, Anne. You really do. Please don't throw in the towel now." We left. It was only a couple of months before all the symptoms began to return to Anne's life and the slide began once more.

While her illness prevented Anne and me from returning to Australia with the America's Cup and to be part of the celebrations, there was certainly still plenty of euphoria across the country to share when we returned. All the talk was of the Cup defence in Fremantle and what a fantastic regatta it would be. Through no effort on my part a potential defence syndicate emerged in South Australia. The man propelling it was my old mate Roger Lloyd, and it wasn't long before he had me on the other end of the telephone: "Jim, I've got a group together and I know we can get the money. Will you join us as Sailing Director?" What else could I say but "yes"—it was my state, and some of my mates, wanting to have a go at defending the Cup. I pulled in Freddie Neill as the helmsman and Dr Mark Tostevin as navigator to handle the computer side of the campaign, then started thinking about a designer. As far as I was concerned there was only one answer in that department: Ben Lexcen. The problem was that he was aligned to the Bond defence syndicate.

After negotiations with Warren Jones and Alan Bond it was agreed that Ben would design the yacht, which would be named *South Australia*.

The fun began immediately. While we were the people paying the bills and buying the design, the Bond syndicate kept us at arm's length when it came to analysing the tank testing and computer data on the yacht. When we finally got the data the boat had been built. We had no time to spend checking the information and we accepted it on face value. As it turned out, what the data showed in theory was nothing like what the yacht was like in practice. We finished up with nothing more than an experimental design from the Bond syndicate, a yacht that didn't like wind or waves. It was everything you didn't want for racing off Fremantle, where the wind howled and the waves rolled.

As soon as the yacht was launched a glaring error emerged: the keel was two tons overweight. We had two alternatives to make the yacht comply with the twelve metre class rule—reduce the sail area, or take the keel off and replace it with a smaller one. We went for the latter. In hindsight it was the wrong decision. *South Australia* was very competitive in the light winds that prevailed for the early part of the Cup defence in Fremantle. But once the winds reached fifteen knots, which they did almost every day later in the season, *South Australia* just lay over on her side and sulked. She had too much sail and not enough ballast.

Part of our deal with the Bond syndicate was to have the use of *Australia II* in Adelaide as a trial horse for our yacht. Our first encounter with the 1983 America's Cup winning yacht showed our yacht to be a shade faster. That was the trend throughout all the trials, but unfortunately it wasn't going to be fast enough. Underneath it all ours was a great campaign with the wrong ammunition.

South Australia—the yacht—was based at North Haven in Adelaide for six months while it was tuned and developed for racing in Fremantle. The location of the base was ideal in many ways, including the fact that it gave us the opportunity to keep an eye on the development of another pet project of mine, the building of the 100 foot sail training vessel *One and All*.

With that project, the America's Cup defence effort, a position on the boards of the South Australian Film Corporation and the *Adelaide Advertiser* and, most importantly, my work as Chairman of Thomas Hardy and Sons, my life was then revolving more around Adelaide than Sydney. Anne and I decided, for the time being at least, we should make Adelaide our home. We kept our apartment is Sydney so we had a base there, and bought a townhouse on East Terrace in Adelaide, an address that once a year had the Adelaide Grand Prix right outside the front door.

My involvement with the *One and All* project was tough because it involved a huge effort in fund raising and organisation. The difference between the dream and reality was a lot of dollars. I took on the role of President at the request of Dr John Young, the plan being for a wooden sail training ship to be built for South Australia's 150th Anniversary. He hit my weak spot because for me one of the most beautiful sights in the world is a wooden ship under a full press of sail. Our presentation to the South Australian Government seeking funds for the project came second to another project, which was for the restoration of a Dutch-designed and built steel ship, *Falie*.

The Government committee assessing the two projects suggested, after rejecting the *One and All* proposal, that we close it down. "No chance," I thought and got straight to my feet in the meeting room.

"Gentlemen, I understand clearly what you are saying and I will go back and say to my own committee that we drop this as a Jubilee project. But I can tell you, gentlemen, that the wooden boat project will not go away. They are a committed group of people." We then conducted a naming competition, which came up with *One and All*. There had been a trading ketch by that name in Port Adelaide many years earlier.

With the dedication of a wonderful committee, and the unselfish contributions of people like my old mate John Harrington, the project was completed, eventually with some assistance from the government. *One and All* went on to fly South Australia's flag on a voyage to Europe then return with the Bicentennial re-enactment fleet which sailed into Sydney Harbour on 26 January 1988. The *Falie* project was also completed for its target, the Sesqui-Centenary celebrations for Adelaide. But as far as I am concerned it looked like an ugly sister when it is seen alongside our Cinderella, *One and All*.

When it came to raising funds it was certainly a lot easier to get support for the America's Cup project than *One and All*. But still, Roger Lloyd had to work hard. Each major sponsor contributed around $250,000 in cash or kind to the campaign. Thomas Hardy and Sons became a major sponsor through donating my time. Among the others were the Sip & Save group of liquor retailers and Australian National Railways. There was another group we referred to as our airline, Air Whippet, which gave us much needed transport. While other syndicates traversed the continent on real planes, we travelled with Air Whippet, the Greyhound Bus Company.

With ours being the first of the new breed of America's Cup defence yachts to be launched we took her to Fremantle for the

12-Metre Class World Championship, which was staged about one year before the actual 1987 Cup match. In one race of that regatta we were racing in close company with the old America's Cup defence war horse *Courageous*, which had Peter Isler at the helm. *South Australia* was just ahead of *Courageous* all the way up the beat. At one stage, while we were on starboard tack, I thought I might just check on the opposition, even though we held right of way.

"Crikey, this is going to be close," I said to Freddie Neill, who was steering our yacht. Then I noticed the bowman on *Courageous*, who was right on the front of the yacht to call the course so they would miss us, got a look of horror on his face. He panicked and ran back towards the mast. I realised that there was no way Isler was going to be able to pull the yacht away and pass across our stern.

"Collision, collision!" I shouted to our crew, at the same time running forward from the cockpit as fast as I could.

"CRASH!" Thirty tons of American twelve metre yacht ploughed into *South Australia*'s cockpit, right where I had been standing.

"Welcome aboard, guys. Now will you take your yacht and play somewhere else?"

The success of Alan Bond's *Australia III* in that World Championship did nothing to help our defence of the Cup. It created a lot of confidence for that camp while we, with our yacht being near identical to *Australia III*, believed the potential was there and it wouldn't take much to find it. The best thing that could have happened would have been for all Australian yachts to be walloped. That way we really would have gone searching for the answers. The old adage that you should never win the lead-up event if you want to win the big one came home to roost once more.

The primary reason for us not keeping the America's Cup in 1987 was because we were not keeping the defence of the Cup as our priority. *Australia III*'s win in the World championship made it appear that the defence would be easy and it was easy street from there. It was also a great pity that the *Kookaburra* syndicate withdrew from the 12-Metre World Championships because they would probably have won the series and forced our *South Australia* syndicate and the Bond syndicate to go back to the drawing board.

Looking back on it all, the very worst thing we did was to agree to a point score system and not use the New York Yacht Club style of arbitrary defender selection. The point score system which the Royal Perth Yacht Club and the defenders accepted could be exploited by the multi-yacht syndicates and didn't necessarily lead to the selection of the best yacht. I believe the Parry syndicate, with its three yachts, did manipulate the system against Alan Bond.

While most people mightn't have liked the high anxiety American system, it bred better boats and crews through tougher competition. The crews of the yachts seeking selection as the defender never knew how long each race would last, so the pressure was really on. If you were behind and the NYYC Committee decided to shorten the course and call the race right there and then it was a mark against you. Some days they sailed full-length courses and on others they wouldn't cover half the distance. At other times they would have starting practice all day long. Towards the end of the American defender selection series everyone was anxiously awaiting the arrival of the yacht club committee, dressed in their familiar straw hats. They would come along and simply say: "Thanks for competing. You're excused," until they finally found their fastest yacht. When the America's Cup came along they were race ready—and in every other match except 1983 they blew us out of the water. Everything the selectors did added up to pressure, and as I always say about competition, you may not like it, but you are always better for it. Whether it's in business or sport, there is nothing better than strong competition.

Our system for the 1987 defence saw what was possibly the fastest yacht, Syd Fischer's *Steak 'n Kidney*, eliminated because it just didn't have enough points accumulated to continue. Obviously there was no way you were going to tell Alan Bond and Kevin Parry to change the rules. I'm sure they saw the points system as an easy way to get rid of the niggling pressure of another competitor. They had eliminated Syd Fischer by using the rules and no matter how much he bleated he couldn't deny he had agreed to the system.

The red light should have come on for all syndicates and the Royal Perth Yacht Club when towards the end of the eliminations *Steak 'n Kidney* went out and beat the eventual defender, *Kookaburra III*, fair and square in a strong wind race. Surely having a boat from Syd's string and tar syndicate go out and beat the hot boat from a $27 million campaign was simply a message saying "don't send me home". You eliminate the yachts that are losing, not the ones that are winning. They should have waived the rules and kept *Steak 'n*

Kidney in the competition, even if it was only to push Iain Murray and *Kookaburra III* up another rung on the competition ladder. Heaven knows the Americans waived the rules often enough in the interest of keeping the Cup in the confines of the New York Yacht Club.

I think there was a certain element of parochialism in the Royal Perth Yacht Club and its two local syndicates having the challenger selection series to themselves in the end. On top of that I got the feeling that Kevin Parry, who headed the *Kookaburra* syndicate, was actually more interested in beating Alan Bond for the right to defend the Cup than actually completing the mission. There was intense rivalry between the pair, something that was reflected in the press conference immediately after *Kookaburra III* was named defender. Alan Bond announced that if Parry didn't successfully defend the Cup he would build another yacht then go and get it back—and I thought "good on you Alan. Fair enough." But Kevin Parry really took it to heart and blew up for all the world to see. I knew straight away our defence was in deep trouble. If he couldn't take that bit of pressure from Alan Bond, then Dennis Conner would eat him for breakfast.

Our *South Australia* team had been the first to become spectators in the defender trials. The wind got stronger and the waves larger as the summer progressed and our yacht became slower, somewhat proportionately. I think at the end we certainly had the strongest and one of the best crews. That point became very apparent when Syd Fischer grabbed a lot of the *South Australia* team for his yacht *Steak 'n Kidney* after our yacht was eliminated from the defender trials.

As always with a campaign like that there were some great times and wonderful memories. On a lighter note, one of the scenes that brought plenty of laughs came when the team left to go to the west for the actual defender series. They travelled from Adelaide to Perth by train, a delightful trip taking in the Nullarbor Plains. The day the train was trundling across the desert it was noticed that one of the team crew had been sitting with his hand out of the window for some considerable time: "What's with holding your hand out the window?" one of the crew asked. The guy brought his hand back in to the carriage and pointed to the white mark that his now removed wedding ring had left on his finger: "I'm going to be away from the missus for a few months so I'm trying to get a bit of a sun tan on the white spot."

A medical scare is no fun for anyone, and for me the rapid loss of strength from my right arm during the defender trials was a scary experience. I first noticed the problem, a sort of tennis elbow, when I began having trouble using the weights during training in our gymnasium. It wasn't long before I didn't have the strength to operate the winches on the yacht so I had to excuse myself from racing. Neil Kerley, the famous South Australian footballer, who was our physical fitness manager and tender boat captain, then noticed the muscles in my upper right arm were starting to wither, so all sorts of investigations started. The pain was intense and acupuncture, among other things, was tried. No one seemed to have any answers.

The big scare came when one morning, while washing my face, I lost the use of my right hand completely. I couldn't call it up to do anything and suddenly thought I had experienced some form of stroke. Much to my relief, I remembered it was your left arm that went out when you had a stroke, not your right. Pride overtook the pain and the discomfort. I decided I had only pulled a muscle and it would be OK in a few days. However, the night after I joined the limp wrist brigade I did discuss my problem with a doctor I knew while we were drinking in a hotel in Fremantle. He was a great help: "I don't know what it might be, Jim. My suggestion is you hold your drinks in the other hand."

When things showed no signs of improvement after a couple of days I decided it was time to get serious about discovering the source of the problem. I saw a physiotherapist in Fremantle, who thought that a chiropractor I had visited the day before the hand went out of action probably accelerated the problem—and I think he was right. I was heading to Adelaide and the physio told me to see a physician while there. That was to ring alarm bells. The thought was that I may have a brain tumour. Neurosurgeons and CAT scans followed. The end result was that the investigations found a disc at the base of my neck had collapsed and ruptured the nerves. I believe the reason for this problem came from craning my neck and looking aloft at the masthead of twelve metre yachts for all those years. We humans are designed to look down, not look up all the time while enjoying our sport. Successful neurosurgery has led to me having 80 per cent strength in my right hand today and that is about as good as it will get. That is a big improvement from when

I couldn't even dial a telephone with my right hand.

For me the ultimate experience that summer in Fremantle was the start of my wonderful romance with Joan McInnes, the woman I had fallen in love with at first sight all those years ago singing at the Hilton Hotel opening in Adelaide. The opportunity to meet her had never presented itself until one night at Perth's Burswood Casino. I was cruising through the casino and I looked across the sea of faces to see one of the greatest supporters of our *South Australia* effort, West Perth restaurateur Thelma Elvin, come through the door. And who should be with her but Joan McInnes. She came straight across and introduced Joan. Instantly I felt like a teenager who had discovered love for the first time. Seeing Joan again confirmed everything I had felt back in Adelaide. This woman really was something special. She didn't have to say anything or do anything for me to know I was in love with her. It was an amazing sensation. I was like a duckling frantically paddling around in a pool as I tried to glean as much information from her as possible without sounding overly enthusiastic. She had been married, she was divorced and she was involved with one of Melbourne's great Australian Rules football players, Barry Breen. "This is just like the America's Cup," I thought. "I've got plenty of competition here."

Joan explained she had been in Perth to appear on a telethon and was flying back to Melbourne that night. It seemed that no sooner had we started talking than she and Thelma were heading out of the casino for the airport. How disappointing.

If ever you needed convincing there is a God and that fate deals the hands in our life then it was evident that night. Half an hour after Thelma and Joan left the casino I looked up and there they were coming back in. The fact that Joan had missed the plane and not gone to Melbourne that night as planned, and that I had decided to remain at the casino for a while longer, was to put us on a collision course that was heading for happiness. I remember the old saying: "Follow your heart wherever it leads you." As far as my heart was concerned, I was gone.

We sat around, drank Margaritas and chatted well into the early hours of the morning. At the end of it all I knew I wanted to see her again. Fortunately for me, Joan's television commitments brought her to Perth twice more during that summer. And each time I saw her I realised even more that I was very much in love.

For the remainder of the America's Cup regatta I was like the cat that had caught the canary. I hadn't actually caught the canary at that stage, but I knew where it was and that was enough to make me very happy within myself. Dennis Conner left Fremantle with the Cup, but for me, being in love was better.

I returned to Adelaide to realise, more than ever, I had Joan in my heart and Anne on my mind. Life at home wasn't exactly what you would call ideal. Things were going virtually from crisis to crisis with Anne, and it was all starting to get beyond me. It was obvious that no matter how much treatment Anne underwent it was only a matter of time before she would slide into her old ways and resume what was a never-ending cycle. While I didn't have any idea what the future might hold for Joan and me, I did know that what little flame there was still flickering away inside my relationship with Anne would eventually go out.

Back at our head office in Adelaide business was booming. I was reminded yet again on my return to head office how well structured the company was, with a strong and dedicated board of directors, efficient management and loyal staff. To say the company was booming was not an exaggeration. While there was a considerable amount of turmoil around us in the industry—there were some significant take-overs—we were continuing to increase our market share. Some other large wine producers were experiencing instability, but we were seen as the tried and trusted company. Our annual turnover was approaching $100 million, a figure that led me to recall that when I first joined the company back in the 50s I had organised a garden party to celebrate us turning over just one million in a year.

The period between the 1983 America's Cup win and the 1987 Cup defence was probably the most frenetic in my life. But it didn't cure my need for travel. Throughout my life, from the time I was a lad, I had a severe dose of wanderlust. Seeking adventure and travel to the unknown were important ingredients in life. When I could afford to be away from business, or when the call came for me to travel for business, I needed no encouragement to go. My travels were seen as gallivanting by some and prompted my long-time friend in the wine industry, the famous Len Evans, to once say to me: "Hardy, you've never done a hard day's work in your life." My response: "It's a poor family which cannot afford at least one gentleman." During the mid 80s I travelled at every opportunity, seeking interesting

277

trips and interesting diversions from life at home. One such trip came my way on 21 June 1985 when, along with six other friends, I boarded a British Airways Boeing 747 in Sydney and headed off on a three week trip where we landed in England, then travelled to France the next day for our tour of the wine country.

All seven of us came from Deerstalkers, a very active wine and food appreciation group that was founded in the cellars at our Sydney office in the mid 60s. As well as being into the appreciation of good wine and food at our monthly meetings, we have always been into the appreciation of good fun, and this trip was no exception. After travelling across to France by Hovercraft we hired two cars and set off on a real voyage of discovery. I don't think there was one major wine district we didn't visit—Champagne, Chablis, Cognac, Bordeaux—you name it, we were there.

It was a delightful trip with wonderful friends, and when it was completed we were reminded how Madame Bollinger aptly described the country's beautiful wine:

"I drink it when I am happy and when I'm sad.

Sometimes I drink it when I'm alone.

When I have company I consider it obligatory.

I trifle with it when I am not hungry and drink it when I am.

Otherwise I never touch it—unless I'm thirsty."

Chapter Twelve

Life's a Roller Coaster

For more than twenty years every aspect of my life seemed to revolve around the America's Cup. It played a significant role in my business activities, my family life and my future. But I did not regret one moment of it. Following the America's Cup defence in 1987 and the subsequent loss of the trophy to Dennis Conner, my life entered a period that comprised almost every level of elation and disappointment one could experience. For most men heading towards 60 years of age this is a time in life when you begin to go through "wind down" mode. For me though it was a time when all my ideas on what my future would hold were changed. My current balance sheet on life would have on one side enormous losses emotionally and within the business, but also a profit that outweighed it all— a future offering a level of happiness and satisfaction I thought I could never achieve.

In business it seemed that everything we touched just turned to gold. Not even the worldwide stock market crash in October 1987 could stop Thomas Hardy and Sons continuing with its expansion towards ensuring it had a role to play in every aspect of the wine market in Australia. At the same time the push was on for us to further develop our market internationally.

Our most recent coup at the time of the crash was the take over of the Stanley Leasingham company, which controlled more than 50 per cent of the "bag-in-a-box" market, the wine cask market. That take over gave us a full hand for the local market—there wasn't

279

an area we didn't have covered. Their business sat very nicely alongside everything else we had: table wines, sparkling wines, fortified wines and brandy. Hardy's had toyed with the wine cask market when it first opened up, but we were a small player and were soon overrun by the big boys. Stanley Leasingham's had elected to concentrate on the cask market and as a result the volume they sold through their big share of the market made it a very profitable operation.

When we took over Stanley Leasingham it was owned by the big American company H.J. Heinz, the soup company famous for having 57 different varieties. With the price agreed our Finance Director, Ian Gray, went to the now very troubled Bank of South Australia and negotiated the necessary finance. There was an interesting set of circumstances surrounding the sale by Heinz, with the company's Chief Executive in America, Tony O'Reilly, keen on having a winery in Australia and the chief in Australia equally keen to sell it. The Australian management won the day then gained great respect from us when Tony O'Reilly stood by our deal after it was signed despite getting a higher last minute offer, which an Australian rival of Hardy's placed through its London office.

The benefit of bringing Stanley Leasingham into our company was twofold. Besides gaining a good share of the wine cask market, the company had a very efficient winery located in the Sunraysia district on the New South Wales side of the border near Mildura. The purchase also brought extensive vineyards in the Clare Valley. Until then—apart from Houghton's in Western Australia—we literally had all our eggs in one basket in as much as our vineyards were concentrated in the regions around Adelaide and at Padthaway in the south-east. That meant that if we had a bad season, particularly with frost in the south-east, we were in a lot of bother with our vintage for that year. Frost is somewhat akin to a bushfire in that it burns off the young shoots and the vines produce very few grapes that year. They usually produced a wonderful crop the following year, but that's a bit late. With us now owning the Leasingham vineyards and winery we had a safeguard against a bad season in other parts of South Australia.

On top of gaining Stanley Leasingham wineries we reinforced Thomas Hardy and Sons' management when Guenter Prass and Mark Tummel joined us. Guenter, originally a winemaker from Germany, had worked his way up the ladder in the Orlando organisation until he was Managing Director then Chairman of Directors. Mark Tummel had a similar rise to be Technical Director. Orlando had a management buy-out that didn't include those two guys. The young turks who took control decided Guenter, who was in his early sixties, and Mark, who was in his late fifties, were too old for the new regime. Wayne Jackson, our Managing Director, went out and captured the pair for our company and they brought with them a huge wealth of experience in the industry. When I say huge, I mean huge. For example, Guenter was the man who introduced Barossa Pearl to the Australian market. He used the German charmat bulk-fermented method to produce a sweet sparkling wine that essentially took the Australian palate from sherry to table wine—it was the vanguard of table wine drinking in Australia. Guenter's initial job with our company was to run Stanley Leasingham while Mark, who was outstanding when it came to production, went into buying and overseeing all packaging for us. There was no question about it, in 1988 and 1989 we were, to use modern terminology, going gangbusters.

Outside business I retained my contact with Joan although her ties to a long-standing relationship didn't allow for any significant social experiences.

Early in 1988 Dennis Conner contacted me and asked for help. He had been contracted to compete in the ANZ 12-Metre Challenge on Sydney Harbour over the Australia Day period in January and could not get to Sydney in time for some preliminary training with his crew. He asked if I would take his crew out and familiarise them with the harbour before he arrived. It was my pleasure.

Following that event—which he completed by unceremoniously running aground on Shark Island in the middle of the Harbour— Dennis then asked me if I would join him in the making of a video on sailing techniques. He wanted me to sail on a yacht with him and I accepted.

We went to the Royal Prince Alfred Yacht Club on Pittwater and while we were rigging the yacht I noticed his gold Rolex watch. It prompted me to tell him I was pretty annoyed because I had given my 1970 *Gretel II* America's Cup issue Rolex to my son David and that some bastard had broken into his flat in Kirribilli just weeks earlier and stolen it. David treasured the watch.

"It really makes me angry to think that some bastard is going around wearing a Rolex with Jim Hardy, Gretel II, 1970, on the back of it," I said.

"Don't worry," said Dennis. "I've got a spare Rolex. I'd like to give it to your son."

I was embarrassed and could only say: "Fair go Dennis. I didn't tell you for that reason. It just annoys me no end. I don't want your watch for David."

Blow me down, a few weeks later my secretary in Sydney received a call from the Customs office. They had a Rolex watch valued at $2000 addressed to David. If I would go to their office and pay $788 in duty I could pick it up.

My secretary called me in Adelaide asking what to do. I wasn't too keen on the $788 so told her to tell the Customs guys the origin of the watch in a bid to get the duty waived. She did just that and they agreed there should be no duty.

David wears that watch to this day. It has "Stars & Stripes '87" on the back, so it was the one from Fremantle when Dennis won the Cup back from Australia.

Some time after David received the watch, when Dennis and I were contesting an Etchells Australian championship at Mooloolaba, just north of Brisbane, I told some people the story of the watch and how grateful I was. Dennis was standing with us at the time.

Next thing Dennis dragged me aside, obviously upset, and jumped down my throat: "Jim, I don't want you telling that story. It's taken me 40 years to get the Big Bad Dennis tag, and you're going to undo it in no time if you repeat that story."

He's a mixture that man.

Soon after the America's Cup I had accepted the position of Vice President of the twelve metre Class Association and our next meeting was scheduled for Yacht Club Costa Smeralda in Sardinia. It had to be one of the best venues on earth for a meeting. When I told Joan I was going to Sardinia she told me she planned to be in London at the same time. I saw an opportunity too good to miss: "Why don't I pick you up in London and take you out to Sardinia?" Much to my delight, Joan agreed. That trip was to result in the strengthening of our friendship. The atmosphere around Porto Cervo, on the Costa Smeralda in Sardinia, provided the perfect formula for two people who were traversing the fine line between moral obligations and a possible romance. Our hearts were to win the day.

At the Association meeting I started to see the emergence of

New Zealand's frustration with Dennis Conner and his failure to nominate a time and a place for the next America's Cup match. That frustration eventually led to the Kiwis lodging the now historic Cup challenge with the 130 foot long monohull, a challenge that was eventually repelled in controversial fashion by Conner and his catamaran.

From the outset I was never impressed with the way the New Zealanders lodged their challenge. To me it really smacked of retaliation from Fremantle when Dennis suggested the Kiwis might be cheating because they were the only ones there with fibreglass twelve metres. What the New Zealanders didn't realise was that the allegations were typically Dennis. They were part of his psyche program. He needles people to take their minds off the subject, and that time it was their fight to become challenger for the America's Cup. Dennis' "cheat" allegation hit the nerve he was looking for—the Kiwis started fighting internally and their on-water performance, which until then had been quite spectacular, began falling apart. Notwithstanding all that, I think the New Zealanders should have had the decency to at least contact Alan Bond when they lodged the big boat challenge and bring him up to speed.

The Kiwi effort resulted in there being a lot of dead race horses around the world in the form of twelve metre class yachts. All the people who bought twelve metres after the Fremantle match—like the Swedes, who bought *South Australia* from us—and believed quite logically that they would be the yachts for the next match, were left holding the can.

The entire 1988 Cup match between the catamaran and the monomaran, as it was called, was nothing short of a huge farce. The public, quite understandably, felt the America's Cup was finished as an event. But I didn't believe that then and certainly don't now. I believe the America's Cup will survive because it is built on history and tradition. It has seen a lot of ups and downs since first being contested way back in 1851, and it will see many more in the future. I guess you could compare it to the Royal Family—it still exists despite having its share of ups and downs over the centuries. I think history will record that the catamaran/monomaran debacle was a turning point in the contest. While few people, if any, agreed with it at the time, it resulted in the introduction of a far more spectacular class of yacht and much fairer rules for the future. For the first time the challenger of the future was guaranteed an even break.

The one pleasing consequence for me was that the 12-Metre Association, being all but defunct because the yachts were no longer part of the Cup scene, decided to spend some of the funds it had on the creation of a new trophy. It was a gesture of goodwill towards the new International America's Cup Class yachts. The trophy, a beautifully proportioned silver loving cup, was to be awarded at future World Championships for the new America's Cup-class yachts to the team that displayed the most friendly competition between foreign countries—a line used in the wording of the actual America's Cup Deed of Gift. It was titled "The Sir James Hardy Sportsmanship Trophy". I considered the title doubly pleasing—as well as being "my" trophy it referred to "sportsmanship" and not "sportspersonship".

Being with Joan in Sardinia was the catalyst my life had been needing for so long. Having someone with me who was a real companion and with whom I could always share the pleasures of social events, no matter the time of day, showed me I had found the formula for happiness I had hoped I would one day experience. But while we were blissfully happy there was a very unsettling web of complications around both of us. We each had commitments and obligations to which we were morally bound. They had to be unravelled if what was then an exciting, blossoming romance was to burst into full bloom. Other people's feelings had to be considered. It was all very complex, but I was reminded of the title of the autobiography of my friend, the great marathon swimmer Des Renford: *Nothing Great is Easy*. I recalled a long-standing piece of advice I had often given others: "Follow your heart."

The date of 11 July 1988 is a date that is in bold print in my life. Anne and I were at our home in Adelaide and all I can say is that nothing was different. Anne's words that night are still with me: "Get out! Get out! Get out and stay out!" In a flash my life over the past twenty years was compiled, compressed then reviewed in my mind. There were two particular messages being repeated, over and over again—I did not want to be a male nurse for the rest of my life; my life was really passing me by. "Get out! Get out! Get out and stay out!" OK, I will.

My departure was memorable. I picked up my toothbrush and little else then walked out the door and into a whole new world. "Where do I go from here?" I asked myself, climbing into the car.

"I don't want to burden friends with this problem." I drove around to the Travelodge Motel on South Terrace and took a room for the night. All the time my mind was racing. It was like a human computer with data going in every direction. I was calculating the consequences of my actions.

I knew I needed time and space if I was going to assess the situation logically and without outside influences. A plan evolved. Hardy's leased a small apartment at Edgecliff, in Sydney, which I had been staying in from time to time. That could become my temporary home. I was on a plane to Sydney the next morning. From then on I was based in Sydney and travelled to Adelaide for board meetings.

Joan was also living in Sydney, but it was "access denied" for much of the time because she was still committed to her relationship. I certainly didn't want to bring any undue pressure to bear on that decision for her. We both thought it best to let things develop with time. And I'm glad to say they did. Joan made the decision to excuse herself from that relationship and from that moment on I was the happiest man on earth.

It seemed only a matter of weeks after I settled in Sydney that I received a telephone call from my son David. Talk about "like father, like son"—his call was to tell me he had separated from his wife, Juliet, and to ask if I had a spare bed in the apartment.

It was wonderful for David and me to be sharing the same home. There were plenty of laughs as we battled our way back into bachelorhood. Our double act extended into sailing—we had decided we should race a Soling three-man keel boat in the trials for the 1988 Olympics.

The Olympic trials were one of the classic "we didn't win but we sure had a good time" regattas. A friend of mine loaned us his lovely old home in Toorak for the duration of the series—so there we were, David, our other crewman, Andrew Crombie, and myself sitting back in this mansion. The high water mark of that stay came the night after we had been out on Port Phillip for our first practice session. We arrived back at the mansion and spread the sails on the lawn to dry, then relaxed over a few cold beers. The next thing we looked out the window to see the entire garden burst into action with a sprinkler system going flat out. There were our sails dancing up and down in the middle of the lawn with the sprinklers fired up beneath them. We didn't know how to turn the system off, so we opened another beer and enjoyed the entertainment.

With us not being the Australian Soling Class representative for the Seoul Olympics I decided a suitable alternative would be to go to the class world championships in Hungary that year. Unfortunately David couldn't make it because of his commitments to the MBA he was doing at the Australian Graduate School of Management, so I grabbed two other Sydney friends, Gary Cassidy and Warwick Anderson. The most exciting thing about this regatta was that it came just two weeks after they had removed the barbed wire entanglements between Hungary and Austria. We were there to see an incredible part of world history unfold, the thawing of relationships between the East and West. We were still very much in a communist country, and they had taken my passport at my destination in Hungary, but it was obvious big changes were coming.

The world championship was sailed on Lake Balaton, a large fresh water lake, and the local sailors did everything they could to make it a success. While very few of them spoke English, and I certainly didn't speak Hungarian, you could sense a relief among the people through the changes they were seeing. At a post-race barbecue one night one of the Hungarian sailors, who had a grasp of English, told me Gorbachev was the first Russian the Hungarians had ever liked. He said the world would eventually realise Stalin's acts when he was in power made Hitler look like a Sunday School teacher. The number of Jews killed by Hitler would represent about ten per cent of the number of Jews and Gentiles who died from starvation in Siberia after being sent there by Stalin.

For me, to meet the Hungarians, enjoy their company, see their country and drink their wine was just delightful.

On the subject of drinking wine, a problem was emerging for Thomas Hardy's. The British weren't drinking enough of our wine and we were losing ground in the market place. Our competitors, particularly Orlando, Penfolds and Rosemount, were doing much better than we were. That situation coupled with the fact that the company had grown dramatically during the previous two decades prompted the call for a Strategic Planning Meeting that we organised at a conference centre in Victoria's Yarra Valley in February 1989. It was attended by all directors.

The end result of that meeting was that two significant decisions were made—we should no longer operate through agents in London but through our own distribution company and, with the development plan for the European Economic Community threatening to block wine imports, we should look to owning a winery in France. We decided that Ian Gray and our Marketing Director Michael von Berg should go to London and France to find our solutions.

In London they interviewed the owners of 40 wine and spirit distribution companies and after extensive evaluation proposed that we bought the majority interest in two companies, Andrew Gordon Wines and Whiclar Wines, then combine them to form Whiclar and Gordon Wines. The reason for their suggestion was that Andrew Gordon Wines were very successful importers of French wine, something which would give Hardy's a strong contact into the French scene should we need it. Whiclar Wines were solid importers and distributors of other wines. We looked at the numbers, agreed such a move would meet our requirements, then struck a deal.

Ian and Mike then moved into France and commenced their search for a winery. They looked at all sorts of properties and finally came up with a small winery located in the south of France, near Beziers. It hadn't made wine for about three years and was very run down. That actually appealed because it would allow us to more easily introduce our efficient production equipment and replace the concrete fermenting tanks with ones made from stainless steel.

The negotiations were tough. The French weren't enthusiastic about foreigners buying their wineries and we had to go through an incredibly lengthy procedure to get the necessary approvals before the deal could be done. Finally it all fell into place, then because we had a company that was rich in assets but poor when it came to readily available cash, we went back to the State Bank of South Australia to borrow the money. We made our first vintage at the French winery in August 1990.

With that winery up and running and being managed by my nephew Bill Hardy, along with chief winemaker Peter Dawson, the goals set at the Strategic Planning Meeting had been achieved in a matter of months and everything was going according to plan. Soon after, Mike von Berg was to return from a visit to our agents in New York, International Vintners, with news that they were interested in buying into a huge winery in Italy, Casa Vinicola Barone Ricasoli—or CVBR. It was located in Tuscany, one of the most beautiful regions in Italy, and had a history dating back 850 years. It was the original home of the famous Chianti style wine, which had been developed almost 150 years earlier by the first Prime Minister of the united Italy, Baron Ricasoli. He blended two red grape and two white grape varieties to create Chianti Classico.

Mike put the facts and figures on CVBR in front of Ian Gray, and both agreed it was something Hardy's should look at. They went to Italy to learn everything they could about the business.

At our next board meeting at Chateau Reynella Ian Gray said: "Gentlemen, here is the big opportunity—the big deal—the big gamble," or words to that effect. He spread out the master plan for Hardys' takeover of CVBR. It certainly looked impressive and I remember saying: "Chianti to me is as important to Italian wine as Bordeaux is to French wine." The sales figures were quite staggering—600,000 cases sold to 50 countries per annum, with 50,000 of those going to America. There were no vineyards attached to the business. It was just a huge winery—and that pleased us because anyone can grow grapes, and wineries can usually buy them cheaper than they can grow them.

Two alarm bells should have rung during that meeting. The first was that the big American liquor company Seagrams had once owned CVBR and had not been able to make a go of it. Then Guenter Prass said: "You will find the Italian culture very different. They are different people to deal with." Looking back on it now, those points were absolutely screaming red lights. But it is easy to be wise after the event.

The enthusiasm of Mike von Berg and Ian Gray for the project, and the numbers we had in front of us, were our strongest guides. I took a vote on whether or not to invest the seven million dollars to take over 60 per cent of CVBR, and apart from Guenter's dissenting voice on dealing with the Italians, the decision was made to go for it. We subsequently made another trip to the State Bank and while we were pleased at the time with the news that they would lend us the money, I now wish they hadn't.

We almost broke even on our first year of trading, then the domestic wine market in Italy collapsed. The rot then spread—the Gulf War and other economic problems in America resulted in our sales plummeting there. In our second and third years of trading CVBR recorded annual losses of around five million dollars. On top of that our profits in Australia were barely enough to cover those losses. We stopped paying dividends to our family shareholders. On the local market we were victims of our own success because the trouble with selling a lot of product is that you require a lot of stock. For example, the one label I am so very proud of, the Sir James champagne, had become such a success that we needed to put down each year what we anticipated we would sell when it was ready for the market place in two years. Holding that stock cost a lot of money. That wasn't a problem until the losses from Italy arrived on the scene. Then our struggle to make ends meet triggered an alarm with the State Bank of South Australia, which in itself was destined for disaster. In borrowing the money to buy our controlling interest in CVBR we signed an agreement stating that our profit would not fall to below one and a half times our interest bill. The alarm bells went off at the bank when we broke that covenant. That problem was subsequently exacerbated by our higher-than-anticipated interest bills, which came as a result of the activities of "the world's greatest Treasurer", Paul Keating. If interest rates had not been so high for so long for the new money we borrowed we would not have been in breach of the covenant, and not struck trouble. We were just one of hundreds of companies in Australia faced with that problem.

Our problems were accelerated by the $3.15 billion financial disaster that struck the State Bank. The new bank management, quite understandably, saw us as one of the companies owing money because we were in breach of the covenant, even though we had never missed a payment. Initially they asked us to find alternative finance and we set about doing that. Then came the straw that really broke the camel's back—the Italian banks also involved with CVBR demanded an additional five million dollars from us to keep the business afloat. The State Bank had little alternative but to cover us for that while we tried to solve our problems with them. We considered floating our company but realised that the Italian performance would not make the shares the flavour of the month with potential investors.

What was frustrating for the directors of Hardy's was that Thomas Hardy and Sons was making sufficient money to pay the interest bills. But the bank continued to put us under financial duress and consequently we were in dire straits. If they had renegotiated the covenant we could have survived, but they wouldn't do that—possibly because the bank was in so much trouble itself. The final ultimatum followed—we had to sell or be sold.

There was no alternative. Thomas Hardy and Sons was put on the market. I was a shattered man.

We quickly found we had various suitors, national and international, but the final decision was for a merger with Berri Renmano, a South Australian company that had very large wine production but few strong brand names. The deal was partly orchestrated by the State Bank, and BRL Hardy was born in mid 1992. One hundred and forty years of family tradition had been demolished in two years. I remained a Non-Executive Director, but the company was dancing to another tune.

Hardy's shareholders finished up losing more than twenty million dollars, something like one-half of their wealth, through the Italian fiasco. I can't blame any particular person. As was so often the case, Ian Gray had put up a proposition and Mike von Berg supported it. But it was up to us, the balance of the directors, to say stop or go.

Deep inside I felt it was inevitable that one day the family would no longer own the business because so many other famous Australian families in the wine industry had been forced into relinquishing control, usually because of a shortage of working capital. But I didn't think it would be my generation, and me at the helm, when it happened at Hardy's. I thought it would probably be something the next generation of the Hardy family would have to contend with.

I managed to maintain my composure throughout this entire ordeal, right until the end. Then it got the better of me. At the final Annual General Meeting of Thomas Hardy and Sons shareholders, I broke down. I couldn't hang on any longer. I wanted to thank Guenter Prass and Mark Tummel for their contributions to the company, but I couldn't. Tears started welling up in my eyes so I asked our Managing Director, Wayne Jackson, to thank them. My son David came out of the crowd at the end of the meeting, put his arm around me and gave me strength.

I felt as though I had been at the helm of a yacht that was in danger of being dashed onto the rocks. We were probably in need of a fresh crew to replace the crew that was aboard because fatigue was setting in. But regardless of that we were trying to save our ship. We were giving all the signs that we could claw our way off that lee shore. At the same time salvage ships were waiting on the horizon, waiting to pick up the good ship Thomas Hardy and Sons. They knew if they could get a tow line aboard they could claim 90 per cent of our ship's value.

If there is any consolation from all this, it is that the name Hardy still stands proudly on the product. It hasn't disappeared and, I'm pleased to say, Sir James champagne is out there doing great things in the market place.

For me many of the dreams I had developed over decades went with the company and the dissolution of my marriage to Anne. I was born in 1932 when things were really tough and in many ways, as I approached my sixtieth year, I was feeling as many people did back in the Depression—this was my own private depression.

I must stress here that while I am not broke today I certainly don't have the financial security I had hoped for at this stage in life. For one, my dream of owning another ocean-racing yacht will not come true. However, if there was one bright point among all this, after my divorce and subsequent financial settlement with Anne, it was that she went on to be healthier and look better than she had for many, many years. I believe she conquered her alcohol dependency.

I soon realised the downside of my life was essentially material—the finances weren't strong. Then I reminded myself this was a mere drop in the ocean that is life and that this setback had been far, far outweighed by the love that developed between Joan and myself. This love unfolded over the years and has blossomed from better to best. We endured the traumas associated with the sale of Thomas Hardy & Sons and through love I was given strength during my emotional lows that came after leaving Anne.

Joan and I began to share more and more wonderful moments together. A special time was Christmas in New York—Joan had always wanted to have a white Christmas in that city, so we did just that. We even caught the train up to Newport, Rhode Island, for a trip down memory lane. It was Newport as I had never seen it—crisp and enveloped in snow.

This was a most romantic interlude and it confirmed that the woman I fell for while she was singing in Adelaide on my fiftieth birthday in November 1982 could fulfil every single wish, every vision, I harboured for a future together.

In April 1991 I could wait no longer. Joan was working at the Channel 10 television studios in Sydney and I arranged to take her to lunch. It was there I proposed. I was like a boy on his first date, overflowing in eager anticipation of the big moment. To my delight Joan accepted. I had won the most important prize I could seek in life. For me there was just one more task—it was then only right that I should go to Joan's father for the final seal of approval. He told me I seemed to make his daughter very happy and that mattered to him. Joan and I married before a small gathering of friends at the Royal Sydney Yacht Squadron seven months later.

Having the woman of your dreams as part of your life brings new priorities and places a fresh perspective on the future. Some people may call this period in my life the twilight years, but for me there is a beautiful twilight at the end of each day and an even more wonderful day to follow. I do reminisce from time to time about how things might have been, but more importantly I look to the future and see happiness coupled with contentment.

If nothing else our lifestyle provides us with plenty of time to do things together and accept some pleasant invitations. One such invitation was to the wedding of Alan Bond's daughter Jodie and that great little America's Cup yachtsman, Damian Fewster, or "Knuckle", as we know him. Regardless of what has befallen Alan these days, and what people might think of him, I consider him to be an exceptional person who gave me and a lot of other yachtsmen a wonderful chance in the America's Cup. He remains a friend.

Despite facing tough times Alan ensured the wedding was a very spectacular affair—but not as spectacular as daughter Susan's wedding at the same waterfront home a few years earlier. That extravaganza was memorable for many things, none more so than when the pontoon, moored at the bottom of the garden which was carrying the band for the dancing, sank at 2 a.m. Down it went, band and all.

Joan and I were also very pleased to be able to be in Perth for the launching of another Alan Bond initiated project—the full scale replica of Captain Cook's *Endeavour*. Alan's financial disasters saw him forced to abandon this incredible ship-building effort soon after construction started, but the man he commissioned to manage it, his America's Cup lieutenant John "Chink" Longley, stood by it with a passion. For Chink it was a dream which could come true and he guided the project from start to finish.

The launching ceremony saw a marvellous blend of old and new—an enchanting time warp. A highlight for me was to meet the old Englishman who orchestrated the actual launching of the ship. He had done more than 20 such traditional launchings, but this was his first new ship, all the others being restorations. His team of men hammered wedges under the hull of the *Endeavour* and lifted it six inches. They then fitted fore and after cradles and sat them on wooden ways which had been given a liberal coating of animal fat.

The entire launching process had me more intrigued than anything else. Its success hinged around a large wooden trigger which was held by, of all things, a piece of the most modern of ropes, Kevlar. The reason for this was that when Kevlar is broken it just dies—it has no elasticity. There would be no shock reaction from this rope which was under enormous load.

A huge crowd was on hand for the ceremony, official guests inside the building and thousands of others lining the foreshores of Fremantle's Fisherman's Harbour. The traditional bottle of red wine was used for the christening. As it burst on the ship's glistening timber topsides the Kevlar rope holding the trigger was hit with an axe. In an instant this 17th century sailing ship was released and on its way. Initially there was a puff of smoke from the friction between the cradle and the ways, then when the cradles got going on the animal fat, it just took off. I reckon it was doing 15 knots when it reached the water—the fastest it will ever go. The whole thing gave me goose bumps, but I couldn't help thinking all the time there was one fellow missing from the official dais that day—Alan Bond. He should have been there as he inspired the whole thing. It reminded me of the day Queen Elizabeth opened the Sydney Opera House. Its creator, Joern Utzon, wasn't there either.

As well as now having time to enjoy life with Joan I am also able to look for new challenges and opportunities. For one, I am working with a group of businessmen on the creation of some small, 40 to 50-bed rural resorts in Australia's wine regions, resorts to take international tourists in particular off the beaten track—away from places like Sydney, Cairns and Ayers Rock. They will be miniature farms and wineries and will provide a look at another side of the Australian lifestyle. This project is quite appropriate alongside my appointment as National Chairman of the Landcare Australia

Foundation, an organisation created to save Australia's rural land and water from further degradation.

My continuing work with the old company is at times difficult, especially with all the new faces, but I must admit, for the most part I still enjoy my relationship with the BRL Hardy wine company. As well as being on the Board I am taking an active role in the promotion of the business as exports of Hardy wines are going extremely well. They are now sold in 43 American states and extensively in Europe. These promotions have allowed Joan and me to enjoy a considerable amount of travel together and one of the most pleasurable expeditions we were able to undertake, where I could combine business and sailing, came in 1994 when we went to America and Europe. I hosted functions for our wines in San Francisco, New York, Washington and Boston and then took in the New York Yacht Club's Sesquicentenary Regatta celebrations at one of my favourite places on earth, Newport, Rhode Island. The high point of that regatta was my induction into the America's Cup Hall of Fame in Bristol, Rhode Island.

Everything seemed to fall into place perfectly for this trip. It just so happened that when the Board at BRL Hardy was planning my involvement in the American promotions the Commodore of the Royal Sydney Yacht Squadron, Norm Longworth, asked me to join him and a squadron crew aboard a 40 footer for the NYYC's regatta. I thought that was a great idea. Then, to cap it all off, I received notification from Halsey Herreshoff, of the Herreshoff Marine Museum, that I was to become the second Australian—after John Bertrand—to be inducted into the Hall of Fame.

As I was a member Joan and I were fortunate enough to be able to stay at the New York Yacht Club, right in the heart of New York. We used the club for a function celebrating the establishment of the BRL Hardy office in Virginia. This office had been a dream of mine since 1970. In looking back over recent times one of the decisions we made at Thomas Hardy & Sons which was undoubtedly wrong was to not grab a golden opportunity and establish our own American office when we bought the Italian Ricasoli winery. Ricasoli was then selling 50,000 cases per annum into America and would have given us the perfect foundation on which to build our business. Instead we changed distributor to a large company, and got buried.

Sure it's easy to be wise after the event, but in hindsight I realise how easy it is to get sucked in by a big company that has all the money and carries enormous power in the market place. They can just sit on an agency. All they are really doing is stopping anyone else from selling your product. They control the market, selling just enough to drip feed you and keep you alive. We really blew that one!

The NYYC's Sesquicentenary Regatta turned out to be a grand affair. It was fun racing with good friends and the event proved to be a perfect path to the induction ceremony for me on the final night, August 5, 1994. It was staged in a huge marquee at the Herreshoff Marine Museum in Bristol—a jacket and tie affair with more than 200 people attending. They came by car and boat—and it poured with rain. I have this vivid memory of women coming off boats and entering the marquee wearing very unflattering wet weather gear that was normally used for sailing. Once inside the marquee the ladies removed the very wet sailing gear and emerged looking glamorous in all their finery, ready for a spectacular night.

The one part of the evening that sparked me was when B. Devereux Barker III stood and proposed the toast to my induction. This same bloke had been the chairman of the protest committee when *Gretel II* was disqualified following that still controversial starting-line incident back in 1970. I couldn't resist grabbing the opportunity when I stood up to respond to remind him that while I agreed that his protest committee had made the right decision back then on the facts they had established, I still doubted the facts. It brought the house down.

With that memorable night behind us we headed to New York then flew to London where I had the honour of opening the new BRL Hardy Headquarters, Hardy House, in Epsom. It was a proud moment for me to see the family name recognised yet again. The office has a staff of 25 and it handles the company's British and European distribution. It is proving to be very successful with strong sales into Germany, Belgium, Holland and Scandinavia in particular. I found it interesting to see we were capturing a nice market for red wine in Germany. While the Germans are very good at making white wine they don't get enough sun for the grapes to ripen enough for the production of quality red wine.

After London we flew to Montpellier in southern France to

visit my nephew Bill Hardy at Domaine de la Baume, close to Montpellier and not far from the great sailing port of Sete on the Mediterranean coast. During the flight Joan and I recalled the brief journey we made to Paris a few years earlier when we stayed with Isdell Rudich, a dear friend of Joan's from Adelaide, who had been living in France for many years. Much of our time was spent with a long-time friend of Isdell, Pierre Cazes, a wonderful old trooper in his seventies. He is an author, former mercenary and big game hunter who always took to the streets of Paris in his old Volkswagen Passatt with terrifying gusto. But it was his parking technique that left us with the most memories . . .

Any parking spot less than 2 feet shorter than his car was a parking space as far as Pierre was concerned. He simply used his little Volkswagen as a wedge, first nosing it in against the car in front and pushing it forward, then reversing it onto the car behind and pushing it backwards. He continued this manoeuvre until the gap was big enough to accommodate his car. We couldn't believe it the first time we experienced the manoeuvre.

"Hey, Pierre, what are you doing," I asked, somewhat astounded by his actions.

"Jeem, Jzhoanie, leeeson to mee. I am parking zee car. Zee car is fitted with zee boomper at zee front and zee bomper at zee back. Zis is what zee boompers are for . . . BOOMPING!"

"OK, Pierre."

When we visited Bill at BRL Hardy's lovely chateau and winery I told him I was planning to enter *Nerida* in the 50th anniversary Sydney to Hobart race and that I thought it should become a family adventure aboard the family yacht. It was my intention to have only Hardys in the crew, and he would be one of them. His immediate response wasn't exactly what I expected. "Jim, I don't want to die." I explained I too had no desire to die then outlined the plans— we would be bringing fathers, sons and cousins together and at long last, get to know each other under exciting circumstances. Bill accepted.

Fortunately his four-year term in charge of the Hardy operation in France was coming to an end so he and his family would be back in Australia (where he would become assistant to the technical director at Reynella) in plenty of time for the big race.

It seemed quite ironic that while I was working on assembling the male members of our family, including son David, for the race, I should receive another great honour. I was named the 1994 Father of the Year by the NSW Fathers' Day Council. For me the award meant I was representing all fathers on the day when the importance of the bond between a father and his children is recognised. Sure the day has commercial undertones but for me it has a special place in any community. The honour allowed me to direct any money raised by the council to the Lorna Hodgkinson Sunshine Home, where Richard lives, and to the Juvenile Diabetes Foundation, which now has a special place in David's life. David has contracted insulin-dependent diabetes. His lovely wife Margie has met the challenge by becoming the Chief Executive Officer of the foundation.

The Fathers' Day award gave me the chance to explain my philosophy on the role of a father. With David and Richard I felt it important that life and not Jim Hardy lifted them to their desired levels. This makes for greater independence. For example I could easily have pushed David into sailing, but didn't, and he is a better person for it. I did not want him to feel any obligation towards my sport.

David is a wonderful son who, especially in his younger years, had to contend with a lot of things a son in other families would not be confronted with. He has come through with flying colours. To me he is as much a mate as a son and I am a very proud father. Some of the best moments in my life were to see him receive his Bachelor of Economics degree and later his MBA from the University of NSW.

Today David, like me, has found love and remarried. Margie is a delightful woman who is proving to be a tower of strength for him as he contends with his diabetes. Professionally David is doing extremely well with a large management consultancy firm.

And Richard—I look back at all the years of frustration, torment and hardship which have confronted him. As a father I am proud of his achievements—his genuine interest in music and football. He is a joy to be with. One needs to be touched by a situation like this in life to appreciate that there's more to it than being superficially interested. I think I am a more compassionate and understanding person as a result of being part of Richard's life.

While Richard couldn't be part of our crew aboard *Nerida* for the 50th Hobart race he followed it with great interest. Our line-up was a bit like the family tree. It comprised my son David—who was a watch captain, my brother David as navigator and his two sons, Christopher and John, and my late brother Tom's three boys, Tom, Bill and Geoff. It made for a great team, but you could never call out "Hey Hardy, give me a hand" because you'd be killed in the rush.

Nerida, as previously mentioned, was the yacht my father built back in the 1930s and, when owned by Colin Haselgrove, she won the 1950 Hobart race. In being restored back to her original, and very complex, gaff rig, she presented plenty of problems for the guys measuring her for handicapping under the International Measurement System rule. There is no provision in that rule to rate a yacht with the classic old, two-piece, gaff rig. This problem was to be minor when compared with the controversy that erupted over the old wooden mast itself, which was getting very tired. Instead of going to the expense of getting a new one I unwittingly elected to sheath it with the most modern material, carbon fibre. I didn't realise this material, which gave the mast great strength, was banned under the new IMS rule for use on masts. After much debate between the club, myself and yachting authorities the sheathing was deemed to be a repair and thus *Nerida* could race in the Performance Handicap division. That meant we wouldn't be eligible for any prizes in the main IMS division—which was fine by me. I didn't really care about the prizes. Being part of such an historic race with eight family members meant much more.

Nerida was not designed to meet the modern safety rules so getting her prepared was a nightmare. There were 83 items on the 'to do' list before we were race ready. Soon though the effort was to be worthwhile.

What a magnificent sight the harbour was on December 26 when it came time for the race. There was a world record fleet of 372 yachts lining up for the 630 nautical mile voyage south.

Our division comprised yachts which had contested the race at least 30 years ago. Being slower than our more modern counterparts, we were given a head start of 30 minutes. It was a downwind leg to the Heads and you could have described our effort as OK. We lost ground because I couldn't set the spinnaker—there was nothing left to hoist it on as all halyards were being used on other sails.

Once outside the Heads we watched in awe as the bulk of the

fleet, more than 300 of them, along with thousands of spectator craft, swept out of the harbour and pursued us. Mind you, the pursuit didn't last long. In no time they had passed us and were gone.

We made the news the first night out, not through any outstanding effort under sail, but through a small navigational error. Numeracy was not one of brother David's great talents but still he was our navigator. He carefully plotted our position that first evening and stood by the radio for what seemed to be an eternity waiting for *Nerida* to be called. Finally it was our turn and David dutifully delivered our latitude and longitude to the radio relay vessel then came up on deck and gave a sigh of relief. I asked how it went and he said "not a problem". Well it was a big problem—we later saw the plotted position that was revealed in the newspapers and on television. There it was for the world to see—*Nerida*'s position was in the middle of the Royal National Park, just south of Sydney. It was as though we were going south by road. Ouch! Our longitude was terribly wrong. But really it was all a hoot—especially after I had told reporters before the race our course to Hobart would see us staying close to shore.

We enjoyed a very pleasant sail down the NSW south coast with the wind generally coming from astern. When we got into Bass Strait it was a completely different story. We hit the legendary Hobart race brick wall—a southerly buster which came through at 20 then 30, then 40 and finally 50 knots. It wasn't *Nerida*'s weather and I decided, because it was absolutely on the nose, we would withdraw from the race and press on using the engine. This decision was influenced by the fact that we wanted to be in Hobart for the celebrations on New Year's eve. Our rate of progress south under sail meant we wouldn't make it. I was reminded of the old adage that a yacht race is only there to get you from one party to another.

We motored for 12 hours into steep and ugly seas then heard the next forecast—another 40-knot plus southerly front heading our way. It was bad news.

As we went into our third night at sea I began to assess the situation. Yachts ahead were reporting headwinds of up to 60 knots, and I knew *Nerida* wouldn't make headway in those conditions, under engine or sail.

At about 4 a.m. while I considered our dilemma, our fate was sealed. A GKW (giant killer wave) roared towards us out of the pitch black night and broke right over the yacht, submerging it for one brief moment. Bill was steering at the time and I was sitting in the cockpit with my back to this wave. As it broke it smashed into my back, hurling me across the cockpit. I led with my chin and it collided perfectly with the end of the tiller. The resulting impact punched my front teeth ever so neatly through my lower lip. Instead of stopping there, the wave continued to carry me towards the side of the yacht. My mind flashed a message: "You're going overboard". But just as quickly my flight came to an abrupt halt, the safety harness I was wearing snapping tight and holding me just inside the perimeter of the yacht. I thumped to the deck in a sopping heap. Torches came out and quickly it was revealed there was no damage to the tiller but plenty to my face. There was blood everywhere. I went below where son David tried to put some sutures on the gash created by my teeth. Everything was so wet they wouldn't stick.

Obviously it was time to seriously assess our situation. The expensive new satellite positioning navigation system I had installed for the race had given up the ghost so I took out the chart and, while holding a rag to my chin to stem the flow of blood, calculated we were only one-third of the way across Bass Strait. There was no way we would get to Hobart until New Year's Day at the earliest. At the same time the chart told me Eden was downwind, or more specifically, behind us and about 14 hours away.

I put it to the vote: Hobart or Eden, and Eden won unanimously. It was an especially popular choice for those who were feeling a little green, including yours truly. I must confess that at that stage of proceedings, while I checked the chart, it was sufficiently rough for even this seasoned sailor to talk to "Ralph" in the big plastic bucket.

While I was bitterly disappointed by not making the distance to Hobart, commonsense had prevailed. Our decision to retire from the race brought to mind a quote from Theodore Roosevelt, which was sent to me by my long time friend, Max Whitnall: "It is not the critic who counts, not the man who points out how the strong man stumbled or where the doer of deeds could have done better. The credit belongs to the man who is actually in the arena (boat); whose face is marred by dust (salt water) and sweat and blood; who strives valiantly; who errs and comes short again and again; who knows the great enthusiasms, the great devotions, and spends himself in a worthy cause; who, at the best, knows in the end the triumph of high achievement; and who, at the worst, if he fails, at least fails while daring greatly, so his place shall never be with those cold and timid souls who know neither victory nor defeat."

We rocked and rolled our way north towards Eden and much to our delight there were 50 race yachts in port when we arrived. Even more delightful was the fact that Joan and brother David's wife Judy surprised us by driving down from Sydney. They heard only two hours before they were due to fly to Hobart that we had retired, so they headed for Eden instead. They drove for six hours straight to ensure they were there to greet us. They booked rooms in a motel so everyone could shower and get a good sleep. It was a great effort by the shore team.

So much for the Hardy family outing . . . and the 50th anniversary Hobart race.

Soon after this experience my interest turned towards San Diego where John Bertrand and the *oneAustralia* team were fighting hard for the right to challenge for the America's Cup. With John giving me the position of Patron of the challenging club, Southern Cross Yacht Club, I felt part of yet another Cup campaign. The *oneAustralia* crew made me feel very proud when, after the world watched their frontline race yacht sink in dramatic circumstances, they rallied and went on to campaign their original yacht as though nothing had happened. Even though they didn't win the America's Cup they had again shown true Australian spirit and won respect the world over. They did us proud.

It seemed yacht clubs were playing an ever increasing role in my life. I had to ask myself if this was becaue I was getting older and not competing as much. Anyway, much to my delight, Hayman Island, that wonderful resort in the Whitsundays on Queensland's tropical coast, formed a yacht club with a view to staging a number of sailing events and I was pleased to accept the position of Commodore. It gave me yet another reason to return to one of my favourite parts of Australia—a region where Joan and I have enjoyed some excellent cruising with friends in recent times.

All these things have become important sidebars to what is a truly satisfying life, a life which today is brimming with the vital ingredients—love and happiness. Mine is a life which has been rich and rewarding. I have had the benefit of seeing it from all aspects; from within my own family as well as outside. For me every experience has been a thread making up a rich tapestry called life.

As this tapestry has formed I have continually reminded myself of one thing: If you don't experience dark clouds, rain and storms there is no way of measuring sunshine.

". . . For all experience is an arch wherethrough
Gleams the untravelled world
Whose margin fades and fades
Forever as I move . . ."

"Ulysses"—by Alfred Lord Tennyson

E MORIBUS SIT HOMO